COUPLING

Coupling

Understanding the Chemistry of Close Relationships

Dr. Daniel Cappon

St. Martin's Press • New York

For Donna
Who is love.

Contents

Foreword

This book is all about love—the bonds formed by choice rather than by family ties. And it is mostly about love between the sexes as a model for all elective close relationships.

It tells you what love is and why it is so desperately needed, and goes into what makes people click, tick, and stick together—that is, the electromagnetism of romance, the chemistry of caring, and the alchemy of love itself. The development of closeness is traced from before the first encounter right through the "living happily ever after" stage or the "repairing" or else "re-pairing" stage, as the case may be. This book will also provide you with an inventory of the one thousand elements that are matched between two people in loving and the secret formula of attraction (and repulsion) between them. This formula is based on my own modification of Carl Gustav Jung's principle of "contrasting opposition" within a person and between couples. This principle says that we are made up of "personages" that stand out in contrast with each other. For instance, the *persona,* the social mask we put on before others, stands in direct opposition to the *shadow,* the dark side within us. You are "together" to the extent to which these personages of the self hold together.

Consequently you will be introduced to the six "personages within us." You'll see how this sixsome relates to its counterparts in your partner and inside the depth of your minds. And you'll see how understanding this sixsome is the key to unraveling the mystery of love.

The magical formula of love is to be found in the finely intuited proportion of the differences that attract and the similarities that provide a common basis for a love match. The culmination of the three stages in the sequence of love—clicking, ticking, and sticking—is the ideal union described.

The purpose of this book is to demystify love so that you can understand what can go wrong in romance and in other close relationships. In order to do that, you are given a tour of depth psychology, so that you can appreciate the effects of perception, motivation, and intuition, and particularly what goes on in the personal and the collective unconscious, peopled by archetypes. That's the heavy part. At the same time you'll also learn how common sense can be used to put together the simpler elements of romantic love—such as sexual attraction, physique, facial features, lifestyle, and habits—with the more complex process of matchmaking occurring below the level of usual awareness.

Thus this book is a blend of pop and depth psychology.

The ideas for this book were inspired by analytical clinical practice with couples who had come to me with problems in marriage and other close relationships. After some years of this experience I seemed to have developed somewhat of a crystal ball. I discovered that by studying a patient, I could predict the nature of the patient's consort, the type of spouse or partner a patient would have, the type of relationship formed or to be formed in the future, and its likely eventual fate. This process of prediction also worked in reverse: From studying the relationship between couples I could divine their past patterns and motivations, as well as diagnose their personalities. I came to see how errors were being made by my patients in terms of love, and how they could be corrected in what I came to call the lean-to or teepee type of neurotic coupling. Although my patients' behavior was very often neurotic, I was able to discern and predict patterns in their behavior—patterns that are pertinent to normal love behavior.

My experience in clinical practice has also convinced me that romantic love is the model on which all other kinds of elective relationships are built. Thus I have included special chapters on the principal laws governing nonsexual relationships such as friendship, play, work, room, and travel mating. And I have even discussed the people one should match for a successful dinner party or for a President's cabinet, for that matter. Having gone that far, why not go a step further? The book ends with an epistemology of love, in which an attempt is made to relate the "laws" governing a love match to the laws governing certain fundamental phenomena and laws of the universe.

As a special, practical feature, each chapter offers at least one self-performed test, so that you may tell (1) whether you are in love, (2) how your persona or image comes across, (3) whether the special person in your life fits you well enough for a love match, (4) to which person of the inner self you give priority in coupling, (5) whether you have made a healthy union, (6) whether your late love is compatible with you, (7) what the diagnosis of your love problem might be, (8) whether or not you have a friendship, (9) how you "fit" in relationships other than love relationships, and (10) how to diagnose yourself and your capacity to love.

In short, the contents of this book may well be programmed in the future for the computerization of coupling. Meanwhile, here is a do-it-yourself guide to intimate or close relationships, an almanac about love.

1

What Is Love?

Romeo, oh Romeo, wherefore art thou Romeo?

—SHAKESPEARE

Romantics don't really want to know what love is, lest knowledge should lift love's pink mist. They're pleased with clever, if negative, slogans like "love is never to *have* to say you're sorry" or "it's never to walk on eggs" or "never to do handstands" except for the love of a child or of acrobatics. Nor is love like a bicycle built for two, although it comes pretty close, as we shall see. Romantics prefer to leave the more positive affirmations to poets ("love's a many-splendored thing") and to such tantalizing rhetoric as "What is love? It's not hereafter . . ." and "wherefore art thou Romeo?"

The love-burnt don't really want to know how it came about that they got hurt, in case it turns out that they had been foolish. Should the love-burnt risk asking the Delphic professionals of the mind and soothsayers what love is, they'd do so with the smirk of one assured that nobody truly knows the answer. Indeed, official oracles dismiss the question with a Gallic shrug at its naïveté.

And so everybody's agreed that love is a deep, bright mystery.

I suspect the reason for this alleged mysteriousness is an unconscious universal conspiracy to keep love shrouded. The awesomeness of the unknown suggests love's divine origin, hence the potency of its promise of healing, happiness, and hope.

Why then attempt to demystify what mankind has been at pains to wrap in veils for so long? Because if love is to fulfill its promise today, we must unwrap its veil and understand it better. It seems that the world's quantum of love is on the shrink. Its quality is declining. The tide of love's ugly sister—hatred—is rising. Indifference, the antithesis both of love and hatred, seems to have taken over where the sisters of love—sympathy, charity, and affection—once held sway. Consequently, more than ever is expected from at least one kind of love, the romantic one between the sexes—epicine or hetero-love as I call it in these pages. Of course, no one love, however powerful it may be, no single human emotional device can bear the excessive burden of great expectations. The result is love gone wrong and hurting the multitudes. Yet the traumatized multitudes must take courage and adopt a superior wisdom that says "if at first you don't succeed, try and try and try again" but do it differently, once you've understood what's gone wrong.

In order to rescue love from its contemporary plight and especially in order to come to the aid of lovers in distress and to those distressed because they cannot love, or think they cannot or will not love, we must lift the pink curtain surrounding love.

Let's begin with a subjective definition. Love is a powerful, positive, and enduring emotion that surges in waves with euphoric crests and desperate troughs, sometimes overwhelming the lovers. To paraphrase real estate agents: Love is the single biggest emotional investment freely made in a lifetime. The biggest financial investments follow in its wake.

However, we shall leave these subjective definitions because it is in attempting to apply these definitions that so many have failed and obfuscated the issue. Let poets and artists continue to give us joy by chasing the elusive nature of these feelings. The mystery of the feelings themselves are safe from scientific scrutiny, for they dwell inside a person. They can never be compared or verified, because there is an enormous gap, a discontinuity, between what we really feel and what we say we feel and what we show we feel.

So let us proceed to the lower and more certain grounds of an objective definition. Love has a triple anatomy. First, in the case of heterolove, there is a set of donors, the dyad of lovers (the I and we). Second, there is a sex-love object, and third, there is the relationship itself (the it), the intimate bond between the lovers. It is this third component—the "it," the cement of a close relationship of sex-becoming-love—that will be called love in this book. This means, among other things, that true love as herein objectively defined is always a two-way street. There cannot be unrequited love. As we shall come to weigh this, there can be an imbalance between the loving and the being loved, for there is usually one who gives more and one who takes more, *at any one time.* But there can be no total lack of reciprocity. Where there seems to be unrequited love, it is either an immature state or else a grave delusion—all of which will be explained presently.

It also follows from this definition that there can be no platonic love between two consenting members of the opposite sex who are able and willing and potentially sexually attractable. For one thing, the original "platonic" relationship was that between an older man and a beautiful boy. Incidentally, this was usually a one-way street. For another thing, friendship between the sexes, as we shall see when we come to consider this particular bond, implies a state of suspended heterolove, sexually inhibited by social exigencies but ready to emerge whenever possible.

I chose the heterolove model in all close elective relationships for several reasons.

First, I found that upon examining empirically the love dyad, the sex-based coupling, certain regularities or governing rules emerged—the laws of coupling, if you will. Then I found that these fundamental features of coupling apply to all elective close relationships, despite the absence of an overt sexual element.

Second, I confess I was more motivated to look into heterolove first rather than into other close relationships because it still is the foundation of family life and because, as mentioned, it seems to be the source of bitter disappointment and hurt on a vast scale.

Third, heterolove has a solid biological basis, accounting for man's sense of incompleteness and the yearning to couple, both as a psychological and ultimately a social imperative. I reasoned that in the millions of years it took to develop the Homo sapiens species, the biological need to procreate and improve the genetic pool by selection of mates must have predicated a corresponding psychological need, ultimately refined into love-mating. The object of the exercise is to produce diversity in the offspring. I admit that in animals, generally the selection is "natural" or random, but obviously in our species such "selections" and survival itself have become artificial; more or less intelligence-guided but at an unconscious, automatic level of awareness. And it seemed more imperative intuitively to secure a complementary mate and thus improve the genetic endowments of offspring than to follow the other rival "instinct" for survival, the herd drive, to which friendship and social defense belong. So the psychology of heterolove must have evolved first.

Also the powerful drive of heterolove fashioned it into the world's greatest aphrodisiac, which greatly potentiates fertility in the service of optimal biological procreation. That is to say that love aids and abets the most fruitful selection process for the survival of the species.

At any rate, it seems to me that love itself, both as the pristine product between man and woman and as an antecedent to the offspring, involved the self-selection of biological progenitors. Prospective lovers have to sift through a thousand qualities and variables before they can click, tick, and stick together—as we shall see in the succeeding three chapters.

This is far too precious a process to leave to randomness and far too difficult to leave to unaided conscious intelligence or to social organization. Consequently, it has been assigned by nature to the intuitive or unconscious selection engendered by love.

While love marriages are not made in Heaven, neither are they made by the spin of a roulette wheel. In fact, the romantic notion of a special, if not unique fit is not far from the truth when one considers the many things that have to fit in the electromagnetism of sex, the chemistry of caring, and the alchemy of love itself.

In the last analysis, I chose heterolove as a model for discovering the quintessential secret of all close relationships not only because it evolved its psychological elements upon a biological bedrock, but also because it worked; because I found that the secrets of the process of selection and bonding that made a match and coupled one human to another lay in the clues provided by heterolove.

And if this book does nothing else but take a tiny step toward making mate selection less random, wasteful, and hurtful, it will have been enough.

THE EMBRYOLOGY OF LOVE

In the sex-becoming-love sequence there is a hierarchy of progressively altruistic attainment, which works itself up from sensation to higher forms of devotion.

At the bottom of the progression is self-centered investment of psychic energy—the *pleasure of sensation* coming from all eight senses: sight, hearing, moving, touching, tasting, smelling, posturing, and visceral satiety.

The second stage is reached when selective aspects of pleasurable sensations or sensuality cluster into *eroticism,* which is a libidinal fixation on sexually arousing sensuality.

The third stage, which is somewhat more sharing and less narcissistic, is that of sexuality itself when at best the objective is *mutual satisfaction* in the most physically intimate acts between adults, namely intercourse. The crowning stage is love itself, when the objective goes beyond the self-centered pleasure of sensation, sensuality, eroticism, and sexuality, and becomes *caring,* in this case for a human being of the opposite sex.

Somewhere along the tree of love there are some main branches between the sensuous titillation of one's own body and mind and giving pleasure and affection to another being beyond one's immediate family. These are the obligatory loves between parents and children and among the latter. One of these branches, the parental-filial, is unique among loves in that it must yield its "object" as an altruistic culmination of its caring. But perhaps parallel to this sex-based genealogy of love, and beyond it in altruistic devotion, is friendship and finally the love of mankind and of still higher transpersonal and absolute values and ideologies, namely *agape* (aga•pe).

In the taxonomy of love based on the nature of the love object there are some less vital branches, such as an investment in objects more remotely animate (animals and feathered friends) and even inanimate (such as filthy lucre).

It is important to see where heterolove lies in this scheme of things in order to see where it came from, where it's linked to compulsory love, and what it might rise to in agape. The reason is that as in all developmental stages, a higher level incorporates the lower stages and leaves behind it large ledges. Thus great love becomes bereft of its basic sensations, eroticism and sexuality, only at its own peril; just as great art, ideology, and agape become bereft of "lower loves" only at the peril of meaninglessness; for instance, an alleged love of God is totally negated by an absence of all the other loves on lower rungs of the ladder.

On a less exalted and narrower range of heterolove development, there are the following classic, experiential stages:

Infatuation or "Puppy Love." Just as play is a preparation for work, so is infatuation a preparation for love. A "crush" is more fancy than real. It's a rehearsal of what I call the *Big Ache,* which consists of a mobilized mixture of surging adolescent sex and affection. It's largely a narcissistic stage of being awesomely in love with love and lost in its wondrous contemplation. Unlike heterolove, puppy love does not depend on feedback for its continued existence, so that it is often a one-way street, unrequited.

There are serious dangers in infatuation. To start, it may elicit a reciprocated but nonetheless infatuated response. This may then be falsely believed to be "it," and become the basis for a larger relationship than it deserves. Worse, it may lead to precipitous marriage and unwanted children, and end in endless grief.

Infatuation may turn out to be a magnificent obsession, like Dante's or Yeats's, not because it has virtue in itself but because its muse may massage the creative juices. On the other hand, in its garb of unrequited love, it often turns out to be a terrible obsession, sometimes comical, sometimes melodramatic, and sometimes tragic.

Quite often the nature of infatuation or of distant if not unrequited love is like that of a therapeutic transference, the attraction felt by patients toward obstetricians, father confessors, analysts, and teachers. Such feelings are best tested by talking them out. Nine times out of ten, when the passion is discharged through confrontation or with sex, the feeling of infatuation fizzles out.

Falling in Love is stage two. At its romantic best it's something like a Berlitz language school immersion course. Perception is distorted by the wish to love so that accurate criticalness and judgment are withheld. Love tends to blind the donor during this stage, but perhaps it is just as well, because without a little bit of blindness no one would fall in love, and because the inner eye may be prescient and behold a vision of its object beyond what is normally and consciously visible. The inner vision may well come to approximate reality.

This stage can go wrong as anything human can. There are people who always *fall* in love but never actually *end up* in love. Their recurrent pattern is usually a neurotic defense mechanism meant to create the illusion without following through with the commitment. In this rather passive acquisitive state the habitual faller-in-love can enjoy a seemingly enriching experience, without actually giving much of himself for any length of time. So he ends up a confirmed bachelor or she a romantic spinster.

Being in Love is a more advanced paradisiac yet active third stage during which men and women are frequently assaulted by the doubts and hurts that constitute the Big Ache. This is when the individuals are intuitively or consciously sifting and sorting each other's characteristics, to see if the click is real, if they match. Meanwhile, their consciousness is enveloped in a pink cloud and their being is deliciously raw and vulnerable. Being in love is a vibrant, enervating state, which many menopausals seek to recapture for the purpose of rejuvenation.

Unfortunately, being in love is a prelude too often taken to be the main body of the symphony itself and celebrated by a marriage that turns out to be premature, because the selection process either has not yet been finished or might have been in error. Many people claim that they've been "in love" with the same person for a lifetime. This term then refers to the magnificent state of a lively, close relationship still fraught with pain, tension, and struggle as well as a wonderful fulfillment. Under these true and tried circumstances being in love is a vital relationship not yet settled and shaken down to the more pacific state of relaxing and taking things for granted.

Mature Heterolove, stage four, is the pinnacle of this embryology. This is when all the fundamental properties of love are experienced and displayed, the ten tenets or commandments to be inventoried below become actualized. This is when the three crucial phases to be described in the next chapters—clicking, ticking, and sticking—have been completed.

VARIETIES OF HETEROLOVE

Theoretically there are as many varieties of love as there are people or at least couples forming a union. In actual fact, unions present a limited number of patterns, both in terms of type of onset and dominant type of relationship.

Onset may be very sudden, as in love at first sight, or very slow as in late-blooming love. Love at first sight may turn out to become as true as love experienced at the one-hundredth encounter if the lovers are blessed with an intuitive clairvoyance that accelerates the click, tick, and stick phases. Antipathy at first sight often proves to be love in disguise. Both will be elaborated upon in the next chapter—Clicking.

Late love, on the other hand, may be a major departure from the norm—so much so that its process reverses the law of attraction of opposites that governs young love. This exception to the rule is large and important enough to deserve a chapter to itself.

Another major dichotomy is a relationship built on neurotic necessity, when the couple has the kind of *need* of each other that forms what I call a *lean-to* union, as opposed to a healthy complementary relationship, built on want, or a desirable coupling. Both kinds will illustrate this work.

One may depict rather lightly the quality of close hetero relationships in the following terms:

1. *Fair-weather love* is idyllic but displayed principally in sunshine when everything in the garden is lovely and the roses are blooming. The first cumulus cloud, however, darkens this light love. Several storms may break its fragile stem altogether.

2. *Rough-weather love* is the obverse, because it comes out when the clouds are darkest and heaviest. It thrives on tension, troubles, quarrels. It's at its best when the enemy knocks at the door. But peaceful times are like a killing drought. Then it turns against itself.

3. *Walking on eggs* is what you're never supposed to do when love rules the household, because if you're intimidated and if tempers are frayed or poorly controlled, the obstacle to affection is almost unscalable. And yet people live like this, with their umbrellas open indoors, ready for a tempest. The delicacy of step when walking on eggs is falsely ascribed to love though it's actually due to an inherent timorousness. Peace is not worth it at that price. And the tempestuous partner, whether contrite or self-indulgent, cannot respect the loved one, or else would exercise self-control.

4. *No-touch love* could be quite comical if it weren't pathetic. Here are two people of the opposite sex, attracted to each other and having intercourse the normal way with normal frequency, yet one of them is physically undemonstrative. The no-touch technique, more appropriate in analytical psychotherapy than in any normal social situation, may go to extremes such as no manual foreplay, no kissing, no embracing, hands flat on the bed during intercourse, no more than a peck at the door. Of course, all these types of love are quirky, but the fact is that people are quirky, and even relatively healthy love can support one quirk.

5. *Sporadic love* doesn't follow the weather, biorhythms or even menstrual cycles. Often it is not even related to the ups and downs of interpersonal relationships or to extraneous events. It is just that one or other of the couple feels affection mainly in spasms—not in the usual waves of tenderness, post-coital or intracoital, but in unrelated spasms with varying qui-

escent periods in between. In these flat periods there's no demonstration of affection and sometimes a desire to be left alone. It is a hard love to figure out and harder to put up with, yet people do. Most often but not always, the fluctuations coincide with inner (endogenous) mood swings (cyclothymia).

6. *Cerebral love* is short on touch and on physical demonstrations of affection. The partner is almost ashamed to show feelings because they connote weakness. Of course, the culprit is usually the man but high-I.Q. women have been known to behave this way and sometimes they're not even that cerebral, merely introverted, or "deep." Yet their thoughts may be more loving and their side of the bond may be steadier than that of the other partner, who is usually an emotional type.

7. *Tranquil love* may be just an end stage (entropic) when the steam has gone out, the passion waned, the security increased, and even verbal communication is at a low ebb, not because the couple is out of touch but because they have little need for words. They know each other. They certainly take each other for granted. This is the kind of coupling that may go on, more or less unchanged, to a golden anniversary. You'd have a hard time imagining that the initiator of tranquility (the other partner is usually restless, at least inwardly) was ever in love, that the turbulence of his love had been weathered away.

So what's wrong with this kind of serenity, you might ask? The world needs loads of it. Maybe. But you can't know that there really is love without the Big Ache, without the waves of tenderness that moisten the eyes, without a lovers' quarrel. The other thing is that one partner in this kind of couple almost always yearns for fire. So the difficulty here, as in all types of bonding, is that rarely if ever do the feelings of *both* people coincide in this dominant tendency unless they have stuck together long enough to come to resemble each other closely.

8. *"Huggling" love* is the opposite of the no-touch cerebral or even tranquil type, in that there's a lot of kissing, hugging, embracing and even holding of hands in the basement, in front of the TV, years after marriage. It's nice and cozy and close, but the "huggling" is often for reassurance from each other, to fortify themselves against the stresses of life and tends to be in varying degrees a substitute for lovemaking. It's fine for re-

capturing the joys of adolescence in love and in foreplay (see the ticking phase when lovers act out the children within themselves); and it's fine for a camaraderie that perhaps surpasses friendship. But sex (not music) is the food of love. It plays on. There can hardly be an excess of it.

If "huggling" is merely the left-hand part to lovemaking, well and good, but if it's the right hand, the major part, it's not so good.

9. *Smothering love* occurs when not only love's natural quality of possessiveness but also its normally accompanying demonstrations of affection are excessive, at least in terms of the recipient's capacity to absorb them. It is said that you can't love a child too much. You can, because you can smother him and sometimes this is an excessive protestation of love, an overcompensation for a basic *lack* of feeling for the child himself. At best, smothering is a self-indulgence. Also, it's difficult to let go when you must, if you love too hard and too much. If this is so with a child, how much more with an adult? For one thing, some adults are not endowed with a child's tolerance for being loved. Some adults have practically no tolerance for this at all. For another, adults have to have room to grow. Yet it's difficult to fault the excessive demonstration of love (relative to the recipient's capacity) especially when the donor feels it is genuine.

I'm sure you can expand upon the kind of open-ended list I've initiated above, which makes no pretense at completeness. And I invite you to have fun and add pet loves to it.

For my part here, just a final word about inequalities, and therefore apparent inequities, in types of love. Every person is endowed with a finite quantum of libido or psychic energy, paralleling physical energy endowment. It is this energy that is invested in the love object and creates the bond called love. Some people's capacity to invest this energy, or even to allow another to invest it in themselves, is quite limited. They may be capable of a love coupling but not of parenting the child thereof. Or they may run out of energy after having two children. Or collapse with some of the vicissitudes of life or fade with the erosions of time crumbling the cement of the love bond. Even if all else is well with the selection process, the description of which takes up the bulk of this book, there may not be enough energy to go around and to cope with the stresses and strains of modern life, inclusive of one's family. There may be a considerable payment in energy spent on love and its consequences. Whether or not it is worth it can be judged, on some suitable scale, from the lives of those who have avoided the commitment and the subsequent devotions, and from how well off you think and feel you'd be if you had gone through life without heterolove and its natural consequences.

THE TEN TENETS OF LOVE

We now come to what may be the practical core of this chapter—namely the physiology or functioning of love, expressed in terms of ten tenets, both subjective and objective, whereby you can tell whether or not love exists. So here, in no particular ranked order, are ten of the most universally experienced properties of love:

1. *Constant companionship.* There is a compelling desire to share the same space, to be in the almost constant and usually the exclusive companionship of the loved one. This is evidence of the feeling of incompleteness that single individuals experience and of their biologically based yearning for union. Parting is more than a "sweet sorrow"; it is a "little death." The poignancy of separation, the quality of its anxiety, is a subjective measure of the tensile strength of the bond. "Did you miss me and how much?" is the habitual test of this tenet. The final test, of course, is death itself and the length, quantity, and quality of bereavement. In great dramatic love, life has no meaning without the other partner; hence Juliet, then Romeo, and then Juliet again are no more (they killed themselves, Juliet twice over), nor are Darby and Joan (they fell dead over each other), nor are the hundreds of thousands who chose to die, one way or another, upon losing their love. Perhaps the chief factor preventing suicide, other than those codified in law or in religion, is the feeling that life is a gift entrusted to the person and not in one's power to dispose of. On the contrary, one has a responsibility to cherish and enrich it, to live it to full potential. Perhaps this feeling is simply a

psychological correlate to biological survival, because the threads of life are otherwise weak and easy to snap. At any rate, it is probably this sense of sin that forbids self-indulgent suicide, along with whatever other responsibility is bestowed or acquired. But there must be millions who have become the walking dead or who have lived an empty-heart existence upon the loss of a loved one.

When in each other's company, true lovers feel very close, literally in touch; in fact, touching may be a compelling desire *("le délire de toucher")*. Another sign is the incomparable feeling of contentment in lying together in bed, whether locked against the powers of darkness in a postcoital embrace of tenderness or just hugging.

2. *Sharing everything.* The compulsion to share is as strong as that for companionship. Sharing refers to all experiences, to good and bad news, to feelings and memories, to dreams, to things treasured, objects possessed in common, like home and children, as well as those possessed separately. "I must tell you" is the verbal component of this desire. Unshared, an object capturing a lover's momentary interest lacks currency; but sharing brings its value to inflationary levels. This communicative aspect is not necessarily verbal. In fact, couples too often dump troubles and trivia on one another. They empty their minds on each other as they would garbage bins. They lay it on each other. And too often they treat each other as parent, friend, lover, spouse, physician, and psychiatrist combined. Not only is such overly verbal communication unhealthy, but it is also a disutility, if not a denial, of love.

"Lack of communication" is a buzz term often used as a signal of early marital breakdown. Its abuse has loosened its meaning, so that it may mean almost anything including a drastically diminished frequency of intercourse.

Most people, however "open" they say or think they are, however communicative or extroverted, in fact rarely talk about important things. Even when they dump in the name of "honesty" they usually manage to avoid the pith of truth.

One may go a step further and state that the more important a thing is, the less it is talked about. But there are interesting variations of personality in this respect. Introverts, because of their better introspection, are more intolerant of small, time-filling talk and more prone to talk about the "deeper" things that matter, while extroverts tend to chatter away.

The quality of sharing in whatever style, whether nonverbal communication, body language, or talk, is a measure of the quality of love. There is, of course, a heavy cultural component here as there is throughout the manifestations of love. In what E. T. Hall calls "high contextual cultures" like those of the older nations of Asia and the Middle East, much less verbal exchange is necessary than in "low contextual cultures" like the North American and European. This is not because people of the ancient Asiatic cultures are tongue-tied, over-restrained or inscrutable. It is because they fully understand each other through habitual modes of nonverbal communication. They don't have to run off at the mouth.

Lovers also can do this, once they share life together, in the sticking phase. They can read each other quickly, not only out of empathy, out of overalertness and sensitivity to each other, but also because they expose a raw receptor surface, as it were, to each other. They have insight into each other's beings. As we shall see in Chapter 4: Sticking, love is built on a beautiful symmetry of shared personages dwelling in the hinterlands of the lovers' minds, so that they know each other literally inside out.

When there's no love left in marriage or when there's never been any love, the couple dreads to be left alone in each other's company, especially shut in together on a holiday. They'd do anything to escape this situation: bring their children or friends along, party day and night.

One of the rather rare circumstances in which sex, as an accurate *amor-meter,* is no measure of love in a marriage, is when a couple can copulate lustily but otherwise have nothing to say to each other when alone together.

3. *Empathy and identification.* This property is an extension of two people being in touch telepathically or, more accurately, intuitively. The fusion of bodies, hearts, and souls, particularly the fusion of personages of the inner self in a love union, leads to full empathy. This also leads to lovers becoming like each other, feeling part of each other. This property resembles the empathy for each other felt by identical twins.

But unlike the empathy between identical twins or the empathy among family members, empathy in love exists between people who were strangers in the beginning. It is not biologically based. In view of this facility for empathy, for an understanding without words, one wonders why the classical lovers in romantic novels so often misunderstood or ˙misperceived each other, with tragic consequence. Perhaps gross errors in communication and in the transmission of feelings occur before the finer tuning that takes place when clicking is finalized. But if there were a lack of empathy and communication between people who allegedly love each other, one would doubt that a true love bond existed between them.

4. *Giving and taking.*   Love, as I said, is a two-way street. Because people vary in energy (libido), dominance, aggressivity, and generosity, one always gives more or at least differently than the other—for a time. But eventually balance must be restored or else the relationship will deteriorate.

Before leaping to the attack of the passive, submissive, ungenerous takers of love, let us realize that it is far safer to give love than to rely on receiving love, for she or he who gives can also take away, but he or she who is a passive recipient has far less direct control.

In healthy love there is a balance, and certainly there is no sexual stereotyping between the giver and the receiver. When an imbalance exists, another paradox arises. The one who is dependent, the one who is incapable of giving or of equalizing the partner's swamping energy, is likely to become more resentful more quickly than the donor. The reason is that you always bite the hand that feeds you because you resent deeply your inferior, dependent position.

5. *Supervulnerability.*   One of several emotional payments to be made for the privilege of love is a strong tendency to be hurt by real or imagined rejection. Being in love is not unlike handing a person (the loved one) a weapon knowing that he or she knows exactly where your Achilles' heel is, that a strike at the relationship will hurt more than anything in the world. In the early days of uncertainty, while clicking is taking place and things are being sorted out, genuine misperceptions, misinterpretation, and mistakes may occur. If the selection proc-

ess goes well, things sort themselves out and wounds heal. Then the Big Ache abates and the lovers feel like superheroes. But once certain thresholds in the ticking stage have been crossed, once troth is pledged and the relationship becomes exclusive, there must be an automatic, perhaps blind, trust placed upon one's partner, for they both know that they can hurt each other. This trust is as necessary as is honor among thieves or *détente* among nations capable of nuclear warfare. And yet things are never equitably balanced or fair. One member of the dyad is always more vulnerable than the other. And one is more capable of inflicting hurt than the other.

Vulnerability is an early test of love. If hurts are not inflicted with malice aforethought, their scars strengthen the ongoing relationship. The fear of hurt hanging over lovers, as soon as they've declared themselves, is much worse than the hurt itself.

One of the chief causes of vulnerability is feeling that one is unlovable or unworthy of being loved. When this is actually true and evident, then it is easier to bear than when the belief is false. Unlovableness is imagined when people feel inferior because they harbor some evil inside themselves (manifestations of their *shadow*) or because in their own eyes they've fallen short of some high mark set by ambition or because of a social gap in their backgrounds. The hanging judge perched on their shoulders cannot be convinced that they're the equal of those who love them. "If only they knew, if only the love scales were to fall off her/his eyes," is the verbally eradicable thought. In short, because its origin is inside the mind, imaginary inferiority is insatiable, a fiend for rejection. What the unlovable—real or imagined—must realize is that opposites attract one another. The bad attract the good, and the ugly the beautiful. Also the "inferior" person must realize that, happily, on a lover's scale of value, the priorities may differ from his or hers. Consequently what seems to be or indeed may be inferiority to you, like big buttocks or a stutter or an inability to think in abstracts, means little or nothing to your lover. Indeed, the very thing for which you judge yourself harshly or for which you feel ashamed—like a stutter—may also be the very thing that charms the eyes or ears of the lover. This gap in judgment between the two widens because the possessor of a real or imagined inferiority dwells on it until it is blown way out of proportion, while the possessor of a superiority tends to ignore it, if not belittle it.

Eventually, as the lovers influence one another, a shift of values occurs with increasing self-acceptance and confidence.

If the inferiority is imaginary, however, and if the person considers herself or himself to be essentially unlovable, things are much more difficult to rectify, particularly if the person with inferiority feelings also possesses a truly lovable persona or social mask. The trouble here is that the sweeter the persona the more horrid the shadow, the inside creature who trots out at night in sleep, like Transylvanian lycanthropes or the willies. Such a person perfumes and powders the persona in an effort to hide the rottenness he feels inside because of this shadow. What such a person doesn't realize is that everyone has a shadow that stands in contrasting opposition to his persona. Inside a King Kong–like creature there's a frail shadow like Snow White, and inside Dr. Jekyll there is, of course, Mr. Hyde. Even if such people realize intellectually that others possess the same kind of inward contrast, even if they know that all that glitters is not gold, still they find it almost impossible to believe emotionally that anyone could be quite so bad as themselves. There's an inverted conceit in this kind of commonly encountered mental set-up with consequent heightened vulnerability.

Now that we're halfway through this rather comprehensive list of love's properties, let us recognize that they are interdependent and overlapping. Yet they do show sufficiently discrete features to be counted separately as criteria that test a love relationship.

6. *Possessiveness.* Heterolove is rapaciously possessive. The first tenet stressed exclusivity and elitism. There may well be an underlying sociobiological motive for this, such as ensuring paternity, the parity of a chosen genetic mix, concomitant responsibility, and ownership. But the fact is that no love except the paternal (and filial in a way) yields willingly its love object. Heterolove holds on to its object like dear life. Hence love tends to be monogamous. Human sex, like that of domes-

ticated animals and of a few wild species, is polygamous; but love, because of its firm exclusive hold on the dyad, renders the metamorphosed sex drive monogamous.

This means that there cannot be multiple, simultaneous love bonds (bonds with more than one man or woman at a time) and that all multiple, swinging, athletic sex performances and "open marriages" are denials of love. They may be all right in a solidly connubial ménage but they are *not* a part of true love, however much the exponents of these aberrant relationships protest. (All minority groups must protest in order to *feel* equal even if they aren't.)

So possessive is love that even time spent on necessary endeavors, like work, is resented, let alone a sharing of deep physical or mental intimacy with another body and mind. Where each other's body (mind and soul) is rightly considered to be an exclusive territory, the possessiveness imperative reigns supreme. If a loving wife is not somewhat disturbed by her husband spending more waking hours with his private secretary than with herself, there may be something lukewarm in her affection.

Yet there is a thin red line between possessiveness, which is not only acceptable but actually a measure of caring, and jealousy, which is unacceptable and destructive. At any rate, both jealousy and utter denial of love's healthy possessiveness are morbid. A touch of jealousy in one's partner is the best cure for a lover who's beginning to doubt whether mutual love still exists.

Although there may not be much *general* trust between lovers, sometimes for good reason, there must be enough to sustain the feeling of fidelity and preserve its implicit monogamy.

7. *Dependency.* This is yet another tithe that one pays willingly or that is exacted by the union of love, which, like any union worth its salt, claims its dues. There is a certain amount of one's self, of one's independence, in fact quite a chunk of freedom, that one must give up when one functions holistically as a love unit, a dyad (a triad or more, if there are children in the established family). One feels and one is socially *attached.* "Do you know where your spouse is?" As a member of a love union, you cannot just pick up and go anywhere

and do anything you want, when you want, because you're tied to the strings of a close relationship. You have to ask and obtain a degree of consent if not outright permission. Generally you act not singly but in agreement; also you report back on independent activities. You even automatically report thoughts and feelings.

Some of this dependency is unconscious. Much of it is consciously and willingly yielded when the realization comes about the surprising extent of subjugation that has taken place; for instance, not being able to go to bed ahead of or later than the other partner. Some dependency is part of the responsibility of a working partnership. But some may be exacted as unwillingly as are union dues or income tax, yet you must not forget the benefits. The giving up of freedom is a tacit *quid pro quo* arrangement. For instance, you tell what you've been up to and you get a report in return so that you needn't wander into the exquisitely painful throes of uncertainty.

Dependency, especially the emotional kind, places a reliance on somebody else always being there, on fidelity and the reciprocation of love—all of which reinforce the vulnerability of love.

8. *Tolerance.* This is an essential property in the physiology of love because it is directly in the service of a cardinal principle governing the process of matchmaking (see Chapter 2: Clicking). As a consequence, there is a dialectical tension, and quarrels break out which are meant to be *constructive,* in the service of a conciliation of opposites, rather than competitive and motivated by the wish to dominate (the battle of the sexes).

The function of these quarrels is to bring about a complementary relationship by bridging the gulf in perceptions, judgments, and values, through tolerance. Love stretches tolerance to the limit of endurance, especially in the sticking phase of living cheek to cheek. No wonder love has to be "blind" in the beginning (during falling and being in love); otherwise a couple might never make it.

Sometimes mutual tolerance is in short supply, or else the differences are too great to be bridgeable. In this case, something has to give and it is generally the bond—love itself. If dialectical tension and quarrels break the burgeoning bond of love, it is just as well because it means that the partners are poles apart.

There are other attributes that go with tolerance, namely persistence or doggedness, and resilience, and they enable couples to stick together. But there must be moderation even in tolerance. Constant bending backwards to please one's partner and continually "working hard on one's marriage" are inadvisable. Once you start "working" on a relationship and once this becomes hard, rather than a joyous, automatic and unconscious tolerance, the writing is on the wall. Usually it is at the end of a close relationship that this happens. Then it's hardly worth trying because you cannot substitute shoestrings for the weathered and hardened cement of love. This is contrary to journalistic matrimonial advice, but it is a fact of clinical experience. Mind you, I'm not speaking of running away at the first sign of trouble. We are talking of turning love into calvary. Constant abuse is a denial of love, even though some physical abuse, even to a degree of battering, is done in the name of love by people overwhelmed by uncontrollable passion.

Holding on at all costs becomes a sign of sickness, bordering on idiocy or masochism, rather than a manifestation of healthy tolerance. What one shouldn't abide are abuse or continuous overtesting by a partner; also indifference, and continuous rejection. The recipient of such treatment is a patsy and is rightly regarded as weak, not merely love-sick but a fool who can never earn respect. While, as you shall shortly see, I don't hold that a high mutual respect is an absolute part of love, it is a frequent and welcome companion to love. And one cannot have respect for a person one treats habitually with indifference (a denial of love in itself) or with abuse, rejection, or constant tests of loyalty. When a person begins to *behave* in this way, however, after a period of loving, either he's run out of it or else he's become sick. This latter situation poses a catch-22 problem. Anyone can be struck down by mental illness at one point in time and anyone can run into an emotional conflict resulting in neurotic behavior. There is no reason a lover would treat this occurrence any differently then a physical disorder and every reason to apply tender love and care. And yet a chronic, persistent neurotic disorder on an emotional basis (*not* a mental illness) is incompatible with loving. Loving is far too altruistic to allow much psychic energy to be lavished on oneself, as a chronic neurotic requires to do. So what do you do in a case like that? What do you do about abnormal behaviors like compulsions to gamble or to drink or eat to the point of ruin, alcoholism, or obesity? In general you do your best, you stick it out for the longest time and as much as you can with love and sympathy. And where it becomes abundantly clear that the person's mental state—say an agoraphobia of long standing—is incompatible with his having much love left, you quit. If there's enough love left, you may then achieve a spectacular cure.

Morally and mentally it makes a great deal of difference if you were aware, however dimly, of the early warning signs of your partner's abnormal behavior before the click of coupling occurred, as opposed to encountering the condition much later during an established relationship. If you had had the slightest inkling of abnormality before you gave your troth, you must have *counted* on it—it must have been what you wanted, however much you've rationalized since then that he or she would grow out of it, that love will heal, that you'll bring about a beneficial influence. This situation is much like a self-caused accident; the only accidental thing about it usually is the extent of injury, not the accident itself. Similarly here, the only unexpected and undesirable factor must be the *extent* of abnormality, not its occurrence.

I'm quite aware that as you read these words, particularly if you're an interested party, you will reject, and even hotly deny them. People in this position always do. But the whole idea in this book is to try to understand. If you have the patience and forebearance to read on and into the nature of the mechanism of love matching you will see why I make these assertions. By the time you come to Passages (Chapter 6) you will see how this works out and how you bear some responsibility for *choosing* someone with potentially abnormal behavior.

Now if there was absolutely *no* sign of disorder or trouble before you decided to stick together (hard to believe!) and if your partner absolutely *flipped* over and became the opposite to what she/he was when you first met, even then your intuition should have told you that this would happen (see the Flipover in Chapter 4: Sticking). You should have reckoned with it. It is only if you're sure that a change occurred in the personality, *not* a flipover or in reaction to you, but a change sometime after you began living together that you're cleared of the original responsibility for making that choice; indeed that you willed to make that match, however unconsciously.

Now the moral and mental question is this: Under which of these three conditions do you stay the longest and attempt to help bring about a change?

1. If you reckoned albeit unconsciously *with* the disorder and made a teepee-type relationship, you're not likely to want out, unless you've been cured or your partner's gone to extreme lengths. It is here that you enter into a real dilemma, though. In order for either of you two to change for the better, your faultily built relationship must loosen up if not break up altogether. Yet you have a moral responsibility to stick because you knew what you were doing (at one level) and why.

2. If a flipover has occurred and if the writing had been on the wall early in the relationship or if the partner's behavior is largely in response to yours—say you've shut off sex and he's started drinking more—you should stick it out and see if you can change yourself in order to correct the situation.

3. If, on the other hand, you're reasonably sure that you had little or nothing to do with a change for the worse occurring late in the sticking-together phase, then your loyalty is being challenged rather than your sense of responsibility and justice. This then becomes a disease or disorder like any other and you've pledged yourself to hold on "in sickness and in health."

Ultimately however, provided the condition is emotionally based, if you've given it a good old college try for long enough, it is better all round to quit than to sacrifice, because by then the chances are that you and the dyad have become a pivotal part of the abnormality in the personality or in the relationship.

9. *Self-sacrifice.* This refers both to an inner, tacit giving

of yourself and to the actual giving life itself. In a massive twenty-five-year study of the willingness to give one's life for someone or something (and as part of my study of attitudes toward death and dying), I found that nearly everyone who was healthy stated categorically that he or she would be willing to sacrifice his life for loved ones. This turned out to be usually one's life-mate—the object of heterolove—and/or its products—one's children. When there were no lovers or children, then one's original family, parents and siblings, would be in first place. Friendship, except when there was no heterolove object, children, or family, came a distant fourth. Rarely was there any object of sacrifice beyond those four. While one can never be sure in the clutch, that those who said that they would behave this way would actually do so, the regularity of this response established a norm of intention, a *mens rea* or mental climate.

This means, among many other things, that people today don't hold their own lives as the dearest objects, that man doesn't live for survival alone. Love object(s) come first. And this is remarkable in an era of disbelief, of weakening religion and of existential anxiety without much hope of another existence beyond the present. Such then is the supreme value placed on love.

But then the willingness to die is the extreme on a range of possible sacrifice. Inside that limit is the willingness to give a lot of one's self to the binding of the union. This harks back to the points made about tolerance and to a major drawback in chosen love, namely a partial loss of individualism and freedom. We shall not argue, in this context, whether the willingness to sacrifice so much for love is good or bad, or whether it is a sign of the times when too much hope is invested in romance, because we'll come to that presently.

Suffice it to note now that it isn't unusual in the social experience of mankind to be willing to give one's life for something that transcends its felt value. Man has always been prepared to sacrifice himself for a greater good, whether this be friendship or his country. Very likely this "instinct" is healthy because it is based on biological altruism, on safeguarding one's own genes, one's culture, or one's species.

Yet the same note of caution needs to be appended here as

we did to the eighth tenent of love, to tolerance. Unnecessary sacrifice, masochism, or futile heroism do not have a place of honor today. A sacrificial response at the whim or the willful demand of the partner is not an integral part of love, either on the part of the one demanding it or the one complying. On the other hand, when real need and sacrifice are in conjunction, the unselfishness of love is truly tested. This is reflected in the verbal habit of lovers when they ask, however idly, "How much do you love me?" The automatic answer is "More than life itself." It should carry the ring of truth.

10. *Uncertainty.* This is one of the most interesting and perhaps paradoxical attributes of love. There are at least three fundamental reasons for a feeling of uncertainty:

First, no one can see into someone else's head and know for sure what is going on there. No two people (not even Siamese twins) can occupy the same space at the same time. You cannot be sure, no matter what someone else says or does, that he or she *feels* the same way you do about what he said or did. Words may help or confuse. Actions do speak louder and truer than words. But both words and actions can be misleading on three different mental levels:

a) At the point of perception (and cognition), when you are the receiver of messages of love, there is so much of you yourself that you put into the message, there is so much wishful thinking, that you are liable to distort these messages either way: You may believe you "see" the same love when it isn't there or disbelieve it when it is.

b) When you give out the signals of love, you may do so not because you really feel what you are supposed to, but for effect in order to get something back; or just because you are supposed to behave that way or for some other motive, which could be quite dastardly.

c) You yourself may not be sure about what you feel, and certainly you can't be sure that you feel the *same* way as your partner, when you give out these messages. A great deal of the actual work of love is carried out largely unbeknown to you. All you know is how you yourself *feel* and you assume it is the same as your partner.

This uncertainty is mainly due to the importance we place on feelings. If we looked more objectively at the bond itself rather than second guess how our partners really feel about us, the uncertainty would diminish.

Second, feelings change. It is their main function to change fast and to act as early warning signals for adaptive responses. Feelings are elusive and unreliable. Their function parallels the quick and initial (short-term) responses of the nervous system, when the body acts by fast reflex. And certainly the feelings of love change. They change progressively in the course of clicking, ticking, and sticking together and they fluctuate with other feelings elicited in everyday life. They also change with mood. Moreover, like any emotion, feelings of love become exhausted unless replenished and they atrophy and decay from disuse or lack of feedback—hence the need for reciprocity.

Third, but overlapping with the first point of the subjectivity of feelings, is the fact that the feelings of love, as opposed to the process itself, are only the tips of the iceberg both in terms of one's own awareness and the partner's perceptions. What goes on underneath is what counts in the long run.

Therefore, uncertainty dominates at least the earlier phases of love and it persists for longer than you think—otherwise love would lapse into a too-tranquil laissez-faire state of taking things for granted, of entropy, without tension, without the real vibrancy of life.

The ability to withstand uncertainty is the most powerful test of mental health, of inner resources and balance. Love itself, the ongoing bond and a mixture of wish, intuition, and faith, counteract this uncertainty.

I know from clinical experience that those who say that they are absolutely sure of their partner's or spouse's love and fidelity—especially those who take each other for granted and have failed to communicate meaningfully for some time—are *always wrong.* When I examine their partners I find that they are usually out of love or that the loving has eroded. Moreover, in such cases I usually get a confession of the same illicit relationships their partners would stake their lives on their spouses or lovers not having had. This is yet another kind of love blindness, occurring in the latter stages of an anemic, atrophic pairing state, when the wish to hang on is father to the thought of love and fidelity and when the partner is the last to know.

Whereas those who say that they aren't sure but they think, feel or hope that the partner loves them and/or that he or she has been faithful, these are usually in luck. In fact, I can tell you with a high level of accuracy, from the manner as well as the over- or underemphasized (or the just-appropriate) degree of certainty exhibited, whether or not the partner will confirm his/her love and/or fidelity.

It is because of this uncertainty that the incessant questions of lovers come up: "Do you love me? How much? How do I know you do?" And those who protest too much either by overquestioning or in the fervor of their response are suspect, if not liars.

Now we're in a position to analyze the components of the Big Ache, that delicious feeling in the guts and heart shot through with doubts and stabbed through with pangs and pains. Its sources are: uncertainty, vulnerability, possessiveness, dependency coupled with the yearning for constant companionship, and the natural fluctuation in the balance between loving and being loved. This adds up to half of the ten tenets of love.

You may argue with the nitty gritties of some of these ten tenets of love and indeed there is nothing original or sacred about any of them. The originality, if any, of this section stems from putting together the pieces regarded by general experience to be attributes of love.

You will have noticed that left this way these ten commandments actually add up to a kind of test of love. (See the test at the end of the chapter.) A test of romantic love includes the status of sex in the relationship.

Love is the world's most powerful aphrodisiac. How else can one explain the familiarity that brings not contempt but continual excitement? Necessity alone won't do it, for it is the mother of promiscuous invention. Guilt won't do it because this sort of moral guilt or the fear of incurring it is out of fashion just now. And yet most couples in love go past the first five years of sexual excitation by an increasingly familiar body, past the seven-year itch, and past the ravages of births and aging; sometimes they go on making love to only one body for the better part of a lifetime.

There are, in fact, only two powerful and genuine aphrodisiacs: love and sex itself. As for the latter, the more you do it, the more you want to do it. The less you do it, the less you want to do it. That is the law of appetites, which applies to drinking, food, sleep, and sex equally. As for the aphrodisiac quality of the Spanish fly (cantharides) all it does is blister the urinary tract. It's all in the skin of the beholder! If it weren't for love's aphrodisiac qualities how would the beholder ever become amorously excited by the beauty in the beast? How could one explain that there is nearly always someone for everyone, whatever their physical shortcomings?

The frequency, intensity, quality, and satisfaction of love-making are the quickest rough indicators of love itself. Sex is an amor-meter.

There are, in addition to the ten tenets, two important mental states commonly accompanying love. The first is happiness, both the active kind that comes from the satisfaction of pleasure and the fulfillment of expectations pertinent to love, and the more passive kind that comes from contentment. On the negative side of an active fulfillment of happiness there is the discharge of tension, which soothes the Big Ache. And on the negative side of contentment is the built-in security of not having to hassle out there and chase romantic rainbows. The happiness of love is a by-product rather than an intrinsic part of love. Yet, to the extent to which happiness is not a fool's paradise, to the extent to which it represents an achievement, a well-built bond, it is a validation of love. Yet happiness is not as reliable as it could be because the capacity for happiness varies too much with the individual.

The other prevalent emotion emerging in love is tenderness. It pricks the dampening eyes when it rises unexpectedly on the crest of love waves. It may be excruciatingly delightful in the postcoital moments. But it keeps throbbing and increasing by increments to incredible levels with each milestone passed, like marriage, childbirth and child rearing. Yet tenderness is also a by-product of love, rather than an intrinsic feature, because its manifestations may be vague or suppressed or disguised (usually by males) when it is taken to be a weakness. In some of the more violent, turbulent, rough yet genuine loves, little if any tenderness is shown. Tenderness is an unreliable index of love for the same reason as is happiness; it varies too much with the capricious endowments of the individual and with his culture.

On the other hand, there is a trio of love associates that comes closer than happiness or tenderness to securing a place within its ten commandments. The commonest and most controversial of these is liking. Yet liking and loving don't always go together because in the family we sometimes dislike the people we love on account of "blood being thicker than water." Furthermore, we tend to dislike some of our own children, despite loving them. We know (most of the time) why we dislike them. The usual reason is that the children (and people generally) who are seen to be most like us, particularly those who share our weaknesses and faults, are the ones we dislike. This conforms to the principle that likes repel. But when we ourselves choose to form a close relationship we are attracted to opposites, or should be. Therefore if we really dislike or come to dislike somebody we allegedly love, and if this happens because the partner is too much like us, especially if he or she shares the very characteristics we dislike in ourselves, we've made a grave error in selection. The catch is, however, that in late love, as we shall see, or in mature love when people have done their growing and are relatively fixed in personality, this law of opposites attracting is reversed in that likes attract one another. The relationship is not complementary, as with opposites, but supplementary—the coupling is not a new creation but an extension of the dyad. So it is entirely possible in this case for dislike to occur. Indeed it is possible, even when the matching is done on opposites, for certain unlikable or incompatible hitherto ignored characteristics to emerge. This may not invalidate loving altogether.

The basic reason likes dislike each other is that they tend to compete, and competitors cannot coexist. They battle for supremacy. This is the real battle between the sexes, when they are not only equal, as they should be, but also resemble each other far too much.

Furthermore, personalities change continuously in an evolving relationship, especially in the accelerated personality change I call the flipover. Then new characteristics may emerge which are disliked. For instance, a dominant female may find that the mouse she married has flipped over and become a lion. She may dislike this situation or the characteristics of this kind of manhood, at least on the surface (otherwise she'd have chosen a lion of a man in the first place) yet she may still love him and the evolving relationship may still be valid and valuable.

Finally, in the transition between ticking and sticking together, especially with the inception of cohabitation, quite a cluster of dislikable, shocking microbehaviors and habits may reveal themselves for the first time. They test tolerance severely. So liking is not necessarily a part of loving.

Trust is also much talked about and generally agreed to be a *must* in a close relationship. But this just isn't so. It is the specifics and degree rather than the presence or absence of trust that make it an unreliable attribute. A lover may generally distrust her or his mate for perfectly good reasons: The mate may be a thief, gambler, drunk, and liar. She/he may, for instance, suffer from the Walter Mitty syndrome clinically called *pseudologia phantastica* or compulsive lying. This does not mean that she/he is untrustworthy in the love relationship. Nor does it mean that such a person distrusted the love relationship, which is just as well, for suspicion of infidelity would be the straw to break the relationship's back. And yet there are lovers who suspect each other of infidelity, sometimes for good reasons, without it destroying the very tentative relationship that may then exist—tentative because of the monogamy of love and its possessiveness.

Once again, this situation is much worse when the reasons for distrust or the suspicions of infidelity are imaginary than if they were real and pushed to the extremes of morbid jealousy or to delusions—which are totally incompatible with love. This trust is a so-so variable.

Finally there is respect. Let me say at once that it is obviously best to have all three associates of love as well as happiness and tenderness than not to have them. It is just a question of their relative power as intrinsic attributes of love. Respect is probably the weakest and least reliable associate of this lot, particularly when it is not earned. There may be no reason why one lover should respect the other, who may be a cheat, a blackguard, or even a criminal. And we all know that all these types frequently have devoted lovers. There may be a severe ideological split between lovers when one of them is of opposing political views, an enemy agent or an Archie Bunker, while the other isn't and does not respect such people. Also, in some cultures like the Asiatic, the woman is supposed to respect her husband no matter what, whether he deserves it or not. This kind of compulsion hardly amounts to the kind of earned respect that ideally accompanies love.

We are left then with ten cardinal commandments of love, a sensitive sex *amor-meter* and some five associates on which to test the existence and value of this bond. Clearly love is possible without one or two of these, so long as the majority of these tenets rules the relationship.

LOVE ON THE SHRINK

There once was a time when people's psychic energy was deeply invested in many different high-level love objects: agape, God, the king, brotherhoods, friendship, mankind and charity, the many faces of power including pomp and circumstance, the majesty of the law, the pursuit of truth and science, fervently believed ideologies, the seven creative arts, the many performing arts and crafts, and so on. The parade of love objects seemed endless. Heterolove was a junior or perhaps a more silent object then.

At present there seems to be an attrition in all those "higher" objects of love. As I have mentioned, when I asked them, people no longer said that they would give their lives or even half their allotted years for the sake of any of those reasons. Indeed such manifestations of higher devotion are rare. Despite little renaissances in arts and crafts, despite annual awards of Nobel prizes for some of these rare pursuits, and despite religious minirevivals, it appears that most of these grand loves are dead. On their ashes has arisen, phoenixlike, heterolove to fill the empty spaces in the human heart.

There are many, many reasons for this state of affairs. With the break-up of the monoelite a fantastic fragmentation has occurred. Religiosity is broken up in almost as many new cults annually as there are new chemical radicals thrown into our environment. The Godhead is weakened by many little gods and by the suspended judgments of agnosticism. Power is broken up, its bases eroded.

Part of this generalized fragmentation of society is that of the family, now reduced virtually to infranuclear bosoms—the one parent homes. And there are, again, many, many reasons for this: devaluation of human reproduction for its own sake, hence the devaluation of motherhood; birth control; enormous social and physical mobility (the average North American moves once in every five years); the emergence of an adolescent force; increased life expectancy; and women's liberation movements. Presently there'll be a man's liberation movement. Then we'll have nothing more to liberate except perhaps our minds.

In the face of this threatened catastrophe we hang on to what seems nearest at hand, which is mostly heterolove, some family love, and friendship. No wonder then that "instinctively" we look to love to make things better, in every way.

We wish that love would protect us from urban stress, work stress and world crises—which we intuitively feel could be solved by more love. But most of all we wish that love would protect our private core from all the vicissitudes of a world crumbling around us. Of course, love can't do all that. So once again, we become our own worst enemy. We are beginning to be leery of love. We avoid it because we feel it has let us down. We erect defenses against it and these defenses do us harm, as some of our physical, mental, and social defenses harmed us. This makes matters a great deal worse, if not entirely hopeless. Without the courage to risk loving again and again, perhaps a little wiser each time, we are left with nothing at all to hope for in our gloom-and-doom forecast. Despite the shortcomings measured against our unreasonable expectations of it, love is still the best thing that's left to us this side of Eden.

A TEST OF LOVING

Part A

Answer each question by checking off one answer only. Add up the score as instructed at the end.

	Yes	Not Quite	No

1. I have an overwhelming desire to be with a person (I think I love) as much as possible.

2. I have an overwhelming desire to share everything (myself and things) with that person.

3. I feel as if I were part of that other person so that I can feel for and identify with him/her.

4. I feel loved by that person (it feels like warmth and being cared about).

5. I feel peculiarly vulnerable to that person, because I know he/she can hurt me more than anybody else and because I am defenseless against him/her.

6. I feel I want to have a reciprocated (give-and-take), long-term exclusive relationship with that person.

7. I feel possessive of the person I care for in terms of sharing intimacy, affection, and time though this does not amount to jealousy.

8. I can tolerate well (and am even attracted by) the many (or deep) differences between myself and that person.

	Yes	Not Quite	No
9. I think (feel) that I am willing to do *anything* for that person, including giving my life for her/his sake.			
10. Although I feel I love that person, I am not absolutely sure of this all the time and am far less sure of my feelings (of love) being reciprocated.			I have no such uncertainties.

Scoring
Score 2 for Yes, 1 for Not Quite, 0 for No. Add all scores up.

Interpretation

18–20	You love well and the love bond is good.
15–18	You are on the way to loving well (or else have ceased to love better) and the bond is promising (or dissolving).
10–14	The whole thing is in doubt (either your loving or your pair bonding).
under 10	Forget the whole thing (unless you've just met).

Part B

	Yes	Not Quite	No
1. The person described (in Part A) is as attractive sexually as anyone I know.			
2. I'm sure that five years of sexual cohabitation will not diminish (or have not diminished) my attraction to him/her.			
3. I enjoy as much giving sexual pleasure as taking it.			
4. Sex occasions much tenderness.			

	Yes	Not Quite	No

5. Sex brings us ever closer.

6. There's nothing I'd refuse him/her sexually.

7. I like him/her.

8. I trust him/her.

9. I respect him/her.

10. Nothing makes me happier than he/she.

Scoring

Score 2 for Yes, 1 for Not Quite, 0 for No. Add scores from Part A and Part B together.

Interpretation

40–35	You're in love and you love well.
35–30	You're heading into romantic love (or you've been there).
29–25	The relationship is in doubt: If most of the score comes from Part A, you've got a friendship; if from Part B, you've got a sexual relationship.
24–20	Very doubtful there's much in it or much left.
19–15	Maybe it's a little bit of sex and/or a little bit of love, but not enough to write home about.
under 14	Forget it.

2

Clicking

*What matters most to each man
has seemingly already been decided for him.*

—SANTAYANA

Let us take the next step toward unraveling the eons of
wool-gatherings that have woven a mystique around romantic
love by asking ourselves specifically how love comes about.
What is the nature of this process that ends in close intimacy?
What are the steps to loving? Through what miraculous transformation does sex become love?

In order to make these stations of the cross of love crystal
clear, we must pursue several moderately difficult lines of
thought.

First, we shall describe the sequence of events in romantic
encounters and thus expose the transitions of love.

Second, we shall propose the fundamental theory of matchmaking, which is the basis of the evolution of all close elective
intimacies, including sexual relationships and heterolove itself.
This theory identifies the nature of the particular force of the
attraction (and repulsion) that moves love along its evolutionary path. The *pirouette* of *clicking,* the *entre-chat* of *ticking*
and the *pas de deux* of *sticking* together are beautifully cho-
reographed steps propelled by the force of attraction. They
lend their names to the ensuing three chapters. Perception and
motivation play fundamental roles in guiding attraction.

Third, we will discern the elements of a love match, and
analyze their discrete components, the molecules that make up

their chemistry. Once again the synchronized eyes of the beholders and the motivations stemming from both personal and collective unconscious sift and sort through these components, ordering them into a priority. This should bring us to the magical formula materializing in the crucible of love. Sex is the forever-reassessed catalyst.

Fourth and last, we shall enlarge our views of this whole process with a comprehensive exposition of the inner forces at work in the course of making a match. A galaxy of coupling stories will illustrate the summary of these ideas. Following these stories will be a test for rating the initial goodness of fit of your own burgeoning love match.

In the next three chapters, we shall penetrate increasingly into the depths of the seemingly mysterious human psyche in order to reveal the *internal* or subjective happenings crowned by love. We shall look at the psychoarchitecture of lovers in order to see how the love bond consolidates between them. This means peering into the relatively inaccessible recesses of the mind, behind the many layered veils, behind the barely ajar doors of the unconscious mind.

And then you will see that the philosopher Santayana, quoted at the beginning of this chapter, was closer to being right than he ever knew, when it comes to love. What society doesn't sort out for the future lovers before they ever meet is determined by the unconscious mind afterward.

Until the dawn of this century marriages were arranged by the heads of the families involved, often with the help of matchmakers. Perhaps for the majority of mankind this is still being done. Now that for many love has taken over from the convention of arranged marriages, is there a real gain in freedom of choice when so much is predetermined by the forces of the unconscious? And are love marriages better matched than arranged ones?

THE SEQUENCE OF ROMANTIC ENCOUNTER

Of course, nothing in real life is experienced in splendid isolation. Events occur holistically and continuously. The stages about to be described are no exception. They are relatively arbitrary steps devised for the purpose of clear description. They may be compressed and accelerated as in true "love at first sight." Or they may be splayed out and protracted into a late-blossoming love. Or they may be aborted. Worse still, they may be regularly and recurrently aborted, so that love is never quite achieved. Or they may not happen at all, hence no love and perhaps no life-mate. There are some dozen steps in all, as follows:

1. Preencounter, when some of the selection of mates has already taken place before they ever met.

2. The pristine encounter, the first opportunity for seeing stars and hearing bells.

3. Acquaintanceship, which may or may not culminate in the sexual phase of coupling.

4. Courting, the inception of a special relationship; also *falling* in love and going steady.

5. Sifting and sorting, an integral part of courting, which really begins with the first encounter but takes place in earnest in this phase of matching oneself, consciously and otherwise, to the opposite sex.

6. Matchmaking, when the parts of two people begin to fit and meld, and the couple is *in love.*

7. Coupling or pairing, when a high level of intimacy is achieved and the relationship becomes exclusive.

8. Mating or the bridal culmination of sex becoming love, the union of bodies.

9. Consorting, when there is a more or less formalized sharing of intimacy, including cohabitation or marriage.

10. Bonding, when the relationship deepens into love itself, the union of hearts.

11. Consolidation or cementing, when the union of souls is achieved.

12a. Breaking or wear and tear, when part or all of the cement of love crumbles.

13b. Repairing or breaking up (and re-pairing), when a reprise of most of these steps takes place for the second (or more)-time-arounders.

As mentioned, in real life these stages may run into each other, with detours, shortcuts and overlaps. By and large, however, they occur in a sequence identifiable by the characteristics of the evolution of heterolove. These steps help orient a couple to where they are in their intimacy.

Before encounter, the future lovers may have a well-worked-out check list or at least an idea of what they are looking for in a mate. They go on sifting and sorting each other's qualities and drawbacks throughout the matchmaking process, guided by surging and receding emotions, yet most matchmaking remains submerged, mysteriously intuitive and unconscious. The proportion of awareness to unawareness is at least that of the iceberg, seven-eighths of whose bulk is as submerged as is the crystalization of love.

Let us now overlay on these twelve discrete steps the three cardinal phases making up the progression of love. As I said, they lend their names to the titles of the next three chapters.

The first is clicking together. This is dominated by the electromagnetism of sexual attraction.

The second is ticking together. This is when the chemistry of caring lays its foundation in all elective intimate relationships.

The third and last is sticking together. This is the alchemy of love itself.

I refer to the electromagnetic forces in clicking because of the often fulminating, sex-promoted attraction between the sexes, which not only causes couples to fall into bed but also sometimes in love, occasionally even at first sight. Some people refer to this sudden occurrence as "the right chemistry." This suggests vaguely that there are perhaps hormonal or other hidden biochemical factors involved. Chemistry *is* involved, to an extent, in animals in heat or when they use their smell and their senses in courtship displays. But in humans, sexual attractions that turn into love are basically discernible and psychological, as we shall see.

In ticking, I have labeled the more subtle transition between sex and love as the chemistry of caring because it is a slower but surer "mass action" during which the physical and psychological elements of the two sexes combine to form the salt and substance of love, that is the bond of the relationship between them. Ticking requires detailed psychological analysis.

I have termed the final phase the alchemy of love in deference to two things: first, because this particularly mysterious precursor of science, practiced by the alchemists of yore, enabled them to dispense love potions while wizards and witches laid love spells; second, because the great Swiss analytical psychologist Carl Gustav Jung had studied alchemists as archetypes in the course of his descent into the "collective unconscious," and Jung was, in a way, the progenitor of this treatise.

I'll assign the first three discrete steps of love (preencounter, pristine encounter, and acquaintanceship) to clicking; the next four (courting, sifting-sorting, matchmaking, and coupling) to ticking; and the last four (mating, consorting, bonding, and cementing) to sticking. The very last, crumbling, only happens when the close intimacy of love becomes unstuck. This chapter will deal only with the first phase—clicking.

THE THEORY OF HUMAN ATTRACTIONS

The universal force, probably based on a universal law, that operates between the two sexes is that opposites tend to attract while likes repel. This is the essence of the electromagnetism of sex and love and indeed it works in all elective or voluntary intimacies.

Of course, the most worldwide contrast is that between the sexes, hence the biologically based attraction of opposites. Sex in all its variety is the procrustean bed for heterolove. In today's proliferations of sexuality, six sex categories may be inventoried: (1) conversational, (2) recreational, (3) therapeutic or rehabilitational, (4) reorientational, (5) relational, and (6) procreational.

Conversational sex is for the relative mutes of this world, the lonely, the isolates, the anomic, the alienated who will not or cannot communicate otherwise. Indeed sex comes handy to conjugal couples who've run out of things to say.

Recreational sex is a way to spend a holiday or to top off

a weekend. It is occasionally a form of sport with its own championship system, notches on a stick, rouge marks on the mirror. Once again, conjugal couples also indulge in this in order to "revitalize" their relationship.

Therapeutic sex, whether as a heart resuscitant, a tranquilizer or a straightener-outer of deviances, may have originated, like everything else deliciously decadent, in California. But it is being practiced in many a parlor.

Rehabilitational sex is what you do after intensive care, physically or mentally, following a real or symbolic heart attack. Its watchword is caution. Too much too early spells disaster, as this writer has witnessed in the Far East when he allowed premature marital reunions of repatriated allied prisoners of war. Just as giving these gravely starved men too much food too early caused runaway vitamin *deficiencies,* so allowing these sex-starved men their women caused intractable impotence.

However, ultimate rehabilitation to human status is impossible without sex.

Reorientational sex is a major threat to the bisexual's spouse who herself is usually only at the level of a "halfway house" to heterosexuality. She will have married the bisexual with the unconscious purpose of being protected from the heartbreaks of hetero infidelity. When in search of cure, the bisexual seeks therapeutic extramarital hetero sex. His spouse panics, for by marrying not quite a man this is precisely what she hoped so desperately to avoid in the first place. This story will be elaborated in Chapter 6: Passages, because it is one of the most important kinds of clinical cases that led me to the discoveries described in this book.

Relational sex is, of course, the variety most promising to combine with love. It is this that St. Paul urged upon the Ephesians (Ephesians 5:33) when he said "so ought men to love their wives as their own bodies. He that loseth his wife, loseth himself." St. Paul, in his wisdom, saw this form of sex as more than merely procreational when he said, "for this cause shall a man leave his father and mother and shall be joined unto his wife and they two shall be one flesh."

Operationally, the principle of opposites attracting and likes repelling applies to a whole range of the man's and the woman's characteristics from true contrasting opposites to subtle differences in quality and in quantity. Also it applies exclusively to the young at heart, to personalities not yet fully matured or fixed. For they need to be "one flesh" as St. Paul put it. They benefit from a complementary union of different characteristics fitting into a whole, the synergistic coupling that is better by far than its two added parts.

The advantage of such a union of opposites is that it can respond adaptively to a whole range of polar characteristics. A cold and calculating man joined to a warm and generous woman will make a blend appropriately responsive with a whole scale of emotions. An introvert and an extrovert melded together will relate better to the outer and the inner worlds than either would separately. The heavy, ponderous guy is drawn to the fluttery girl; the deeply profound to the scatter-brained. They offset each other's strengths and weaknesses. You can easily figure the gains in such unions. You can also see how these psychological and social advantages are grafted on to the biological ones because opposites and differences in personal characteristics favor corresponding genetic differences so that the zygote, the child, will show a rich diversity in endowment.

Perhaps the most controversial quality in terms of the undesirability of stereotyped differences is strength of character or dominance, especially in females. Although it seems to be true that "strong" women, depending on the degree of their motivation, tend to choose and to be attracted to weaker men. This usually leads to a faulty match. Most "strong" or even dominant women, whether of the Scarlett O'Hara willful, spoilt-child kind or those of more rounded strength, deep down wish to mesh with a man who is at least a peer in strength, if not a tower. If they don't carry out this inner healthy urge because of some past happening, because they've been put off by some rough and tough man like father or because they've downgraded men and seen them as emasculated or emasculatable, they are making an error. Inevitably they come to despise weak men and begin a protracted campaign to stimulate them into escalating and violent actions against themselves (the females) in order to prove their residual masculinity.

For instance, Bonnie was a big, business-oriented girl who had rejected her dominant, successful businessman father because she couldn't please him and be like him and also because he couldn't control his drinking wife, her mother. She chose a soft, tender, loving man, who looked like a bear but behaved like a mouse—a man who worshipped his mother and honored females, so a man out of sync with the times. And as soon as she got him wed to her, she began to whip him up, to test his "strength," his masculinity, his temper. She told herself that she wanted to shift him from his passive role and most especially that she wanted him to dominate her, to keep her down and especially to keep her honest and faithful.

Like most men of this kind he didn't see why he should abandon his principles, his pacific attitude, his gentle honoring of woman, and turn into a brute merely to please his wife's whim. So he resisted her escalating challenges. The relationship reached an impasse as it nearly always does in this sort of case, when neither party gives in. She wanted to become submissive but needed a stronger man to submit to. Yet she liked and loved Dennis for what he was in all other respects—nice and kind and unlike her. He didn't want to dominate her and flex any kind of muscle to do so, and thus compromise his principles. They solved the standoff by each retreating halfway in their respective positions in order to save their marriage, barely a year old.

Usually the type of strength such women need in a man is different from their own. They require a man with the silent, quiet type of strength to offset their own motor mouth, or the physically competent man to contrast with their intellectual competence, or a socially charismatic man to complement their own personal gifts in one-to-one relationships.

The principle of contrasting opposites is reversed when it comes to matured, older, fixed people who are usually beyond the reproductive period. They are grown already and biologically fulfilled (or not) so that there is no advantage to growing more quickly together in the cocoon of a love union, any more than there is a purpose to their possessing different genes if these aren't going to mix into a fetus. Moreover, older people become short in the tolerance for differences. So the golden rule here is the obverse of contrasting opposition: namely likes attract and opposites repel. In a union of likes, there are usually sufficient variations on the same theme for supplementarity of characteristics; that is, the couple tends to extend their virtues (or shortcomings) in the same direction. We shall discuss this major reversal of the cardinal theory of attraction between people in the chapter on Late Love (Chapter 5).

Meanwhile, we must add more flesh to the bare, simplistic skeleton of contrasting opposition. Clearly, if everything were radically different in the two coupled people, their total energy would be absorbed just in tolerating one another. It's not for nothing that common belief has it that compatibility rests on common interests, attitudes, and concordant behaviors rather than on differences. Moreover, cultural and social groupings, based as they are on family life, could not survive and thrive unless there were sufficient homogeneity between the sexes.

Consequently, the magical formula of compatibility in a love match (or in any other close elective relationship) rests on a *proportion* of similarity or commonality related to differences, contrasts, and oppositions. Probably if all the "elements of love" were accounted for and checked through consciously, even the "opposites" who attract each other are more fundamentally alike than they are different. This magical formula, this proportion of similarities as against differences rests on three crucial factors:

1. The absolute number as well as the intensity of both opposite and like elements. The degree of tolerance for differences even in love is not infinite, nor is the tolerance for boring sameness and for competition among likes infinite.

2. The priority given by both men and women to certain characteristics depends on the person's motivation, perception, intuition, and value system, both consciously and unconsciously. What's more, this order ranking of characteristic differences must somehow coincide or at least be congruent in the couple. So that, for instance, if it's important to a dark woman to be attracted to a fair man, not only must it be reciprocal (important to the fair man to be attracted to the dark lady) but the value of this feature of physical attraction must also be

roughly equal in the two, so that the approximate level of priority is roughly the same. This means, among other things, that other factors like intelligence or kindness or social status need not be different or contrasting on a polar range.

3. The range of opposites, contrasts, differences or heterogeneity, incongruence, dissonance or discordance, is more manifest than the range of similarities. In short, differences are placed in the *foreground* of the relationship.

Consequently, the foreground of heterolove is *dissortatively* matched, that is, it is made up largely of differences. Yet the effect is symmetrical, symphonic, and symbiotic. The two opposites balance one another. They are harmonious and reciprocally beneficial to one another.

On the other hand, the commonality, the similarities, the likes or the homogeneity, the congruences, consonances, and concordance are placed in the *background* of the relationship.

Consequently, the background of heterolove (hence of all elective relationships modeled on it) is *assortatively* matched; that is, made up largely of sameness, which is implied, taken for granted, quietly unobtrusive.

In fact, the personal choice, both conscious and unconscious, favors foreground opposites; whereas the "givens," the geographically dictated choices made by the nature of things, and by society (rather than the person) favor similar backgrounds. This spatial arrangement, more than anything else, gives the person the illusion of choice, because personal preferences are manifest, as I said, in the foreground. This too is where "love" has changed the structure of professionally matchmade or arranged marriages.

Love as a matchmaker should work better in the long run both biologically (genetically) and adaptively, because the matchmakers and social structure in the past favored sameness or homogeneity. Not only did they do this so as to preserve social order and the homogeneity of classes, but also in the false belief that compatibility was exclusively based on commonality, at least of place and station in the world.

If it's true that contrast rather than sameness rules the foreground of love, you may argue, why does folk intuition lean on commonality of interests and does not fully acknowledge the obvious attraction of opposites?

This is an awkward question to answer, although it does not invalidate the basic theory and countless observations that support it. The attraction of opposites has been recognized as well as the attraction of commonality. In fact, most memorable characters of literature are based on the play of opposites, and many great loves, like Heathcliff and Cathy's in *Wuthering Heights*, are based on this rule.

Popular opinion shifts according to observed imbalances rather than reflecting the magical formula of balances or emphasizing contrast. For example, if contrasts in a couple are so excessive that the lovers cannot cope, people say "No wonder! They have *nothing* in common." Not true, of course. Even casual examination will show that they have a lot in common—if you count the one thousand "elements of love" that I will talk about shortly—but not enough. If, on the other hand, a couple is so much alike that they compete and quarrel to establish dominance, people merely say that they're unsuited and don't get along. When the attraction of opposites works well, and is obviously in balance, people are always astonished and say "Yes they're great friends or very much in love, yet they're so unalike, really opposites."

We shall elaborate on this rule of "opposition" in Chapter 10: Why Love? when we'll see how this law of attraction finds universal grounding in the laws of nature. Meanwhile, let's note just one more thing—namely why commonalities are part of the silent background of coupling rather than the foreground.

It is because what is usually said to be *the* background of a person, namely the variables of the social profile, such as race, religion, and so forth (we shall enumerate them presently), are usually quietly and implicitly matched *assortatively*. Moreover, as mentioned, they are already sorted out before the first encounter, geographically, by where you happen to have been born and live, and by culture and society, rather than by yourself.

So, in summary, when we say that opposites attract one another in sex, love, and all elective relationships, by this we mean:

1. Some preferred, important opposite characteristics attract one another. They are given a high priority by a variety of conscious and unconscious motivations.
2. Differences usually lie in the foreground of a relationship.
3. Differences are probably, in the overall, less numerous and/or intense than the similarities that lie usually in the background of the relationship.
4. The magical formula of love depends on a proportional balance between a dissimilar foreground and similar background. When this rule is illustrated by an exceptional reversal and some elements of background, like race and religion, differ in the coupling, the appropriate overall proportion must nevertheless be maintained. Thus "cross-cultural marriages," like religious or racial or ethnic intermarriages, constrain the individuals in their personal choices of other differences such as in personality, as we shall see, because there are limits to the available psychic energy even when in love.

In terms of the sequence of encounter, as mentioned, most of the "givens" of the background are already taken care of by the location and circumstance of the first encounter. At the first encounter, in fact practically at first sight, there is a quick, psycho-osmotic sorting of the foreground and background proportion of opposite and like elements that is carried out by personal prejudice, that is, by predetermined psychological preferences. The *givens* of the social profile are accepted and confirmed as similarities, unless social barriers are to be deliberately broken. The attractions work their electromagnetism usually via sex. During progressive stages of acquaintanceship there is a deliberate sifting through of the "elements of love." Some are matched, others are discarded; the magical formula is being checked out intuitively. At the end of this phase, if there is a click, an initial match, there's a falling in love and this ends the phase we're here considering. In the next two phases, in ticking especially, there is a finer sifting and rearrangement, a recording of priorities and preferences, and a final matchmaking when the deeper elements of love are being fitted. In the last phase, sticking, there is a final adjustment of this ratio, as the union is cemented into love.

At this juncture let's look at what happens from the moment of first contact onward. The forces of attraction are mostly unconscious, so that when I see couples who have gone wrong in their marriage and I take them back to the very beginning, to their first few encounters, they hotly deny their intuitive perceptions, which should have warned them of the shape of things to come. Yet I've come to learn that once couples have clicked well enough to proceed down the bridal path, via ticking together, they *did* have a pretty perspicacious view of each other, even if they shielded this from the conscious mind. Otherwise they wouldn't have clicked. And I find usually that the very things they complained that they had never seen in the first place, are precisely what clicked into place and fitted their personality needs *at that time.* As we noted before, in these circumstances people shout out, "Oh, I swear I didn't know that she/he was going to turn out like this . . . all that came out later!" Sometimes, rarely, it is true, especially if later is *much* later, like years, and if real changes, actually a flipover of personality, had taken place. However, most of the time *everything* had been (pre- or subconsciously) intuited practically from the pristine encounter. So that when I persist in retracing these initial steps, however obscured by "blind love" or more likely by blinding sex, gradually the truth comes out. Yes, those qualities were dimly recognized and registered somewhere in each other's mind and somehow processed ("Oh, he/she'll get over that . . . I'll help change him/her . . . it's not important," etc.). Only if the clicking phase was abbreviated to a very short acquaintanceship and courtship stage, virtually to love at first sight, or only if they met in a highly romantic and faraway situation, such as on a cruise or on a foreign trek, not on familiar grounds where information abounds, only then may there have been insufficient opportunity for mutual psychic penetration, for the inaudible vibrations emitted instantly on contact between people.

The great Irish poet William Butler Yeats once said that in wise love, each partner divines the high secret self of the lover and refuses to believe in the mere daily self. It's a noble aspiration, but Yeats's own tormented love life, which can best be described as wallowing in unrequited obsession, attests to its impracticability as a coupling commandment. Still, he struck a resonant note with the idea that there's more to coupling than meets the eye. Divination, instinct—call it what you will—is at work in mating, right from the first chance eye contact across a crowded room.

In other words, *what the eye doesn't see the psyche senses.* Each of us, whether we are aware of it or not, has a highly individualized list of the qualities we consider essential in a potential partner. Some of them, such as appearance, social position, or intelligence, are fairly obvious and we're aware of their presence or absence in a person right from the start. But others—kindness, generosity, or integrity, for example—often aren't fully revealed until the relationship is well under way. However, when two people "click" anywhere between first encounter and courting, each of them has already "divined" that the other has the particular set of qualities he or she is looking for.

Knowing why you're looking for certain characteristics puts you well ahead of the game. There's little doubt that part of what attracts you to someone—physical appearance, intelligence, achievement, grace, charm, or style—is obvious. But when you catch sight of a stranger across a crowded room and feel a surge of interest ("I'd like to get to know that person standing by the punch bowl" is the common thought), you're unconsciously taking note of more than just externals. The man next to him may be even better-looking, but, somehow, he doesn't have the same appeal. The reason is that your unconscious sorting and sifting matchmaking mechanism comes into play.

So, what the eye doesn't see, the psyche senses. But while you may trust your intuition (that first surge of interest across a crowded room just *may* be an accurate indication of ultimate compatibility), you should also be warned that all of us have a propensity to see what we're looking for, in the sense that we project the qualities we want or need onto the other person.

For example, Tanya, a good friend, continually acts in this fashion. She's an attractive, unattached career woman in her early thirties. In one recent incident she went to a Christmas party given for a business associate. She's successful at what she does, and was deliberately looking for a man to reflect her own sense of self-esteem. Intelligent, powerful, and wealthy were the adjectives running through her mind. How did her antennae scan the room?

Two men were standing by the punch bowl. One was of moderate height, graying at the temples, and showing the first signs of middle-aged spread. He was wearing a three-piece suit of gray Harris tweed, neatly pressed, and a pair of impeccably polished Gucci loafers. The other, a Warren Beatty look-alike, was as tall, dark, and handsome as the first man was nondescript. But Tanya hardly noticed him, because the effect of his matinee-idol good looks was lost in the implication of his attire—blue jeans and cowboy boots.

Her own bias—she's a conservative person who places a great deal of value on externals (in fact, her solidly bourgeois background has made her a bit of a snob in the direction of the status quo)—drew her toward the man in the Harris tweed suit. Her upwardly mobile snobbishness blinds her to everything but what she's searching for. Had she stopped to inquire, she would have seen that the blue-jeaned Adonis, one of the most accomplished lawyers in the city, had so much self-confidence that he didn't need a three-piece suit to signal his status.

Nevertheless, she set out to meet the middle-aged businessman. He turned out to be married, but randy anyway, and only interested in a little hanky-panky away from home. She left the party disappointed.

How many people haven't made the same mistake? It's not unusual to approach someone at a party who seemed interesting from afar, only to discover that the person is an excruciating bore. It's a natural human failing. Each of us wants to see the characteristics we prefer in other people and the degree of distortion we bring to our perception is often just a direct reflection of how desperate we are to find a mate.

While the psyche senses the algorithms of the heart and soul of the other person, and while it sorts them out quickly and intuitively so that it can even scan the future and predict flip-overs in character, its insights rely heavily on its windows. And the senses are the windows of the psyche, which processes all informational inputs in subliminal or entirely unconscious perceptions. Before falling in love and letting the perceptual blinds down, there may be very little time for the exercise of sense and sensibility. In fact, it is this input, the eye of the beholder, that accounts in the electromagnetic phenomenon of falling in love. The better the perceptual acuity, the better the perspicacity, the truer the qualities (quirks and negatives) perceived, the healthier the ensuing relationship.

People vary in sensory profile, in the preference and competence of their eight senses (vision, hearing, touching, moving, smelling, tasting, sense of position, and visceral satiety). They also vary in their degree of sensuousness. Consequently what one sees in another person, particularly when emotional reactions accompany the visualization, is not only what is really there but also what you project from desire and what you interpret (truly and falsely) from past experience. Moreover, as the psyche churns away from first to last impressions, it consciously revisualizes and reevokes the sounds, touch, and sensations of pristine and subsequent impressions. The whole thing is recapitulated and remolded unconsciously in sleep dreams and semiconsciously in daydreams. In all these processes the preferred sensory pathways and perceptual competence play an important part.

The "sex" appeal may be visual, auditory, tactile, or kinetic, and evoke sensuous pleasure, like an electric tickling sensation. In the direct exercises of the senses during the encounter, and indirectly in recalling the person to mind consciously in wake and sleep dreams, arousal of both passion and feelings takes place.

What ends up in the eyes of the beholder is modified by past experiences and wishes. This is where motivation and perception come together. In the course of this confluence, in the "eye of the beholder" you may have a brilliantly unimpeded insight into the very soul of another person, fall in love at first sight; or you may look and become instantly antagonized but eventually fall in love or more usually you may react with indifference. Or else your mental state may so cloud your perceptions as to introduce grotesque distortions. It is thanks to perceptual distortions that the beauty may come to love the beast and that some of the ugliest people may find a mate who sees beauty in them. Did Esmeralda see the beauty in Quasi-modo, the hunchback of Notre Dame? Puck certainly played havoc with a female heart, falling in love with an ass's head in *A Midsummer Night's Dream.*

Real or distorted clairvoyance at first encounter may account for the phenomenon of love at first sight. All is perceived as if in a time machine; the sorting out of clicking and of ticking are accelerated and concentrated into one eye-blink or one touch. The ideal image of the opposite sex is rapidly matched to one's self. Dreams and aspirations and commonality, magical formula and all, click. And the clicking can be heard and seen in starry eyes from miles away. In healthy people, psychologically ready and available, in ideal situations (not on rebound from a love gone wrong or a marriage) love at first sight can be valid, lasting, and good.

The instant antipathy at first sight to which I have just alluded is often a warning sign of the shape of a turbulent love to come, especially when it is due to violent opposition. The clash and shock occur as a result of finding someone utterly different from oneself, possessing the very characteristics one didn't dare to display oneself but always wished one had. Love then comes as a surprise and is worth having. But if the antipathy is due to likenesses, to envy, disapproval, and competitiveness, it augurs badly even for a late love between matured and rigidified persons who have already come into their own.

Now let us rewrite the scenario of first encounter. You find yourself staring at the man by the punch bowl and are powerfully attracted to him. The feeling is or seems to be physical, although if your mind were really dissected then and there or subsequently in retrospect, you'd offer as the points of attraction a mixture of physical and mental qualities. (And it would make a difference as to what their proportion is and which dominate. Subsequently this will provide the clue as to what motivated your attraction.) But for now, he caught your glance, as in a candid camera, however surreptitious you were. You think you see a response in his face (it looks like it's coming from the eyes, but research of man and animals shows that most of the significant signals come from *around* the eyes and especially the mouth region). Anyhow, he (or you as the liberated woman) take the fateful step forward: "Hi!" The respective voices electrify each other. Soon there is a touch. Sheer magnetism. Soon or presently ("Let's get out of this place!") you are caught in the electromagnetism of sexuality but distinctly tinged with romanticism. You know that this isn't just sex. What's happened? What is the mysterious force that's thrown you together? If you are young in heart and mind, if you've still got growing to do, the main thrust of that force is contrast, differences, opposites of the characteristics and qualities you are (mostly unconsciously) seeking. You are fair, he's dark. You're slender and small, he's big. You're angular, he's round. Your eyes are deep set, his bulge. You're beautiful physically in one way (feminine), he in another (masculine). Now this is all physical, just to make an obvious point. In real life, as has been mentioned, the up-front qualities you and for that matter others can see, are a mixture of physical and mental. For one thing, rightly or wrongly you associate physical with personality characteristics: the strong jaw, the tender eyes, the sensuous lower lip. For another thing, you cannot yet see anything but the physical; the psychological is more covert and takes longer to reveal. And for a third thing, you may tend to physicalize or even sexualize people and in doing so you associate certain physical characteristics with certain intimates past or present, like parents, siblings, friends, and the intimates of your imagination—the movie stars, teachers, and school seniors on whom you've had crushes. So that by the time you start clicking you've sensed that his warmth complements your coldness; his decisiveness your hesitancy; or her generosity your mean streak; her social perspicacity, your inability to judge people; and so on.

So here is a fantastic sexual attraction—the thunderbolt striking—anticipating a love union, which itself is analogous to a zygote, the product of two different genetic endowments.

Before we move on, you might care to challenge this theory of opposites attracting and its operation in the unconscious. You might doubt that intuition divines *all* the outer and inner elements of love that stand in opposition or contrast or possess a measure of difference. You might say to me: How do you know? How can you be so sure that this is how it works? Especially, how do I know that the psyche senses by a sort of psycho-osmosis whether or not two bodies (in sex), two hearts (in love), and two souls (united) will be in sync; whether the yin will fit the yang? Or is it only a theory?

To which my answer is that every time I retraced the lovers' steps with them, every time I looked to see what happened in the beginning, it was the same story of preferred opposites that made the clicking. But more than that, after some thousands of clinical observations I began making predictions based on the principle of contrasting opposition. If I were given details of the personality of an individual and/or the person's life history, sometimes if I was only given five consecutive sleep dreams, I could predict what sort of person that individual would be or has been attracted to. I could predict what sort of mate or spouse the person had or was going to get. Often I would be in a position to meet this mate, lover, or spouse. The accuracy of prediction was high. With practice I began predicting, equally dramatically, from facts given the other way around. Given knowledge of the nature of a love relationship, the type of dyad, I could not only deduce the details of their personalities but also what kind of life experiences they might have had—the life patterns that led them into choosing their mates the way they did. In fact, I was getting better than the more highly paid psychics.

Now here comes a crucial point. The accuracy of my crystal ball as a clinician varied in direct proportion to the neuroticism or faultiness in the personality I got to investigate or of the relationship I was told about. With faulty characters or relationships—what I call the lean-to—I could pinpoint *details* of the characteristics sought by one person and found in the other. For example, I could tell that a certain lady would choose unavailable men, or men who would let her down, hurt and reject her, or weaklings who would lean on her but whom she would progressively test, despise, and discard. But the more normal or healthy the personalities, the truer the love, the sounder its foundation, the better cement between the uprights of a healthy union as opposed to a lean-to, the more difficult it was to predict details in healthy couples. There are many reasons for this, but the main ones are that:

1. The more normal the person, the wider her/his range of reactions;

2. The more neurotic the person, the more predictable his/her priorities in the attraction to other people (they stem from neurotic motivations), and

3. the choices they then make are of *false* opposites, like Jack Spratt and his wife. Their mates are obverse, that is, opposite sides of the *same* coin, like the compulsive slob and the compulsively neat or the bisexual and his only heterosexual mate, a woman uncertain of her femininity.

Only the general theme of attraction of "opposites" and the general "package" of opposites rather than specifics were predictable in the normal case.

Consequently, we learn from the abnormal how the normal works not only because we are more interested in its workings because we want to correct it, but also because the abnormal is simpler, more repetitive and much more predictable.

THE ELEMENTS OF A LOVE MATCH

Let's now take a brief look at the nature or at least the classification of the type of check list we carry with us, consciously or unconsciously, when in search of love. Then we'll see how and presently why, certain characteristics are given priority and how these click mutually in two lovers. We can best do this by following through the sequence of encounter in order to see when certain elements or classes of elements emerge and then dominate the choices made.

Even before the encounter, the presorting is made geopolitically and socially. That is, the random chance of geography and social groupings will predetermine the ten or so variables of the social profile of the lovers about to meet. This will be largely an *assortative* preselection; that is, the social niche of the future lovers favors selection of *similar* characteristics in terms of their specific backgrounds.

What are these givens of the social profile? They are mostly manifest externals: namely age; race; ethnicity, hence cultural-religious affiliations; social class; marital status; occupation; degree of urbanization; schooling; and sex, of course.

"Well," you'd say alertly, "so lovers are not really opposites in everything, right?" This is where we modified the nature of the law operating as a force of attraction. As stated, the given *background* of the two lovers is usually similar, forming a solid basis of commonality. It is against this common solid background that the *foreground* of physical and personality differences or contrasts are absorbed and transformed into a love match.

Sometimes either the situation of encounter, the nature of the environment, or more likely the *motivation* of the would-be lovers favors cross-cultural or socially dissortative unions. In other words, an attraction across relatively socially restricted territories—racial, social, cultural, age, or what have you. This choice absorbs considerable psychic energy. In this case there is not enough energy and tolerance left in the coupling for differences in the foreground—differences of temperament, lifestyles or personality. You notice that Romeo and Juliet had to cross this kind of chasm and the very opposition of their families fueled their love. But then they were similar in all other vital respects. They were both of princely blood, of the same race, ethnic group, town; both young, beautiful people; both romantic, vivacious and foolhardy. They had to be because their families' opposition was strong enough to take up their whole energy and in the end their very lives. One suspects that had they overcome the obstacles in their cross-marriage, they would have found too little internally and personally to keep the spark of their love going—too little contrast. So in a complementary love relationship, the attraction comes not only from the contrasts usually found in the foreground but also from the magical formula of commonality and contrasts distributed over background (the givens, the externals) and foreground (the acquired, the internals).

At the point of encounter the package of elements that dominate, apart from the visible aspects of the social profile (age, race, etc.), are the physical or physique attributes, the spark of intelligence, some aspects of lifestyle and some of the more superficial aspects of the personages of the inner self—the persona or social mask and some of the habits of a person. These packages then make their mutual impressions.

1. Physique

The wisdom of genetic diversity calls for one coloring, the fair and freckled for instance, to be attracted to the opposite, the dark; and for one body type, the ectomorph (lean and hungry look) to be attracted to its opposite, the endomorph (more roly-poly) or the mesomorph (the athletic).

Physique comprises height, weight, frame or body type, coloring, the shape of the head and face, the general impression of looks, and that elusive quality of presence, so related to charisma. Moreover, physique as well as persona and presence may often cast their shadows before them so that sometimes, long before the actual encounter, a person may have irradiated a powerful and seductive image by reputation, report, or visual preview. The tall, dark stranger entering a room may well instantly subdue males and females to his compelling presence. Yet, as we shall see in the next chapter when we discuss the personages of the inner self, it will take only one kind of person to truly match him. She will have to be as luminous as he is dark, as sunny and uncomplicated as he is somber and complex. And inside, their respective shadows will have to be as opposed as their *personae* are on the outside.

Equally, the beauty queen is not your everyday lover's cup of tea. On the contrary, few men feel powerful enough to assault the regal citadel of beauty and then they do so only to prove their own strength, as she is to learn later in the loveless, chilled, and saddened tower chamber. Indeed, any God-given gift like beauty, intelligence, or talent, tends to create a forbidding situation. Their awesomeness introduces too big a gap between gifted people and mere mortals. Also the cultivation and care of extraordinary gifts leads to narcissism, to excess psychic energy spent on the self. Hence the beauty queen's capacity to love is impeded. She then is inclined to be unloving, hence unlovable. This explains the tragedy of loveless isolation, as Marilyn Monroe and countless others no doubt discovered. The only feasible match is between equally beautiful people though the nature of the beauty may well contrast. Yet each magnificent gift is liable to render its bearer to be too self-absorbed and narcissistic to be able to give enough love to another. A better match would be one between, say, a highly intelligent person and a quite ordinary partner with an extraordinary inner gift of selflessness. When this happens the world asks: "I wonder what she or he sees in the other person?" Little do they know! Alas, this kind of intuitive wisdom is relatively rare, for one star is usually overimpressed only by another and not by the less shiny attributes that are needed in such a case.

2. Intelligence

The manifestations of sparkling intelligence are perceived early in most encounters. Sometimes they actually precede the encounter when they are talked about and form part of one's reputation. The level of intelligence is tacitly assumed from information about the level of education achieved by the person, by the level of occupation, status, and wealth. Its spark scintillates in speech. But first and generally early impressions gathered from verbal skill alone are highly unreliable. There are any number of glib, verbal, and yet dumb people; just as there are a few taciturn intelligent ones. Sometimes one is fooled the other way: Still waters do not always run deep, and strong-looking silent men may cover up both weakness and dumbness.

However this may be, perceived intelligence is an important characteristic evaluated early in a relationship. Generally, like everything else, it is overvalued by those who either are or think they are short of wits. On the other hand, intelligence tends to be undervalued by those who have an abundance. This latter factor, as well as obfuscation by sexuality, is what makes for the classical coupling (conforming to the principle of contrasting opposition) between a highly intelligent man and the dumb blonde. And then there is the tougher situation in which an intelligent who is also gorgeous woman finds herself—that this combination puts off a lot of men who feel threatened by her.

All too often I have come across the intelligent woman, beautiful in looks or not, who does the classical male number and marries (usually when young) a gorgeous but dumb man. The marriage never seems to work. Either we get the clash of assortative narcissistic pairing or else the man eventually becomes "emasculated" by the woman's superior status, earning power, or just brains.

Often intelligence, as well as power, is seen by women in general rather than by those with super intelligence, as an extension of the male phallus. Thus intelligence is falsely perceived as a male attribute—not something woman are expected to *exhibit,* even if they possess it. Only if a male lacks intelligence when compared with a woman, as just mentioned, does *he* see this as a lack of phallic power.

Sparkling intelligence preeminently visible in the foreground in early encounters tends to be matched disassortatively (high I.Q. mixed with somewhat lower I.Q.) in accordance with the principle of opposites.

Fortunately or otherwise (again depending on your viewpoint), the *general* intelligence level (the quiet type) is not usually seen as a foreground feature unless it sparkles, as mentioned, in early encounters. Then it is usually treated as a background feature, a given endowment, hence it is selected assortatively, that is, matched largely at the *same* level. And yet psychobiological improvement in the human species depends on diversity and favors a mix. Does this mean that basic biological needs are, after all, not supported by the psychology of contrasting opposition? Yes, they are but in a more subtle way. It is the *components* of intelligence—like verbal and performance I.Q. and like grasp, insight, mathematical and logical reasoning, and so forth—the specifics, rather than the general level of intelligence, that are matched in subsequent encounters and in terms of opposites or contrasts.

In other words, couples are usually fairly equally matched in *general* level of intelligence but *differ* in *traits.* So that, for instance, somebody who is mentally agile, quickly perceptive, verbally and socially intelligent, will tend to be attracted to somebody else who is ponderous, deep, logical, and perhaps with special intellectual gifts even if he/she is somewhat socially dense. The end result, as in all such matchings on this principle, is an enrichment when both the relationship and offspring benefit from different sets of intellectual qualities.

3. Lifestyle

Lifestyle is a person in action. It comprises all his preferential and habitual microbehaviors gathered together into an overall bundle, dominated by a single or a couple of characteristic behaviors—like being a vegetarian or a mogul or a bohemian. This predominant behavior that ties up the others into a bundle and gives them its name is styled by the person but influenced by his culture. The resultant lifestyle is then cast in the image of its possessor. And this image is related to the ideal self.

A lifestyle, perhaps more than anything else other than psychogender or sexual identity, gives us individuality—the male jock, the femme fatale, the high urbanite. Yet lifestyle, more certainly than anything else, is sacrificed for the sake of coupling, which inevitably alters the lifestyle of both partners and creates a joint style. The only time when two partners may revert to their individual lifestyles or create a new one is when they agree to live separately together.

4. Personages of the Inner Self

Three of the personages of the inner self or the people who dwell within us surface in the clicking phase, namely the *persona* (the social self), the *hominus* or *femina* (the man or woman who turns us on, both sexually and emotionally), and the *ideal self.*

The persona and the image of the hominus/femina may electrify and magnetize from the moment of first encounter. Of course, these images may shatter if one of the would-be lovers finds out that the social mask (the persona) hides very different and disagreeable personages behind it. Equally, the relationship may terminate if a would-be lover finds her/his hominus/femina not to coincide with the real man/woman. Illusions that make the picture fit when it really doesn't, play an important part in errors of judgment in the initial stages of encounter. The sexual fog blurring judgment and the blindness of falling in love may well lead to illusionary projections of the hominus on a man who lacks the characteristics a woman wants to believe he has. Similarly, a woman may seem to resemble a man's femina, but on closer acquaintance the illusion vanishes. The discovery of such an error or of what really lies behind the persona, in the unguarded moments of togetherness, may come too late. But on the whole, as we shall see, a couple intuits perfectly well the usual alignment between these surfacing social aspects of the personages of the inner self and the deeper more concealed ones, so that when the latter emerge they come as no surprise.

In the ordered course of romantic events, the details of lifestyle, the manifestations of the ideal self and the hominus/femina, reveal themselves somewhere between acquaintanceship and courtship, though they may make an indelible impact upon first impressions.

I mentioned that the process of a love union parallels and resembles that of a sexual union in procreation and that the resultant love match is like a zygote, the fetus.

When the two gametes meet, the paternal and the maternal, they each yield twenty-three chromosomes (genetic packages), which when put together create the human endowment of forty-six chromosomes for the zygote, the new creature. But each of these genetic packages, each chromosome, has some three to five thousand discrete genes determining the specific characteristic of the offspring. So that in the biological union of but one cell from each parent (the sperm and the ovum) to make a new cell, an average of one hundred thousand discrete characteristics from each parent are matched. They determine the child's biological inheritance.

The same sort of union takes place in love matchmaking. There are a set of ten social profile packages—the physical attributes, the various aspects of intelligence, lifestyle, manners, personal habits—and some six packages of deeper personality composites that have to be matched. Each of these packages contains scores of discrete characteristics. When it comes to sorting them out during clicking and ticking, there may be perhaps a thousand different characteristics that meld in a love union and determine its psychological endowment. Clearly one cannot go through all of them—ethnic grouping, coloring, height, quickness of grasp, racy and risk-taking lifestyle, mild manners, hygienic habits, honesty, charm and 987 more—with a check list in order to match them perfectly. Even a modern geneticist cannot yet do that with prospective genes. So, as mentioned, a lot is left to chance or to covert sorting out. But all these characteristics become eventually manifest in a lifetime.

What we present of ourselves to others—physique, persona and lifestyle—makes an overall *image* in the eye of the beholder that is usually difficult to dissect. Part of the reason is that the overall effect is what counts. Part of it is that the actual image is like ink blots or clouds upon which we tend to project our perception. We make our own closure on many open-ended or vague impressions. But mostly what we do is give priority and emphasis to what we *seem to see* in terms of what is important to us in the first place, unless the quality perceived is objectively very striking.

But there is a complication here. How can you judge what somebody else sees in you? How do you know how you come across, the impression you create? How do you ever put together what you actually are and represent with what you feel you are and what you put on (persona) and what you wish to be (ideal self)? Obviously the perceptual distortions you occasion in presenting yourself form a breeding ground for amplified perceptual distortions others experience upon seeing you. Anything you can do to reduce such distortions focuses the picture. For instance, you can identify some of the important characteristics of your persona and see how you are likely to come across to others. To this end I have inserted a test (How You Come Across) at the end of this chapter.

At this point I have to add a final complication. This is the *quantity* and *duration* of opposites that attract.

Only a few of the packages of characteristics displayed at encounter are permanent and unalterable. Race, ethnicity, culture, height, and complexions do not change over time, but others like social status, occupation, persona, and lifestyle do. Many qualities like dominance or honesty have a quantity.

In the course of acquaintanceship, the sensing psyche divines not only a number of characteristics that attract or repel, that fit or not, but also a range of quantity and of duration. A rich entrepreneur may fall on bad times and become a pauper. And if a man is that keen on a woman's virginal figure, he is still well advised to take a peek at her mother.

Thus the psyche's antennae must carry out an exquisitely accurate estimate of the quantity and duration of the other person's characteristics, particularly those held to be of paramount importance. Moreover, for clicking to occur, this estimate is mutually carried out and must be found to fit. However complex this process may appear in the course of matching themselves to each other, a couple continuously calculates, albeit unconsciously, all the factors inventoried here and more. No wonder the results are often in error. No wonder that most selections have been made apparently at random, through trial and error—an emotionally costly and wasteful process.

But once we extract this information from the psyche, once it becomes conscious and describable and calculable, the combination of computer and informed lovers can do a much better job than was ever done before by matchmakers.

5. The Place of Encounter

Where you are depends on who you are. Not everyone can be having tea at the White House or sunning in the garden of Buckingham Palace or manning the barricades of freedom fighters or spying on the Galapagos bird life. It is in this sense that the places of encounter tend to be assortative, "birds of a feather flock together." The place of encounter and to an extent that of subsequent meetings, particularly those taking place by chance like meeting at parties, in clubs or at political rallies, constitute the physical and social environments that are largely predicated by the chance factor of geo-socio-politics. Thus where people are to meet is the locus of those preencounter selections that determine the basis of commonality for would-be lovers, because that is the place where the background elements of love, particularly the social profile, tend to be prematched.

Clearly, some environments are highly erotic, like the singles bars, pleasure cruises, and skiing vacations. Others are charged with expectations and aspirations, like set-ups, whether by professional or amateur matchmakers, and even blind dates.

Where and how you meet tends to set the subsequent events in a relationship to a considerable enough extent that often had the same people met under different circumstances and in different environments they would have had a different relationship or perhaps none at all.

In normal times, especially in large urban environments, the question of meeting the other sex is extremely critical, particularly for people who are no longer in school. High schools, colleges and universities are our society's largest if not its most successful marriage bureaus. But once you have gone past them, the meeting places and choices narrow abruptly to workplace, neighborhood, casual and market places, including clubs and holiday sites. The hunt can become desperate and Mr. Goodbar lurks around every corner. This is one of the most pathetic and pathogenic aspects of our alienated urban life: Half the lonely hearts are seeking the other half in the lonely throngs of the city and most of the time they do *not* find each other. "Where are they?" is the constant cry of people in search of love mates and friendships.

It's clearly harder for older people and those on the second or more time around than for the younger singles. And it's my distinct clinical impression that there is a difference between men and women seeking marriage: Generally men are the more marrying kind. A woman released from marriage in her late thirties is less likely to seek it again than a man, unless she's got no children.

The single most important social and physical design lacking in our current North American urban life, therefore, is the meeting place for intimacy, for making close relationships, both for romantic love and friendships. Europe and some of the other continents are more fortunate. In the first place, people there are not as nomadic; they are more traditionally stable—topophilic. In the second place, they have special environments and social structures, such as the English pub, the Continental cafés and the Asiatic and Middle Eastern professional matchmakers and an extended family to serve this purpose.

In my younger optimistic days as a clinician, I used to say to perplexed patients and others, "Don't worry! As soon as you become *psychologically available* for love; as long as you become free and accessible to intimacy, you'll find your match waiting on the threshold." And indeed, it seemed to be miraculously so. On hundreds of occasions when I could help liberate the woman from unavailable men or the man from rejecting women, there would be someone there, with open arms, however much the body had aged in the wasteland of emotional knots. But in more recent years pessimism has set in because I have seen psychologically available beautiful people whom nobody seems to want. Not for wont of their looking, either. They seemed to look in every nook and cranny and there was nobody there. And yet I knew that their counterparts were there also because I sent them out there myself. Perhaps matchmaking would have been more serviceable than analytical and group psychotherapy!

To the question "Where should I look?" I've always answered and still do, "In your own backyard." And by this I mean that the tight private network of family, friends, and neighborhood is still the best. People who get desperate about the opposite sex forget that one's own sex is a perfect medium for meeting the opposite sex—one's brothers, sisters, brothers-in-law and sisters-in-law, and male and female friends know others, including members of the opposite sex. More on all this, in its more critical context later, in Chapter 6: Passages, where the specific love problems in the life cycle are discussed. For now let us settle this critical element of the situation of encounters by offering an approach to it and a quick guide.

There's a technique for reading an encounter, and here's how it works. Notice all the things that have conspired to bring you together with another person. Do they suggest similar lifestyles and habits, which are a good barometer for eventual success? Did friends introduce you? Did you run into each other so often at the local supermarket that you began to say "hello"? Or do you belong to the same tennis club?

Common sense suggests that the closer you are to home, the more likely your chance of a fateful encounter. If you're a North American, you're not as likely to fall in love with an Argentinian as with another North American. If you're a church-going Roman Catholic, you're not likely to "click" with a Mohammedan. Similarly with most of the other factors making up what we call the social profile.

A famous entrepreneur once observed that there are really only two thousand people in the world, and it's easy to see what he meant. Our social status, careers, and outside activities tend to guarantee that we'll meet the people most like our social selves. In other words, in terms of whether a good match will result, the situation in which the encounter occurs is almost as important as what you bring with you in your head.

Every situation has its own particular set of circumstances and risk that establish the atmosphere of an encounter between a man and a woman. For example, when Theresa Dunn went looking for Mr. Goodbar, she hardly expected to be murdered. She wanted to get laid, plain and simple, no strings attached. But in her search for sexual freedom she forgot that very few things happen by chance.

Singles bars tend to be characterized by sexual hunger and vulnerability tinged with despair. If two people are desperate enough to go searching habitually for each other in singles bars, their encounter will reflect loneliness, eroticism, promiscuity and sheer fear, to say the least. There's a strong element of anonymity, which not only increases the risks of rape or brutal murder, but also reduces the chances of having a well-matched social profile. So if you pick someone up in a singles bar, don't expect it to be the beginning of a fairy-tale romance. The right elements of magic just aren't there.

A lot of this is basic common sense so I will not bore you with the minute details. Instead, I've constructed a kind of Michelin Guide to meeting people; one to three stars for good, better, and best. The chances for a successful click increase with the number of stars because the number of givens has varied accordingly. As I said, it's just good common sense, like winning at cards. Although there are times when bluffing pays off, generally, the better your hand, the better your chances.

I've differed from Michelin in one significant respect. I've listed the situations that should be avoided, the "turkeys," if you will. These objections aren't based on morality. It's just that one's experience suggests the odds aren't good enough. The chances that any one of them might lead to a meaningful relationship are so slim that I feel it's better not to try. Save your energy for the situations that have some possibility.

To be avoided: Singles bars, pick-ups at movies, parks or on public transportation. The anonymity means there are real risks in terms of safety. And there's absolutely no guarantee that there's any commonality of interest. (The encounter can be modified by habituation—for instance, mutual interest with someone who has shared a commuting vehicle for a long time, or with whom you ride the elevator regularly.)

Good	*Benefit*
Neighborhood stores, bars Package travel tours Same apartment building† Communal (or co-op) living Parties, other festive occasions	These situations provide similar socio-economic profile and lifestyle, plus a lack of anonymity.

Better	*Benefit*
Camping Clubs, both sports and social Night school classes Hobby, craft centers Community centers, YMCA, YMHA, etc.	All of the previous, plus a definite guarantee of common interests.

Best	*Benefit*
Friends Family acquaintances Workplace Church or synagogue School (high school or university) Neighborhood (the girl or boy next door)	All of the previous, plus lifestyles that already interact.

Moving right along the steps of intimacy, there are a couple more packages of elements or characteristics to be matched,

---

†*On same apartment building, sharing a house* or *communal living:* Paradoxically, dating in such environments has a way of backfiring—there's too much close surveillance in too smothering an environment to allow for the gradual rapprochement to familiarity that is natural in the development of love. In fact, there's a reversal in that people who are already on familiar terms but are really strangers seek to become close. And this doesn't work too well.

beyond the details of lifestyle and the more private attitudes of the persona that unfold as one progresses in courtship. These are habits and family relationships. They are gross behavioral externals, yet they count a great deal, especially in the cohabitative phase. How much does it take to love a man who speaks with his mouth full of food at the table, has unsavory and unsanitary personal habits and a couple of sexual kinks? How about a woman with a motor mouth and a monomania for neatness and cleanliness?

As we shall see, such habits may be unimportant or even unobserved in the eyes of the beholder even before they were blinded by being in love. Or else they may matter but not form a serious obstacle. Or else they may demand much more of the magical formula of opposites that attract and similarities that blend in order to absorb them. Indeed such habits, hang-ups, eccentricities, as well as would-be in-laws and faulty ties like being mama's boy or daddy's spoilt girl may tax tolerance to the limit, as much as would big gulfs in social profile like cross-racial, ethnic, or religious marriages. The given quantity of personal psychic energy is limited so that absorption of jarring habits and adverse family relationships may exhaust it before there can be any exercise of tolerance of opposite characteristics, however desirable and attractive they may be.

To all of which must be added the possible curves and zigzags in lifestyle, like a square city man attracted to a ruralized flower child; and the even more redoubtable aspect of public opinions and private attitudes of the persona. Consider in these terms the bright-eyed Trotskyite views of a bearded long-haired young man who does not believe in baths and showers though he may be a vegetarian and who also does not want to make a child, who may be perversely attracted to a conservative banker's daughter with traditional views on hygiene, politics, economics, health, and procreation. No matter how large any one gap, it may be bridged by love, as we know from love matches between beauties and beasts and between saints and sinners—but only within the mutual limits of mental endurance and tolerance, and depending on the composition of other opposites whose *distance* and *number* must then be reduced, and on the solid congruence of similarities.

A further and crucial key to the importance given to the discrete elements of each of these five packages (social profile, physique, lifestyle, and habits) is provided by the dynamics of perception and of motivation, that is, by the internal psycho-architecture of the couple.

One of the crucial attitudes, private and public, that cannot afford to stand in opposition in the clicking between couples is their desire to have their own or other people's (adopted) children. This didn't used to be such a problem before the epidemic of marital breakdown, zero-population-growth principles, the downgrading of homemaking (and of most other jobs and careers) and especially vasectomies and severing the fallopian tubes. But now it is. This problem is accentuated by the ground swell of male liberation. Men are no longer blindly devoted to "the little woman and the kids." They think more of themselves. When they come to an age, say thirty-five and over, when they have already "done their bit" with two plus children and a marriage behind them, they may be extremely reluctant to start it all over again, even if the woman is much younger, sexy, attractive, good, and loving.

Similarly women who have "done their bit" or else those who have no intention of doing it, of having children, may fall in love with men who, for valid reasons apart from macho, want children. The impasse may be physically as well as psychologically impossible enough to annihilate a most promising relationship. Where the social situation (financial, ex-marital, number and age of kids already produced) is not overwhelming, this problem, especially if it turns out to be just on the surface, may be reconciled in the ticking together stage. Otherwise it might be prudent to turn away, if it's not too late already.

THE INNER FORCES

As already stated, the overall effect of the inner motivational forces molding perception is to select from the one thousand elements a person possesses an internal check list of the quantity and quality and durability of characteristics given priority for a good fit. The real miracle of love is not that this is possible from the point of view of one person but that it coincides with a set of duplicate perceptions and motivations, hence a

similar order of priority in the other person to be equally fulfilled by the first person *and* at the same time.

The only reason this coincidence of needs and wants *can* occur is that everyone is (biologically) the same, some people are
(psychologically) like others, yet everyone is unique. In this respect, especially in the fit of opposites, lovers are inverted mirror images of each other.

There are three overlapping orders of motivations arising
from three relatively separate locations of the mind: the biological, the collective unconscious, and the personal or experiential unconscious.

We have already introduced the psychobiological motivation in terms of the universal law of attraction of quantified
dualities allowing a proportion of tolerable distances between
differences against the commonalities—the magical formula.
The purpose of this juxtaposition of opposites is a union, the
blending of two heads, hearts, and souls that are better than
two single sets of them; and generally the two sets make four,
including the zygote of love (the "it") and a progeny. What we
have not yet mentioned is that in time, after the many constructive quarrels in the service of the tolerant adaptations of
love, there is a *successive approximation* between the lovers.
Not only does their union achieve its own superior "personality," its integrity, but the disparate, complementary, apparently incongruent elements standing in polar opposition move
toward each other. Consequently, for example, an ultra-ratio-
nal man may soften toward spirituality and the supernatural,
while the woman who was inclined to be a psychic believer becomes less gullible and more hard-nosed. The extroverted
partner becomes more introverted and vice versa; the people-
lover becomes more cynical and an idea-lover and vice versa;
the colder, warmer, and so forth. Ultimately in the sticking
phase, the two coupled people resemble each other, much as
a faithful old dog resembles the little old lady who owns him.
This is the basis for their tacit understanding, transcending the
need to communicate verbally in established coupling.

The second order of motivation arising from the need of the
collective unconscious to pair up its imagery is the central part
of ticking.

But the third order of motivation, the one that arises from

personal experience, must be more than adumbrated at this time because without it we cannot fathom the full significance of clicking. As mentioned, it gives us a handle for understanding why certain contrasting elements are given high priority in attraction, why others are given lower priority, why others still are ignored, while yet others must be congruent or matched in similarities.

The unconscious context of experiences allows beauty to form in the eye of the beholder. It accounts, to a point, for one's sexual "type," for why a woman may seek, deep down, for instance, a dominant or a tender man rather than an intelligent one. It accounts for why a man may seek a scatter-brained or vivacious, or stable or creative woman, rather than a physically beautiful one. Indeed it may account for attraction between different races, cultures, or age groups, thus upsetting the usual order of similarities among geopolitically destined couplings.

The personal unconscious is also where all hell breaks loose; where the biggest errors are made when intuition functions faultily and when instinct is lost and neurotic relationships are formed, or when a vacuum may be created and no close relationships become possible.

The personal unconscious determines choices in elective relationships, which nonetheless are built on the old family patterns. This is when we "choose" types of lovers and friends who duplicate the kind of relationships we have had in our original family. These early-life formative experiences predicate not only our choices and patterns or subsequent behaviors in intimacy but also the prejudices we carry (the desires or wants, if you will) in relation to the product of these relationships, for example whether we wish to have children, and how many children. To give another example, if you are a neglected member of a large family, you're not going to be keen on having many or perhaps any children. If you've been a lonely only child, you may want to have lots of children. If you've been a happy member of a large family, you may want to replicate that situation.

Let us state firmly at the outset that a vital part of these motivations, albeit unconscious, are rooted in culture rather than strictly in personality. It is virtually impossible to disentangle many of the cultural from the strictly personally experienced motivations because we spend our lives, from the first moment of birth, in a cultural context. Hence everything personal is modified by culture.

Supposing a woman had an overbearing father whom she secretly loved but outwardly rejected and actually disliked, she may be motivated to become attracted to the opposite of her father figure, say to a soft, passive man. Now her culture may also be heavily patriarchal, favoring females marrying men in the image of their powerful fathers. In her attempt to escape this double jeopardy she may go in either direction. Or much worse, she may go in *both* directions by serially seeking dominant and passive men and being satisfied with neither; or by seeking apparently dominant males who are really inwardly passive (still, probably no good); or by seeking apparently passive males who are really inwardly dominant (which might just be all right). The only way she can resolve this conflict is to go with both the deeper personal motivation *and* the cultural demand and relate to a fatherlike figure.

Generally, in cases where a strong personal motivation is in conflict with a cultural ethos, the former wins the unconscious ground. And when a woman is in doubt because of an unresolved father complex, which means that deep down she is attracted to that type of man but behaviorally rejects him, she will make less of an error if she allows herself to be attracted to the original father figure than if she chooses someone in violent contrast to him. If, however, she has resolved her father attraction inwardly by really discarding that type, she is free to relate to another kind of man.

All of which shows you how complex the personal motivations are in determining the hominus for a woman. Obviously, exactly the same kind of considerations apply to the man in relation to his mother complex and his femina.

Learning what causes us to act in a certain way is a difficult task. Untangling this intricate web of motivation can often take the patient work of an expert. But since we're dealing with just one aspect of motivation—why we're attracted to another person—our task is simplified. We also have a solid starting point. Once we recognize that the more noticeable characteristics we find attractive in members of the opposite sex depend upon certain past experiences, such as how we were brought up, or how we related to our family, or how much we're subliminally influenced by our image-conscious culture, we can begin to understand what we might expect in a relationship.

Let's look again a little more closely at motivation. Motivation forms our attitudes and preferences. For example, a man who had an impoverished childhood might either crave luxury, or reject money totally and become a militant Marxist. But it's his motivation—either to overcome the deprivation of his childhood by acquiring a fortune, or to somehow validate his past by saying material things never mattered anyway—that forms his attitude toward money.

Motivation also determines our attitudes or preferences to people. It's just as easy for a deprived child to become a jet-setting playboy pursuing beautiful women as an extension of his lifestyle as it is for him to become a connoisseur of art. One pale Anglo-Saxon I know always falls for dark, voluptuous women because he imagines they're erotic, in contrast to his thin, blond mother who was cold, religious, and undersexed.

A well-balanced individual is motivated to seek a healthy match. But many people look for mates who will feed their neuroses. The difficulty is that neuroses aren't so easily cured. If there is something inside our own heads that's causing us to mismatch, it's not easy to summon the insights and courage to tear the scales off our erring eyes, especially without undergoing the hazardous and protracted journey of full-blown analysis. The task is further complicated by the fact that in most situations one explanation of motivation, such as a father fixation, is never enough. Motivation works on many levels and one problem leads to another. In seeking safety, we put more and more barriers between ourselves and satisfaction.

Consider the story of Erica. She's thirty, the child of an upper-class English family and the product of the right schools. Even though she had the brains to be a doctor, which is where she felt her vocation lay, she was shuffled off to teacher-training college because medical school wasn't considered appropriate for a girl from her background. At twenty she fell in love with a scholarship student who was studying to be a flutist. Her father disapproved and the relationship failed.

Erica felt the class system was ruining her life. She left for North America, taught for a few years, and ended up in Washington doing advance publicity work for a highly placed political candidate.

At present her healthy good looks, ready wit, and outgoing personality make her an ideal person for the job and win her a lot of friends. Her social life is active and sports-oriented. Tennis, sailing, and skiing are regular pastimes. But the men she mixes with on a day-to-day basis are just casual companions. Her heart belongs to someone else.

A year ago she met a late-middle-aged urban planner to whom she took a liking. Actually he reminded her of her grandfather. Erica has never forgiven her father for breaking up her love affair, nor has she forgiven the musician—a man her own age—for succumbing to her father's pressure. In fact, over the last few years Erica has begun to believe that her grandfather was the only man who ever really loved her.

Other than this familial resemblance and his loneliness that implied a neediness Erica would like to fulfill, the urban planner doesn't have a great deal to offer. He isn't as bright as Erica, nor is he handsome or great fun to be with. So although she encouraged intimacy, in the beginning Erica was frank about the fact that she didn't love him. She didn't want to hurt him by continuing to see younger men, and she wanted to absolve herself from unnecessary guilt if she decided to break off the relationship.

And yet gradually she fell in love with him, while his response had remained at the level of gratitude for her interest and companionship.

This strange situation is the result of many complicated motivations. The man fulfills Erica's need for security because she recognizes that his advancing age makes it unlikely that she'll be displaced by another woman. Deep down she also likes the idea that people will talk about the relationship, which makes her feel different—a little bit like a star.

As for him—well, on the surface, it's obvious. What older lonely man wouldn't be attracted to a lovely young girl? Still, if he does love her in return, he risks the heartbreak of abandonment at a time in life when he'll need her most of all. While his loneliness didn't bring happiness, it did provide a certain security. At this stage of his life, becoming dependent on a love that might be withdrawn at any time would be foolhardy

The harsh reality is that this relationship becomes a vicious circle. The tension of unrequited love is what sustains Erica's interest; the moment he lets go of his defenses, the moment he demands or nags, her affections will wane. Each of them is feeding off the other. She flatters his ego and makes him feel comfortable. He provides a sense of security and a certain notoriety. But their respective reactions of gratitude and frustrations are far from ideal. It's not the beautiful symmetry created when two equals fall in love.

SUMMARY

Now that we understand that our own psychology as well as the circumstances of the encounter influence our reaction to people, is there a way of knowing that we're attracted to people for the *right* reasons? In other words, is there a general rule that applies to all of us in our quest for a lasting and healthy relationship? The answer is yes. It harks back to the law of contrasting opposition, the magical formula of balance between the dialectical tension of opposites and the easy comfort of basic commonalities.

It seems to be a universal law of nature to seek balance, which man has recognized almost since he began to think.

Aristotle called it the "golden mean," the ancient Chinese talked about yin and yang, and the seventeenth-century English philosopher Sir Thomas Browne added a new wrinkle when he advised that those who endeavored to abolish vice destroyed virtue too. In other words, said Sir Thomas, the whole world is constructed on the basis of polarity and the very essence of life is contained in this conflict between opposites.

The advanced scientific knowledge of the twentieth century has only confirmed what our ancestors seemed to understand intuitively: the "fearful symmetry" produced by the fusion of opposites is basic to life. Now we can see it in the tiniest microcosm, the atom, where negative electrons and positive protons move about in a state of equilibrium; in the positive valency of sodium coupling with chlorine's negative ion to make the salt of the earth; in the split-brain discovery of medical science; in the odd and even number system of mathematics and binary system of computers, to name just a few examples. But perhaps Sir Isaac Newton said it best in his second law of thermodynamics: For every action there is an equal and opposite reaction.

Newton's law is a cosmic truth, but for Carl Gustav Jung, cosmic truths were simply grander manifestations of individual truths.

Jung believed that the human psyche, like the universe, is composed of many contrasting qualities that must be kept in balance. His studies of human nature indicated that people were never completely good or completely bad. Like Camille, a "fallen woman" who uses men for money and success, we all have a hidden side. When Camille falls in love, she sacrifices everything, including her life, for the man she adores.

Perhaps we're all so fascinated by tales like this because we intuitively recognize that they contain gems of a universal truth. Dumas's book *La Dame aux Camelias* served as a basis for the classic Garbo film *Camille,* and Verdi's eternal opera *La Traviata.* The book caused a scandal when it was published; who would dare suggest that a disreputable courtesan had any redeeming qualities? But Jung would hardly have raised an eyebrow, since Camille confirmed his theory that every surface characteristic is unconsciously balanced by its contrasting opposite. In other words, hearts of gold lurk behind even the most depraved exteriors.

So what does this have to do with coupling? Only that Jung's theory of balance can be observed in why people are attracted to each other. Just as a depraved exterior is often balanced by a heart of gold, so, for example, a seemingly rational, unfeeling scientist can be attracted to an intuitive artist for more than the obvious reasons. If it's a deep and lasting attraction, his motivation is healthy and can be seen as a drive toward establishing an equilibrium that he lacks within himself.

Jung believed that ideally each of us should contain an equal amount of all the human characteristics, but none of us is perfect. So when we're lacking a characteristic we unconsciously seek to have it balanced in our mate.

The essence of my argument is that people with opposite characteristics attract because they balance and complete each other. Similarly, likes repel because they already have the qualities and do not need them from others, with whom they would only compete. By borrowing from someone else, we can extend ourselves to include the whole range of any characteristic—reason to intuition, aggression to passivity, introversion to extroversion. In other words, happy coupling with a better half can make each of us a more complete whole.

Recognizing that there must be certain elements of contrasting opposition in any relationship—the yin and the yang— means that we must be careful to distinguish between real opposites and apparent or seeming opposites. Jack Spratt who could eat no fat and his wife who could eat no lean may have had very little garbage, but it's doubtful that their relationship was a healthy one. Both of them were obsessed with food, just as obsessively tidy people and slobs are both neurotic about neatness. Like the capitalist and the communist who are both possessed by thoughts of money, they're opposite sides of the same coin, and not true opposites.

The real problem with pairing based on compensating neuroses instead of healthy balances is that the partners become like parasites, feeding off each other (whereas healthy coupling is commensal, mutually and beneficially supportive). Instead of growing together toward a self-actualized coupling, neurotics lock themselves into support systems that shrink up the possibilities of life. In fact, psychiatric practice demonstrates that more often than not, when one partner conquers a neurosis, the other shows up for treatment because he or she can't cope with a well-balanced mate. We have come to call this type of coupling a lean-to.

In this chapter I've shown that we're attracted to people for some reasons we do understand and for some we don't, and that our reactions to people by the time we meet them are already prejudiced by our own psychology, as well as the circumstances in which the encounter takes place.

I've also outlined the basic criteria for intimacy: that opposites attract on a deep psychological level, but that in order for that to happen there must be a solid backround of similarities. Healthy couplings are characterized by a balance of characteristics. Lack of balance distinguishes nuerotic lean-tos. Given these guidelines, we can begin to move more deeply into our psyche to discover whether our attractions are healthy and conductive to a deep and fulfilling relationship or whether they reflect inner imbalances that we should work toward correcting.

In the next chapter, I'll identify those aspects of the psyche that need to be kept in equilibrium and show how they can become unbalanced. I'll also begin using the term unconscious in another way. Up to now, we've been talking about unconscious motivations that relate to our own personal experiences. But starting in Chapter 3 I'll discuss motivations of the collective unconscious, which are universal and apply to everyone. These determine the attraction or repulsion between people at a much deeper, more significant level.

A TEST OF GOODNESS OF FIT OR CLICK

This is a test of how well you might actually click with a person in whom you are currently interested. Check off one response from each of the three possible responses to each question.

Part A

The person to whom I am attracted

1. Is much older or younger than myself	Somewhat older or younger	About the same age
2. Belongs to a visibly different race	A different race but not visibly	The same race
3. Belongs to a very different ethnic or national group	Somewhat different	The same
4. Belongs to a very different social class (two or more notches)	Somewhat different	The same
5. Has been considerably more (or less) well) educated (by 5 years or more of schooling)	Somewhat more (or less) educated (less than 5 years)	About as well educated as I am

6. Has a very different level or type of occupation than myself	Somewhat different	The same level or type
7. Is much richer or poorer than myself (moneywise), by over $16,000 per year income or over $100,000 savings or inheritance	Is somewhat richer or poorer	Is at the same level
8. Belongs to a very different religion than the one I practice (e.g., Christian and non-Christian)	Either different religion but one of us does not practice, or practices different denomination of the same general religion	Same religion or its degree or lack
9. Belongs to a very different culture than I (e.g., European vs. Asiatic)	Somewhat different	No difference
10. Was brought up in a very different physical environment, (e.g., city vs. rural area)	Somewhat different, (e.g., downtown vs. suburbia)	No difference

Part B

The person to whom I am attracted is

1. Very different from myself in physique (height, weight, body frame)	Somewhat different	About the same

2. Very different in skin complexion and hair (light vs. dark)	Somewhat different	About the same
3. Very different in degree of energy possessed	Somewhat different	The same
4. Very different in the kind of persona presented (outgoing vs. ingoing)	Somewhat different	The same
5. Very different in temperament, (e.g., fiery vs. placid)	Somewhat different	The same
6. Very different in terms of attitudes and opinions—social, political and otherwise	Somewhat different	The same
7. Very different in terms of lifestyle, (e.g., trendy vs. traditional)	Somewhat different	The same
8. Very different in terms of interests, (e.g., physical activities vs. sedentary)	Somewhat different	The same
9. Has very different manners and habits, (e.g., polite vs. rude, or rough vs. refined)	Somewhat different	The same
10. Has very different family relationships and ideas about children than my own, (e.g., close family vs. distant, or wants vs. doesn't want children)	Somewhat different	The same

Scoring

1. Score 2 for each response in the first column (in each group of 3 per question)
   Score 1 for each response in the second or middle column
   Score 0 for each response in the third or last column
2. Add your score, totalling A and B separately and then together.

Interpretation

Overall (A and B)

35–40   You seem to be too far apart and are in for some quarrels over differences you may not be able to reconcile. Not compatible.

30–34   You've got to be extremely flexible, generous, adaptive, and in love to be able to make it. Doubtful.

25–29   Too far apart (still). Try another (you've got a maximum of 1999 potential partners left).

20–24   You're on the limits of the compatibility of opposites. If you're young at heart and in the head, adaptive and willing (in love), you might make it after initial difficulties (quarrels).

15–19   You're in the orbit of the magical formula for ideal sex and love, provided the proportions are right (i.e., the subscores A and B, following).

10–14   You are a bit too much alike unless you're older (in heart and mind) and fully matured.

5–9   You are at the limit of the compatibility of likes. The only way you can make it is if you're older (second or third time around) and looking for a comfortable complementary relationship. There will be some quarrels due to competition.

0–4   Far too much alike. If you are strongly attracted or think you're in love, you're narcissistic (i.e., in love with your own image). If it's mutual, you're a couple of narcissists. The relationship can work only if neither of you changes for the better (e.g., increases his or her capacity for true love). If that happens (a flipover), the relationship will fall apart.

The Subscores (Magical Formula)

1a.   If your total score is under 25 and over 19 but most of it comes from Part A (background, the givens), you're too far apart for your own good. Try someone else.

1b.   Buf if your total score (19–25) comes mostly from Part B (acquired characteristics of personality), you have a possible but difficult relationship, especially initially.

2a.   If your total score is 15–19 but comes almost exclusively from Part A, you're in for a tough time—too much energy to go into reconciling background difficulties. It takes exceptional people to make it (heroes).

2b.   If your score is 15–19 but comes mostly from Part B, you've probably hit the magical formula. Congratulations. Stick with it.

3a.   If your total score is 10–14 but comes mostly from Part A, you may have enough differences to keep you engaged in the relationship; but why try when there are other easier ones?

3b.   If your total score is 10–14 but comes mostly from Part B, you have too many similarities unless you're very mature and don't need this relationship to grow in.

4a.   If your total score is 5–9 but comes mostly from Part A, you may have enough differences to keep you busy if you are very mature, older and seek a complementary relationship, but in that case why try?

4b.   If your total score is 5–9 and comes mostly from Part B, you're too alike, unless you are very mature, older and seek a complementary relationship.

5a
&b   If your total score is 0–4 wherever it comes from, you're too much alike, whatever your age, maturity and marital status. If you insist on this relationship and if that's mutual, you're in for a narcissistic (self-loving) sickly coupling. If only one of you feels strongly, forget it.

A TEST OF HOW YOU COME ACROSS

Check one response from each set of responses.

Part A

1. a. I try to disguise my height by several inches.
   b. I'm content with my height the way it is.
   c. I'm dissatisfied about my height but don't do anything about it.

2. a. I try to disguise my weight or body contours (shape).
   b. I'm content with it the way it is.
   c. I'm dissatisfied about my weight, body shape, and so forth, but don't do anything about it.

3. a. I style my hair, to suit my face and fashion.
   b. I take ordinary care of my hair.
   c. I don't bother much with my hair, though I should.

4. a. I cap my teeth, or take great care of their appearance.
   b. I'm only concerned with the health of my teeth and gums.
   c. I neglect my teeth, though I shouldn't.

5. a. I change the color of my hair or take great care of the texture of my skin and the looks of my face, hair, and nails.
   b. I only care about the health of my skin, face, hair, and nails.
   c. I tend to neglect most of these, though I shouldn't.

6. a. I use makeup studiously and/or I take great care of my muscles.
   b. I take ordinary care of my face and body.
   c. I tend to neglect them, though I shouldn't.

7. a. I use artificial devices to enhance my "sex appeal."
   b. I do not use such devices.
   c. I'm dissatisfied with my physique but do nothing about it.

8.a. I dress for elegance in order to make the best impression possible.

  b. I dress to suit my mood or convenience.

  c. I don't pay much attention to how I dress, though I know I ought to.

9.a. I take great care of my clothes, shoes, hats, lingerie, undergarments.

  b. I treat them only as utilities.

  c. I tend to neglect them, though I shouldn't.

10.a. I try hard to look several years younger (older) than I am.

  b. I let my age show.

  c. I'm not happy with the age I look but don't do anything about it.

11.a. I wear quite a lot of different jewelry, adornments, or unusual watches or striking eyeglasses.

  b. I treat these merely as utilities.

  c. I pay no attention to such things, though I am expected to.

12.a. I am aware of my posture and maintain a good one.

  b. I make no special effort to keep up my posture.

  c. I ought to correct my posture but don't.

13.a. I am aware of my physical presentation and presence (or its effect on others) and try to enhance it.

  b. I take it as it is.

  c. I am aware of a lack in my physical presentation and presence (or it tends to be ignored) and don't do anything about it.

14.a. I am aware of the way I walk and carry myself and always try to use these to good effect.

  b. I walk and carry myself naturally.

  c. I know I ought to correct my gait and carriage, but I don't.

15.a. I exercise strenuously and try to exude health and vitality.
   b. I'm only interested in being healthy and not how this impresses others.
   c. I ought to exercise and gain energy, but I don't.

Part B

1.a. I am aware of my movements, body language, or nonverbal communication and try to make them count with others.
   b. I am sort of aware of these but don't use them to a specific social purpose.
   c. I am aware of being gauche or awkward or rigid in movements or stultified in body language or poor in nonverbal communication but do nothing to improve these.

2.a. I try to cultivate a certain manner and social behavior (like suave, smooth, cool, etc.).
   b. These are displayed naturally according to my mood and circumstances, without my manipulating them.
   c. I have been made aware of certain deficiencies in my manners and social behavior but have done nothing to rectify them.

3.a. I smile whenever appropriate or touch people or shake hands warmly.
   b. I only do so when I feel like it.
   c. I tend to shy away from this, though I want to.

4.a. I always try to maintain eye contact when face-to-face with other people.
   b. I only do it when I feel like it.
   c. I tend to look away, though I'd like to hold other people's eyes.

5.a. I'm always extremely careful about any and every odor emanating from me, whether by mouth, clothes or other, and swamp them with appropriate deodorants instantly.
   b. I only do this when the odor is offensive.
   c. I tend to forget about that, though I well know I shouldn't.

6.a. I modulate my voice very carefully so as to give a good impression, and I tend to do this in private also.
  b. I let my voice go according to my feelings.
  c. I tend to grate, be strident or monotonous but don't do anything about it.

7.a. I wear clothes, textured materials, hair styles, drive cars, and generally indicate a lifestyle for a certain effect (such as virility or femininity, out-of-doorsiness, elegance, opulence, etc.).
  b. I do these things to please myself.
  c. I would like to do that, but I don't—not because I can't, but because it's too much bother to concentrate on it.

8.a. I want to come across as a certain kind of person, such as attentive, polite, charming, good-mannered, kind, seductive, and do all I can to bring about that impression.
  b. I have no such interest, though I may have some of these qualities.
  c. I would like to impress people in a certain way all right, but I don't know how and can't keep it up even when I try.

9.a. I always try to sound, intelligent and deep and prepare myself accordingly.
  b. I don't much care how I sound, though I care how I am.
  c. I would like to sound like that but I can't keep up with it.

10.a. I try to look intense or very attentive to another person and always remember his/her name.
  b. I don't make any such efforts.
  c. I try but fail.

11.a. I have a distinct and studied signature.
  b. My signature simply evolved.
  c. I would have liked to make it striking but couldn't.

12.a. I try to come across as having good taste in food, clothes, clubs, traveling places, interior decor, and companions.
  b. Whatever taste I have is for me rather than others.

    c. I would like to develop such tastes and I have enough economic means to do it but don't know how.

13.a. I follow fashions in most things so as to be with it.
    b. I only follow fashion when it coincides with my taste.
    c. I should like to follow fashions, but I fail to do so.

14.a. I try to be sociable, outgoing, and care what others say or think, and generally I'm more aware of others than of myself.
    b. I have some of these tendencies without trying very hard and I have some of the opposite tendencies also.
    c. I am not sociable, outgoing, or aware of others, but I would like to be.

15.a. I try to be more objective than subjective, and to see everything and judge everything from other people's point of view rather than my own.
    b. I only do this when I judge it appropriate.
    c. I try but fail.

Scoring

Score only once for each group of 3 questions. Score +1 for a, 0 for b, −1 for c. Thus you should have scored 30 times with a number (+1, 0 or −1).

Interpretation

25–30   You try too hard to be somebody you aren't and you're driving yourself close to the brink.

20–24   You're (still) trying too hard to impersonate somebody else or to acquire a top persona or social mask. Are you sure it's worth it?

10–19   You're trying to bend backward your basically introvert nature and change into that of an impressive extrovert. Unless you absolutely need to sell yourself this hard, ease up somewhat.

5–9   You're going in the right direction—selling what you've got.

−4−+4   You're either very lucky to be so well endowed by nature, both physically and mentally—or you're too darn smug.

−5−−10   You're extroverted but don't show it. If you know it, you're too indolent to act accordingly. Try harder.

−11−−20   You must try and reconcile yourself with your basically introverted, bland persona.

−21−−30   You're either kidding with these answers or you must do something about your image.

Subscore Test Results

You can subdivide your persona, or social self, and the image you're trying to create into two major categories—the physical and the psychological impression. The former is largely represented by Part A, while the latter by Part B.

Thus you can gauge from your subscores where you succeed or fail the most.

Part A

11–15   Either you've got a very unfortunate physique, appearance, and presence and are trying against odds to overcome it, or you're oversold by TV ads and superficialities and want badly to sell yourself the same way.

5–10   If you're not terribly well endowed physically you're certainly trying valiantly to overcome it. Presumably you've really got to do it.

−4−+4   You're lucky in looking good, and wise to rely on what you've got.

−10−−5   You should seek some cosmetic, fashion, or motivational advice with your image because you seem to need it.

−15−−11   Either you're super narcissistic and physically self-conscious or a defeatist or both.

Part B

11–15	Either you've got a very unfortunate persona or psychological image and attitude, or you're an overambitious perfectionist who is trying too hard, or both.
5–10	You probably grew up under adverse circumstances, which didn't favor your "personality"—and you're trying valiantly to overcome your faults. Good luck!
−4–+4	You're lucky to have developed a good persona and wise to use it the way it is. Or else you've misjudged yourself.
−10––5	The odds are somewhat against you and you should probably seek some help with your image. Either you expect too much of yourself or you're worse off even than you think.
−15––11	You must be putting yourself down.

3

Ticking

*For any given (primary) colour the eye simultaneously requires the
complementary colour and even generates it, if it is not already present.*

—WILENTZ

The ticking phase of sex becoming love comprises the
latter period of courtship, the actual coupling that cements the
relationship and, often enough, sexual mating as well. By now
the couple has decided to invest more time in the relationship
and eventually to elevate the status of the relationship to an
exclusive one. This decision reflects the fact that love is monogamous and that it is well worth giving up variety in seren-
dipitous sexual pleasure. If mating ensues, sexual intercourse
becomes lovemaking, an entirely different attitude and feeling
from just having sex. Ticking may culminate with intimate
consorting and eventual cohabitation.

It is inevitable that we keep reassessing the role of sex
throughout the succession of its transformation into love, because it puts its eradicable stamp of uniqueness on this particular elective close relationship.

Sex sparks clicking; making love fuels ticking; and love itself, the world's most powerful aphrodisiac, oils sticking together.

Sex is much like a university degree. When you haven't got
it you become extremely frantic to get it. When it is within
reach your ecstasy climaxes. But when you've really got it,
when it is all yours, you wonder what the fuss was all about.
For some people, though, sex has a different academic flavor.

It's more like school examinations. Even when you've passed, you're haunted by the recurrent traumatic dream of sitting for the examination in a cold sweat. And the lengthening interval between passing those exams of sexual success does little to abate the blue funk that comes from a deep-seated fear of failure, inadequacy or unworthiness.

I call this phase ticking for three overlapping reasons. First, it hosts the transition from *falling* in love into *being* in love. Despite being starry-eyed and blinded, one has an innate if superficial curiosity to find out what makes the other person tick. There is also a corresponding fascination with what makes oneself tick in response to or in initiating the partner's response. This psychologizing interest parallels outwardly the intricate events going on inwardly under the curtains of the unconscious. It is this curtain we must now lift so that we might see what actually does make the couple tick.

Second, this phase is dominated by complex emotions. It is ruled by the ticking of the heart, whereas the clicking phase was ruled more by the senses and by intuition.

Much as we value emotions, they are mercurial, unstable, and prone to distortions. They mislead perhaps as often as they lead rightly. We learn to rely on them. But when things go wrong, when there is a flaw in the personality, when there is a pattern of errors in the clicking, in what and who attracts us, we must unlearn to rely so heavily on emotions. The main function of emotions is like that of the central nervous system, to advise us quickly about what's going on in the environment so that we may act accordingly. This type of information is built for speed rather than accuracy in adaptation. Also, the adaptive responses evoked by emotion, like reflexes of the nervous system, are not very discriminating or specific. Important details are overlooked. Specific adaptations happen subsequently, more slowly. In the body, the hormonal or endocrine system corrects the mistakes made by nerves. Analogously, thinking corrects the work of perception in clicking and of emotions in ticking together. After all, emotions emerge from a myriad of sources bubbling in the mud flats of the unconscious. In the ticking phase we tend to ascribe them to the burgeoning object of love. But they may well belong elsewhere. They may be displacements from the past, from previous hurts and blessings in the original family life, in school, work, social relationships and especially in relationships with the self.

The primary processes of the unconscious, taking place in the imagery of our creative self—the processes we are about to reveal—are often modified or translated faultily into secondary thinking, into false interpretations of feelings. This is where big mistakes are made—in the ticking phase. So we must try and discern intelligently these algorithms of the heart.

This brings us to the third reason for using this word, for we must listen to the ticking of our own heart and our head as well in order to find out what's going on inside.

One of the cardinal things going on there is a continuation of sorting out contrasts and differences contained in the archetypal images of the self and fitting them in the coupling process. So now we must meet these people within us and see what they're up to. And see what makes them tick in unison when they are bonded in a love relationship. It is this mysterious ticking of inner beings that provides the formula for the chemistry of caring, distilled out of sexual attraction, on its way to loving.

PERSONAGES OF THE INNER SELF

There are six levels to the inner psychoarchitecture of this city of Ur—the human psyche. They are represented by different symbols or personages of the inner self, which are progressively archetyped.

This internal architecture is symmetrical and built on the same principle as that governing coupling. In other words, the personages *inside* us stand in contrasting opposition and it is this very arrangement that is reflected *outside* us in coupling.

There may be no particular magic in this sixsome or the sixological (numerical) aspect of the persons within us. But they tend to oppose each other and relate as three pairs. They may also be seen (symbolically) to relate to the trinity of our physical, mental, and spiritual nature.

The deeper-dwelling personages especially are more archetypally represented than the more superficial; that is, they are symbolized by images that have been with mankind for eons, ever since mankind has known itself, so that accordingly these images emerge from the collective unconscious. Like ghosts of the distant past, they seek to become reincarnated into the "bodies" or personages that are formed during one's lifetime. So these archetypes relate to and find expression in the personal unconscious. And ultimately, like the haunting ghosts they are, they seek to emerge from the deep cavelike darkness of the unconscious into the light of day, into the external world, where they find expression and imprint in a coupling relationship. Thus the sixsome not only vitalizes coupling with their ghostlike spirit, but they actually determine the ultimate nature of the love match.

When these things come out, whether as feelings, imagery, dreams or in behavior, the trick is to have a "rosetta stone" so as to read them correctly, to know what they mean and whence they came.

Herewith the rosetta stone of the six people dwelling within each human:

The first of the people inside us is the *persona*. This is the public and social self, the image we act out, the mask we put on in the presence of others. The persona is more than clothes, makeup, toupees, girdles and silicon breasts. Though it is the most visible part of this self, externalized in behavior, in public and semiprivate attitudes, and especially in lifestyle, the persona is deeply imbedded in the unconscious, in the hidden layers of the psyche. Consequently the persona is the archetypal repository of the typical symbols or masks of humankind. Yet the persona relates and adapts to the realities of the environment.

The second personage is a more spiritual aspect of the self; it is that which we would like to be, the *ideal self.* It contains one's most private dreams and aspirations, our ultimate goals and purposes.

The third is equally spiritual and closely related in that it is the ideal mate, the man (*hominus*) or woman (*femina*) who turns you on automatically, electromagnetically. Archetypally they may be represented by any of the sexier Greek, Roman, or even earlier gods. The woman (femina) is the Helen of Troy in whose quest man will risk anything for any length of time. The man (hominus) is the knight in shining armor.

All these three creatures of the inner self we have met already because they play an important part in clicking.

The fourth personage stands in sharp contrast to the persona. It is, in fact, its exact opposite. Even more so, it is the other side of the ideal self-image. It's called the *shadow.* Its archetype is Mr. Hyde, the beast within us—the id-driven earthbound animal self; as dark and ominous as the ideal self tends to be luminous and celestial. Meeting up with one's unconscious, shaking hands with one's own shadow, is one of life's most awesome experiences.

Let me not mislead you. The shadow is called that because it dwells deep in darkness, not because it is always sinister. It tends to be the ugly, animalistic part of the self because we usually put our best foot forward and show our nicest side. Then, we keep the obverse beast within us. But, as we've often pointed out in these pages, man is a creature of necessary contradictions and perverseness. So that when we put our worst foot forward and show the worst side of the self in the persona, the shadow is lovely.

On the fifth floor, as it were, there dwells an older being, in the sense that she/he has been there longer than the others, especially insofar as she/he relates to the personal unconscious or the individual's life experiences. This is the *eternal child,* the *puer aeternus* or *puella aeterna* (eternal boy or girl). This is the irrepressible spirit of the child we were; more important, the child we might have been; ultimately the child of nature, to whom nothing is impossible. It is the little boy a woman sees in a grown-up man. She falls in love with him so often that Eros himself is thus symbolized as an impish angel with a fatal bow and arrow capable of piercing any heart. It is Puck who performs the same function in *A Midsummer Night's Dream,* when among other contrasting opposites, he unites the beauty and the beast as well as night (Oberon) and the morning glow (Titania) or Diana and Apollo. And finally the eternal boy, when he persists within us, is Peter Pan; the girl is Wendy, who doesn't quite succeed, presumably because of the greater momentum of her gender to gain maturity.

The one sensory quality of the eternal child is kinetic freedom, which is so intense that the child is no longer earthbound. Unlike Prometheus or Adam and Eve, who have sinned and been punished by becoming gravity-bound, the child within us is free in space and time. He levitates. And his continuous existence inside us is celebrated by levitation sleep dreams, when we float freely on top of vales and hills. Indeed this philobatic (space-free) propensity is the one that has given us wings, in hang-gliding and flying, no less than the inspiration to create animated or real creatures to rise above the earth, like Superman or the astronauts.

The eternal girl, though she shares with the boy the same propensity for irrepressible freedom, symbolized by a bird and actualized by a soaring ballerina, also possesses a gender characteristic. She is a coquette, a charmer with not quite the same innocence or lack of guile as a boy.

The eternal child stands in contrast to both the ponderous persona, bound heavily to conventions, realities, and responsibilities; and to its obverse, the Plutonian cave or hell-dwelling shadow, where Hephestus (the god of the underworld) symbolizes man's most certain nature—his sinfulness. The eternal child is both convention and conscience free. His prescientific curiosity could lead him to pull wings off insects, not sadistically but innocently, to see what flies do when they find out that they are reduced to a toddler's creeping, crawling, walking, and wingless state. The eternal girl may seduce the pedophile, father or son, not pervertedly, but in presocialized innocence, in order to see what might happen.

The sixth and last personage is the most mysterious and undefinable of the lot—the *anima,* the soul, the repository of all that's spiritual in man or woman. Curious enough, Jung, a Swiss patriarch, seems to have forgotten to give gender identity to the more superficial dwellers of the psyche, for he omitted the hominus and *puella aeterna,* the woman's viewpoint of those images. Yet he separated what is surely sexually inseparable—the human soul—into the male soul (animus) possessed by a female and the female soul (anima) possessed by males, thus emphasizing a total gender duality. Inasmuch as the anima is the inner mortal cornerstone, it cannot have a gender. It is the most remote part of our earthbound, biological, and human nature; the only place where man and woman are truly joined in total sameness. The anima, therefore, stands in contrast to the shadow; however base the latter, the former remains lofty. It contrasts with the persona; however tough and realistic the latter, the rational hardheaded side, the anima is enfolded in beliefs and bathed in the mystique of numinosity. The anima is the locus of real religion, that is, of man's deepest solicitude. It breathes inspiration over all universally valued creativity.

In the microcosmic reality of the psyche, no less than in cosmic reality, nothing exists separately. It is the intellectual function of human intelligence that requires separate analysis for the sake of study, understanding, and utility. But the real world is holistic, all together. In the psyche the integrating force is the *self*. This is the whole ball of wax; all that's inside, subjective, and real and all that's personal but outside, objective, and equally real. It is the cement of this sixology.

The development of language reflects these truths intuitively so that the modern idiom "getting it all together" means just that: the self exercising a benign rule over the close and happy cohabitation of these persons within us; also the dyad or couple pulling themselves together. For that to occur in good balance, for a healthy harmony to exist, these internal characters may contrast but not conflict with each other, for they must make a coherent whole; similarly in coupling. Unhealthy, unbalanced minds lack this integrity because these inner persons are violently opposed to each other and because the self is out of touch with them. These personages of the inner self are like loose marbles when they step out of their boundaries in the unconscious; when they break the inner mental barriers and invade our conscious behavior by acting out their unruly nature. Then we are "out of our minds."

In fact, if there were such a thing as "a nervous breakdown" or, more proper, a mental breakdown, or if the description of "something snapped in my mind" meant anything, it would amount to the tension between conflicting and contrasting personages of the inner self breaking when they are too far apart and the integrating force of the self not being able to hold them together.

Remember it is easier and simpler to describe and illustrate the somewhat abnormal or extreme example, as related in *The Strange Case of Dr. Jekyll and Mr. Hyde, Sybil* and *The Three Faces of Eve*, than the smoothly functioning normal case.

Thus, to make the point, I shall often overemphasize the difference and lean toward the abnormal end of the spectrum. But the overall idea remains valid at both ends.

Now that we've just been introduced to these six personages, let us do three things. First, let us familiarize ourselves with them a little more. Next, let us see how they determine coupling in general. And finally, let us see what specific roles they play in ticking.

The persona then is Farrah Fawcett, the sex symbol; Scrooge, the miser; Richard Nixon, the President—the facade we all possess. The persona is polished by image makers, the Madison Avenue crowd. It is broadcast by the mass media, proclaimed by the doctor at the bedside, the lawyer in court, the academic or cleric on the podium or pulpit, the con man on the street, and the hardnosed investigative reporter on the job. Don't let's think the persona is just an empty package. Good manners, charm, style, presence, and charisma can be an accurate reflection of the inner person and not be donned merely on professional or social occasions. In fact, the normal healthy man's inside is pretty close to his outside look, even if he is a complex, multifaceted *gemini* type.

One of the things that makes the persona hard to read is stereotyped images, particularly sexual stereotypes in North America. If the perceiver of a person resembling such stereotypes also lacks the perspicacity to see through the persona right through to the shadow, a great many opportunities are missed.

For instance, there was a man who liked to sing and dance, who played the piano superbly but played no sports and was perfectly helpless with a hammer or saw. In fact, he couldn't change a light bulb. Neither could he cook an egg, because he was born with a silver spoon in his mouth. Moreover, his father died young, before he could pass on masculine skills, whatever they might be. Though he appeared not at all effeminate, he was suspected of misorientation in that direction, particularly because he was also a loner. Accordingly he was given a wide berth by most women, except one, an only daughter, the apple of her father's eye. Her father was a typical jock, a sportsman, a do-it-yourself, the whole bit. The woman was good with a hammer and saw and good at sports, but a feminine softie deep down. She could see the toughness in the fiber of the man's anima and fell in love with him. In the end he did the better cooking while she did the hammering and the TV hockey watching. He also learned to change bulbs and he proved to be superb in bed. And he was by far the dominant member of the coupling despite his deceptive appearance and the wise nodding of knowing acquaintances.

The persona, "the clothes that maketh the man," is what stands revealed at the initial encounter and for a while thereafter. But we all know that "all that glitters is not gold." It does not take special psychological sleuthing skills to see beyond the social mask. But there are people who tend to be overimpressed by externals, by superficialities, by the tree without seeing the wood. This may be because of a heavy cultural emphasis on materialism or because of early deprivations or a persistent poverty of spirit. Sometimes a penchant for the mere persona is somewhat pathological, as the following two people will show.

Barbara is thirty-two years old, the executive assistant to the president of a large corporation. She's intelligent and attractive, although inclined to be dowdy in the way she dresses. But she's extremely competent at her job. In fact, aside from her painful shyness, her main problem is her terrible taste in men.

When you talk to Barbara about growing up, there's one experience she always remembers. Every time her younger brother Tom entered the room, her parents seemed to forget about her. She tried to gain their attention by helping out around the house and bringing home report cards filled with A's, but nothing worked. She remained the dutiful daughter they took for granted. It was witty and charming Tom they adored.

Barbara knew Tom was a fraud. He cheated on exams and embellished his schoolyard stories with exaggeration. But Barbara sensed that Tom's need to lie about who he was hid a weakness she could control. By doing his homework and chores, and just generally covering up for him, she made him dependent on her and gained the upper hand.

All the men Barbara has been involved with become reflections of Tom. She gravitates toward witty and charming con men who have a flair for telling stories and a propensity for dishonesty. But they are popular at parties, and indirectly give her the center stage she's always wanted but never had. As well, their weaknesses satisfy her long-standing unconscious need for control.

Or take the case of David—there seems to be one in every crowd—a self-effacing pussycat who is consistently attracted to women with acid tongues and personalities to match. Spending an evening with him and his latest lady is like finding yourself cast in a TV sitcom: David and Gladys, the henpecked husband with the harridan of a wife.

Why, one wonders, would anyone be motivated to seek a negative persona in a mate? In this case, David was the middle son. His older brother was brilliant, cutting, and manipulative, and his younger brother was a bully. He himself gave his parents no trouble and became a social worker, but he never believed they were as proud of him as they were of the other two—a successful lawyer and a college athlete. His consistent attractions to women who combined the worst elements of both brothers was an effort to compensate: If he couldn't be like his brothers, he'd have a woman who was.

The ideal self is usually well hidden in the preconscious. It becomes manifest when mousy Norma Jean becomes Marilyn Monroe or a skinny boy becomes Robert de Niro. But it is virtually impossible that the short, fat, bald man you met at a party sees himself as a Kennedy princeling politician on the stump. Yet sometimes an outsider will sense the idealized self-image inside another person before she or he does, hence the Pygmalion myth. Eliza Doolittle was unfair in charging that Professor Higgins made her over, as a fair lady, in his own image. Her falling in love with him helped. But, in fact, Higgins transformed the flower girl, Eliza, into her own ideal image—the toast of London.

The reason Walter Mitty got nowhere is that he lacked a stable ideal self—he had too many of them. Possibly that is why comedians like Peter Sellers, unlike Charlie Chaplin—the tramp—can impersonate so many different characters.

The ideal opposite sex, or love partner, the femina (a man's ideal woman) and the hominus (a woman's ideal man) are highly charged with sexuality. But they are not only instant turn-ons; they also evoke more permanently romantic feelings.

Because this personage possesses biological, hence transpersonal, significance, the roots lie in the deeper collective unconscious; and the image is archetypal, as mentioned above. However, these ancient images, the femina in Venus, Helen of Troy or Cleopatra, and the hominus in Hercules, Adonis, the knight in shining armor, or Prince Charming, are modified by modern culture, the film factories, and transformed into Greta Garbo, Marilyn Monroe, and Sophia Loren, or Elvis Presley and Superman. Then these obvious sex symbols get further transformed from movie and football heroes to the girl and boy next door, where they're often tinged with an incestuous touch (all in the family) or with a touch of school class.

But while the *image* of Superman might whet our erotic fantasies, Superman in the flesh might not seem so appealing. The essential thing about the hominus/femina is that they're *ideals;* they don't snore, complain, or have jungle mouth in the morning. They're composed of glorified aspects of mother/father, sister/brother, girl/boy next door, romantic hero/heroine, and movie star. They represent not so much what these people were but what they might have been. Still, the hominus/femina we're in search of influences every encounter we have with a member of the opposite sex.

Both images are strongly affected by culture. In our society, they result from the collective efforts of Hollywood and Madison Avenue combined with the sexual freight left over from literature and myths. A normal North American male inundated with images of the Dallas Cowgirls as a feminine ideal won't become feverish at the sight of a Hottentot woman with a ring through her nose. Nor is an urban woman who thinks Robert Redford the sexiest man she's ever seen, likely to curl her toes at the vision of an Eskimo man spearing a whale. An Eskimo woman would have a different response. Her conditioning would make her receptive to the hunter's physical appearance, and her unconscious mind would connect hunting prowess with the "masculinity" of a good provider.

Since it's shaped before puberty, which for many of us was pre–women's lib, the hominus/femina tends to correspond to the more traditional concepts of masculinity and femininity. Because most of our historical assumptions about sexuality were established in a patriarchal society, they support the view that women should be passive and men aggressive. These ideals permeate the whole body of our literature and mythology, which play such a large part in the formation of the hominus/femina. So it will be a long time before these archetypes change, and the deep dark recesses of the mind are absolutely free of their past influence—before we're completely comfortable with the idea that women can be independent, aggressive *and* sexy all at the same time, and that it's not only permissible but desirable for men to cry.

This is confirmed by the attention that problems with male sexuality have attracted in recent years. The impotence epidemic, in particular, indicates that many men have trouble fitting the "new" woman into their idealized sexual images, or feminas. As much as their intellects may approve, when they find power instead of passivity, many of their psyches can't cope, and their bodies act accordingly. It's an unfortunate fact that such problems can't be solved overnight. It will take more than a decade of social change to erase the archetypal conditioning of centuries.

In a similar way, women are inclined to respond to power, for power is an effective aphrodisiac. In Western society the hominus tends to be the matinee idol, the tall dark hero of romantic novels, or the knight in shining armor who will whisk the fair damsel away into worlds of unbridled passion. In many ways this is the male image peddled by the enormously popular Harlequin Romances. The current success of these books is evidence of the durability of a hominus image.

Both the hominus and the femina represent the ideal mate a man or woman wants to make love to. When a man says "she's my type," he's talking about his femina, and if this vision of his dreams strolls into a party one night he's bound to fall head-over-heels in love at first sight, like Rhett Butler for Scarlett O'Hara. It's the "it" of sex appeal, the old "oomph" for her and the new "machismo" for him.

Both images depend heavily upon the relationship children have with their parents. If the reaction against the parents is violent, the hominus/femina is likely to be constructed as a parental opposite. A boy with a cold, dark, and aloof mother, who always felt emotionally starved, is likely to have a warm, loving, and blonde femina. Similarly, a woman I know who had a rough, tough, and rugged but philandering father fell for slim, wispy, and aesthetic men. But sometimes this idealizing image rests on false premises, and completely throws a relationship out of whack, as the following story illustrates.

Because she was so beautiful—tall, slender, and blonde, an Elvira Madigan type—it was easy for Donald to imagine that she was the girl of his dreams: soft, romantic, and feminine. In fact, in many ways, she was. But she was also extraordinarily talented, intelligent, and determined to succeed at her career as a fashion designer, all of which suggested a drive that didn't fit with his concept of femininity. Still, there was a very strong sexual attraction between them, so they decided to spend a weekend at a romantic old inn outside the city. The first night was like a scene from a movie—champagne, a candlelight dinner, the works, but with a difference. Unlike our image of Hollywood heroes, Donald was impotent.

Donald was a man who believed wholeheartedly in women's lib. And yet he now realized that his psyche just couldn't cope with a woman who really was his equal. She was just as intelligent and successful as he—in fact, she probably earned a shade more money—and when they got into bed she was equally aggressive. She *looked* like his ideal woman, the one he'd dreamed of making love to. But somehow, when he'd constructed the scenario in his head, he'd imagined that he'd be more in control.

This is another example of how much love is beyond our control. It's not a rational process. The battle of the sexes is still being fought with an out-of-date rule book. We all know it. But how do we cope until the proper revisions are made? They're now part of our intellects, but they must work their way down into our unconscious where the mysteries of love actually abide.

The eternal child is also archetypal in that it rises from the marshes of the collective unconscious, from the childhood of the human race, because of the miraculous transition from child to man and woman. But the essential childlike qualities are retained: spontaneity, wonderment, acceptance, impishness, irrepressibility, and curiosity. And these qualities transform the archaic image, through cultural adaptation, to modern and personal ones.

And we know from Freud's study of sexuality, from the *Lord of the Flies* and *The Turn of the Screw,* that children or their spirits are not always innocent. Indeed, to learn how evil a child can be when reverting to nature as the characters from these novels did, one would almost believe that we are born in sin or at least steeped in perverse libido. In such cases the eternal child stands more in contrast to the ideal self and even the shadow (which might then be gentle and kind as the child is nasty and cruel).

As a result of the admixture of the collective and personal experiences of the past, the eternal child within us stands in contrast to the adult self and, often enough, in contrast to the child we have actually been.

A man who likes to play practical jokes, like that lovable urchin Puck, might have been a quiet and dreamy boy. His *puer aeternus* just represents a longing for the carefree innocence of childhood, which he's now free to demonstrate in a way that corresponds to the man he has become. So, as I said, the eternal child is a composite of the child we were, the child we'd want to be, and the child that never was.

The desire to become children again follows a primary law of biology, which is that the history of the individual repeats the history of the race. Or, in more scientific jargon, ontogeny repeats phylogeny. Children are like primitive man. They believe in magic, fairy tales, and ghosts, just as their ancient ancestors believed in evil or benevolent spirits who controlled the wind, the rain, and the sun. Allowing the child to play a part in an adult relationship means that each partner somehow becomes part of the much larger framework of mankind. We go back to our spiritual origins. It's a mysterious and perhaps a slightly difficult point, but I make it because I feel it offers just one more nuance to the beauty and complexity of love.

In the best couplings, the eternal child skips in and out like sunbeams dancing on the water. Both partners play sister and brother, father-daughter or mother-son, and this is healthy. As we've already suggested, the more varied the roles partners can play with each other, the more vigorous the relationship. Playing house with your mate can also be a good preparation for parenting, but if there's too much childishness in the relationship—the coy little girl who talks baby talk to her husband all the time—there's an undercurrent of incestuousness that may be unhealthy. In short, if the eternal child within allows us to play out all its potentials in coupling—adults as children at play, the man as father to his "girl," the woman as mother to her "boy"—all's well. But if the relationship is fixed incestuously and one-sided or lopsided, it's not all well—it betrays the rigidity of a neurosis.

On acting out the eternal child, whether this comes down to baby talk or just the tenderness they show a child, the couple is engaged in a full dress rehearsal of parenthood whether they know it or not and whether they'll stage it eventually or not.

The myth of the omnipotent North American male encourages partners to play the roles of father and daughter, but now that women have realized the high cost of dependence, I suspect that this will become a less dominant part of male-female relationships and assume a more realistic function as one of the many games people can play. Still, I wonder what will become of one couple I know. They've been locked into these roles for several years and, although the husband doesn't seem to notice, the signs of strain are beginning to show.

Timothy is an aggressive outdoorsman, an avid squash player, hunter and all-round athlete. His wife, Linda, appears to be fragile and delicate, a woman who's always ailing, like Mimi in *La Boheme*. They have no children. Although Linda would like to have a job outside the house, Timothy won't allow it. So she passes the time cooking and gardening and spending the generous allowance Timothy provides.

Why would a man be so determined to force his wife into the role of a Dresden doll rather than flesh-and-blood woman? Why is his need to play father so strong that it's suffocating any *real* emotions and needs that exist within the marriage? As a boy, Timothy overheard quarrels between his parents that focused on sexuality. His mother was an asexual woman, but his father insisted on exercising his "conjugal rights." Timothy was powerless to protect his mother.

Now that he's a man—powerful and established—Timothy can avenge his mother through his wife. He treats her as his mother wanted to be treated. But Linda is a different woman.

I strongly suspect that she's playing the part of the ailing and asexual creature because she knows that that's the woman Timothy wants. But how long can she sustain the role?

It's a difficult situation. Timothy is so obsessed with fulfilling his own needs that he's ignoring hers. If she revealed to him the passionate side of her nature, he'd be shocked. So she may be forced to find the kind of sexual satisfaction she needs outside the marriage.

The he-man myth runs throughout our society like a subterranean stream. This means that the eternal child is a part of the psyche that's less easily displayed by men, because it's considered not "masculine" to be childlike. For women almost the opposite is true. Girlishness is not only socially acceptable, it's often considered downright sexy, because it suggests that the male is the more powerful member of the couple. *Playboy's* Playmates have always had the appearance of overdeveloped girls-next-door for that very reason. In addition, their enormous breasts suggest mother. A man with the inclination could probably fantasize that he was ravaging his mother and his daughter, both at the same time.

And let's not forget literature and the movies. The sexual fantasies of many of our creative men seem inclined in that direction. The myth formed the basis for one of the earliest novels in the English language, Richardson's *Pamela,* and reached an apex (or nadir, depending upon your point of view) with Nabokov's *Lolita.* It is suggested that Lewis Carroll lusted after young girls, and that this is what gives *Alice in Wonderland* its particular charm. Louis Malle recently added some fuel to the fire with his brilliant film *Pretty Baby.*

On the other hand, while most women would admit that the character of Tom Sawyer is an appealing one, few have lusted after him as a sex object. Yet there are some women who are attracted to predominantly childlike men, and we might wonder why, since it tends to go against the grain of social conditioning.

Too often the relatively asexual woman can only accept a man when she relates, like a proud mother, to the boy within him. This is particularly so in cultures discouraging aggressive eroticism in women. In some cases, this is healthy. If, for example, a woman was burdened with responsibility and didn't have much fun as a child, she might be inclined to respond to spontaneity before all else. Perhaps she developed the persona of a bland and serious woman, and she needs a fun-loving imp to show her the other side of life. Only through him can she become the child she never was.

If you feel that you have too great a need to play out the parts suggested by the eternal child, or that you're consistently attracted to the childlike qualities in members of the opposite sex, then it's worth examining why. Your need to find a father or mother figure might be at the root of your faulty relationship. In searching for someone who will take care of you, you may be running away from the responsibility of being an adult. And until you grow up or allow your mates to be autonomous, you'll always have lopsided relationships rather than the beautiful symmetry created by two balancing equals.

But it is with the shadow that the contrasting opposition between the people inside reach their dichotomized zenith and therefore, perhaps the greatest dynamic. The shadow is not only Freud's id or animal self, contrasting with the ego, which is the adaptive civilized self, or all that the persona isn't; the shadow is the repository of all that's to be hidden in man's mental cave, good or bad. It is a microcosmic Hades though it may well shelter a Persephone or an Orpheus or a saint (in a whore's or a pimp's clothing) no less than a crippled Hephestus, a vicious Cerberus, or the hound of the Baskervilles. The primitive and modern seven arts abound with archetypal shadows indicating their procrustean bed in the collective unconscious. These archetypes are then adopted, as it were, by the personal unconscious, related to one's own life experience, and carefully repressed and locked deep inside us. When a personality flipover occurs—and this may be predictable if the relationship between persona and shadow is distant, conflictual and unstable—it is the shadow, Mr. Hyde, that takes over. This is when the bland banker's clerk, loyal for a quarter century to his master, turns crook overnight; when the roué takes over the man of high morals; when a judge turns criminal. But don't forget, it can happen the other way round, as the history of so many saints testify. Both St. Augustine and St. Francis of Assisi (my favorite sinner) were virtual sociopaths in their youths. To prove the existence of the shadow we need not go to R. L. Stevenson's extremity of Mr. Hyde.

In vino veritas means that when the niceties of the persona are stripped off by wine, the dark side stands revealed in contrast. Like all simplistic dicta this only tells half the story; for the wine reveals the half regarded by the self as inferior, while sobriety tells the equally true half, the persona. This is the core of inherent human contradictions. Will the real self stand up, please? They both are: the somber, sober man and the gay drunk; the plain housefrau and the *heterai,* the seductress.

It is not only in the cups that shadows are revealed but under any condition that lops off the inhibiting layers of frontal-lobe gray matter. For instance, laughing gas in the dentist chair or during delivery shows a spark of the cosmic joke in the most humorless person. When I gave this gas routinely to stutterers in order to see if they could be persuaded to talk normally, I found out that universally they laughed at the puniness of human concerns and affairs. Moreover, they laughed at our miniscule planetary dwelling place, the earth, for they were levitating in outer space, not unlike fliers twenty miles above the earth or astronauts one hundred miles or more away experiencing the "break-off" phenomenon.

Perhaps the most comical and melodramatic of the unashamed exhibitions of one's shadow occurs late in the second stage of a delivery when in her disoriented mental state the woman tells the naked truth, often to her obstetrician's chagrin. She releases part of her shadow in no uncertain manner but covers it up subsequently in a blanket of amnesia, when everybody helps to cover her embarrassment up again by laughing off her previous ravings.

The shadow comes out at night regularly in sleep dreams and haunts insistently the person who has totally forsaken and cloistered it. But in good mental health, the shadow contrasts only to a degree with the persona so that they form a smooth continuum, which is part of a complex personality. The shadow is exposed only partially and fragmentally to consciousness, and to intimates in behavior, except in extreme events of mental dislocation and stress.

And let me add this: When you meet your own shadow and

recognize it, from a dream or a composite of your extravagant impulses, it is awesome to behold—an unforgettable experience. The intensity of that encounter can only be compared to meeting your own shadow in another person in a prospective lover or friend. This is then apt to start the chemical mass action of love. The interplay between personages of the inner self in coupling explains many a long-acknowledged fact. For instance, when you say of the other person "He brings out the worst in me!" what happens is that his persona brings out your own shadow. In fact, that's how and why couples are matched through the attraction of opposites in the first place: His titillating devilment spurs your shadow and this enables you to become better in touch with yourself. In the end, through continuous contact and after many quarrels, if the initial attraction to a shadow proves important enough to sustain a relationship of love, his persona will be tamed by yours. Your own shadow will color your persona much more and you will not only *come* closer *together* and become more like each other, but you will also *be* more together within yourselves.

So the acerbic shrew has a mousy shadow, just as the mousy man has a streak of strength usually displayed as an indomitable stubbornness. They play a balancing game between the private and public selves.

The novelist Robertson Davies once said that to discover what a man fears most, you must look at what he tries hardest to hide. These are the qualities of the shadow, all the moral disvalues such as dishonesty, faithlessness, or cruelty. The less they fit with our persona—the image of ourselves that we want to present to the world—the more we'll try to keep them hidden, yet it's not hard to discover what qualities people harbor in their shadows. Just ask them to think of the worst sins they can imagine. The answers—brutality, perversion, dishonesty, and so on—will lead you straight to their shadows. Remember, nobody, but nobody can be as good as gold. At best you can only be as good as a gold alloy.

Still, as mentioned, the shadow doesn't always have to contain the undesirable elements of our personalities, just the ones that for one reason or another don't fit with our persona. Books and movies are filled with characters—criminals and ladies of the night, for example—who have been forced by circumstance into social roles (persona) that obscure the true decent people hidden away in their shadows. From his councils to the Prince, one would guess that Machiavelli's shadow was as honest and honorable as his dishonesty was apparent and skin deep.

As stated, in a well-integrated person, the differences between the shadow and the persona aren't particularly extreme. On the other hand, in neurotics they're often diametrically opposed. When this is the case, there's too much stress beween the persona and the shadow, and they sometimes trade places in what I call a flipover.

As already mentioned, this flipover has befallen many of the Christian saints (St. Francis and St. Augustine, for example) who experienced road-to-Damascus style conversions but were really just playing musical chairs with their personas and shadows. In fact, many of the original followers of Christ were ripe for a flipover, and He just seemed to provide the catalyst to get it going. Like Mary Magdalene, they were people whose unsavory personas harbored saintly shadows.

The best writers seem to have grasped this concept intuitively, and by applying it to a coupling they've come up with some of the most fascinating relationships in literature. When the personas and shadows of two people complement each other, they're drawn together like iron to a magnet, and they acquire universal appeal because we all sense the underlying truth upon which the attraction is based. Take Katharina in *The Taming of the Shrew*, for instance. She's the wild and fiery bitch who is "tamed" into a submissive woman. Petruchio's plan could only succeed because he was astute enough to see that, in her shadow, she was a tender, loving woman. But, of course, Petruchio could only conquer Kate because she, too, understood intuitively that they were complementary. His normally easy-going persona hid a high-tempered shadow, which he deliberately manipulated to conquer her.

Still, we might wonder what forces are at work when someone is so strongly attracted to the qualities hidden deep within the shadow, when other characteristics are more obvious. This usually happens when a person has had a long history of oppression. He or she lives out a rigidly enforced social role—

life at the persona level—and this kind of oppression forces the qualities of his or her shadow to go deeply underground where they fester. Such people look for a mate who will release these hidden qualities.

In order to keep peace with her widowed mother, for example, one woman I know (we'll call her Mary) succumbed to the pressure to become a perfect little lady, the soft and pretty clinging vine that her mother's iron-handed discipline demanded. Just as her mother's persona (a perfectly polite society matron who did everything exactly to the letter) disguised the she-wolf underneath, so their family home—an impeccable example of feminine frilliness filled with flowers, organdy, and chintz—acted as yet another form of sheep's clothing. In this hothouse environment, there was no place for any of Mary's "natural emotions" (shadow) to escape.

Given this situation, it's not too surprising that Mary's burgeoning sexuality had to find its release in wild masochistic dreams. Because her mother had made it clear that sex was "dirty," Mary felt a need to be punished for her "natural inclinations." Her guilt was so acute that, subconsciously, she began to look for a man who would be able to keep this horrible person that she knew was lurking inside her—a harlot, in fact—under control.

But what kind of man would satisfy Mary's unconscious need to be brutally dominated, while simultaneously meeting with her mother's approval? Certainly not a macho sportsman, or a sadistic criminal type. For Mary, the solution lay in a gentle, soft-spoken bookkeeper with a keen distaste for pornography. Nevertheless, he was a man who seemed to experience an almost erotic delight in reading about brutal crimes, and even animals didn't like him. In other words, despite his misleading persona, this was a mean man whose mere presence forced Mary to continue keeping what she feared most about herself deeply hidden away.

This fascinating interplay between the shadow and the persona makes many literary characters eternal. We can all see aspects of ourselves in the conflict—even in characters such as TV's Archie Bunker. His popularity rests largely on the blending of his persona and shadow. He's a bastard on the outside, a loud-mouthed bigot who never stops complaining, but inside he's an angel. He loves his wife, family, and country, and of course, he married Edith, the dear, kind, and gentle soul who wouldn't hurt a fly. She's his perfect opposite, though we seldom get a chance to see the devil inside her because it would probably undermine what little faith we have in our idealized image of human nature.

Now do you see the deep-lying reasons, beyond economics and justice, for why a well-married couple *is* a fundamental and equal partnership? They each contribute psychologically exactly half to the other, just as they do to their offspring.

Finally, the anima lives at the level of the psyche that we commonly call the soul. When two people feel that they are "soul mates," their animas fit. And if everything else has also fallen into place, watch out for a powerful, passionate, and seemingly larger-than-life love affair. The notion of anima derives from the spiritual nature of Homo sapiens. Its archetype shares wings with the eternal child. But these are not the wings of a bird, the wings of levitation that free the body and enable it to soar, gravity unbound, beyond our little planetary spaceship. They are the wings of angels and archangels, which enable the divine quintessence in mankind to leave the body and experience the purity of light and the enormity of time and space that is cosmic consciousness. They are the wings of the dove, the Holy Ghost. This is the stuff that the deepest solicitude and wonderment, hence religions, are made of.

No matter how much we dissect the parts of love, if its mystique is contained in any one personage, it abides in the anima. This is the vaguest and most asexual part of the psyche. It's the force that's at work in most of the great romantic novels and poetry, a sense of empathy between two people that seems like a kind of cosmic connection.

The love between blood brothers should illustrate this point. Although some have chosen to see undercurrents of homosexuality in passionate friendships between members of the same sex, I disagree. In most cases, it's the mating of animas. Anthropologist Robert Brain has studied the relationship between love and friendship and I think his analysis of the Biblical story of David and Jonathan reinforces my point that the anima is asexual. When two men are blood brothers, he says, their friendship epitomizes emotional and disinterested love and stresses the importance of inner attitudes of loyalty and trust untouched by sexuality.

The same is true for men and women, although sex becomes part of the scenario. A few people—those with a dominant anima—sense the soul-mating immediately, and sex becomes almost a religious ritual celebrating its existence. But for most people sexuality becomes a way of moving down deeper into the anima. And when the earth moves, the anima has probably been reached.

This may be a highly romantic view of love, but it's the one to which I subscribe. So, if I may, I'd like to jump ahead again, and tell you the story of one couple I know who were immediately attracted at the anima level. They've been married for two years now and have recently produced a son. John had been a prominent physician, a large bearlike man who was driven to aim for the top. A future in high government office was often mentioned in connection with his name, and there had seemed to be little doubt that if things went according to plan, that was where he'd end up. At thirty-five he had two children and the perfect politician's wife: attractive, gracious, and committed to his career.

Marianne, the new woman he soon came to love, was thirty-two years old, an accomplished actress who, he later said, looked like his vision of Cathy in *Wuthering Heights.* She tended to behave like Cathy, too—wild emotions, drastic ups and downs. But they were all part of what she knew was essential to her work. Inside she was fairly strong.

They met at a cocktail party. She was impressed by his mind and his manners; he, by her beauty and charm. He found her sexually attractive, but he wasn't a man who played around. Her policy was no married men and, in any case, her feelings were sisterly. Still, they thought they'd become casual acquaintances.

Several months later, they met by accident in the lobby of an out-of-town hotel. He was attending a conference and she was about to start shooting a film. Since they were both alone, dinner seemed perfectly natural.

By the end of the evening, each of them recognized a powerful attraction. He found himself telling her things he'd never told anyone about his lonely childhood as an only child. Although at the peak of her career, she found herself revealing all her secret self-doubts. He was desperate to go to bed with her, but didn't suggest it. She knew she couldn't stand to share him with his wife and family.

Thus began a year-long friendship. They'd have dinner about once a month and offer each other lots of support against the various highs and lows in their lives. Their feeling for each other grew and the sexual tension became acute. Finally, Marianne couldn't stand it anymore. After deliberately having too much to drink one evening, she announced, "Let's have an affair."

It wasn't that simple, of course. They ended up in bed, but John was impotent, and he continued to be so every time they went to bed. He knows now that he was incapable of giving Marianne anything less than all of himself, but at the time the results were devastating to both of them. He became hostile. They stopped seeing each other and John threw himself back into his work.

Marianne was heartbroken. Six months passed. She tried to get interested in other men, but none would do. John refused to see her. Then one day she heard that he'd left his wife and resigned from his post. But still she didn't hear from him.

It wasn't until two months after that that she saw him. He walked through the door of a party thrown by mutual friends. He came right over and took her hand. "Let's have dinner," he said. The rest took care of itself.

The course of this love affair was very much the result of two animas longing for completion. It defied reason. It could not be worked out at the sexual level (hominus-femina). It was very much like Cathy Earnshaw's impassioned cry to Heathcliff: "We are one."

Wuthering Heights is a widely romantic and many would say unrealistic novel, but it has continued to captivate generations of readers because they intuitively see its universal truth. When Emily Brontë created Heathcliff, she was giving birth to her own demonic anima.

But everyone isn't equally prone to such rash behavior. In most people—the result of living in an age that has elevated reason to the status of a god—the anima is weak. Nevertheless, some people still carry about an aura of spirituality, which is the mark of a strong anima. Artists, for example, who somehow seem to be part of the mysteries of life, have strong animas.

The numinous quality of the anima is what allows great writers to create such convincing characters. They can see directly through to their heart and soul, and once that's understood, everything else falls into place. Tolstoy's anima is what allowed him to create Anna Karenina, and to write convincingly about the complexities of her love for Vronsky. It has often been said that Tolstoy's male characters are all aspects of himself, so there's a good reason to assume that Anna is his soul mate, the feminine projection of his anima, the woman he longs to meet on a spiritual plane.

One of the most common problems of male sexuality, the madonna-whore complex, is related to the anima. When a man is capable of "screwing a whore" but can't "make love to his wife," then he's experiencing a split between the femina and anima. The anima in this case is endowed with the characteristics of the Virgin Mary; the mother, the ascetic ideal, who is worshipped rather than sullied by physical demands. The femina becomes the sex object, a victim of almost sadistic abuse, which is the part of himself he keeps hidden in his shadow. A healthy man, of course, is well-balanced enough within himself to see the madonna and the whore as different aspects of the same woman, depending upon circumstances.

By this time, it should be becoming clear that a great deal of what we find attractive about a mate functions in our mind at the level of myth. Much of it is not innate, but due to the influences of culture and history on our unconscious. Love is an art, and just as artists use patterns of objects, actions, or events to awaken a particular response in their audience, so people are in fact collections of patterns that have the same effect on each other. When the patterns fit together as they do in a work of art, or like the pieces in a jigsaw puzzle, then love results.

MATCHING THE PERSONAGES

In elaborating these personages of the inner self, I gave you a preview of how they match and mate in love. Clearly what happens is that at least one or other of the personages inside is seen to exist or is actually replicated in another person who thus becomes strongly attractive. In fact, the essence of the attraction, the secret of this deeper chemistry of caring, is the discovery that part of oneself—one's femina, shadow or anima—is actually fully three-dimensionally alive in another person. This is also the very essence of opposites attracting, namely that the persons within us who stand in contrast to what we feel we are seem to become catalyzed by other people's manifest selves, by what they feel they are and seem to be, and vice versa. This explains not only the necessary dualities and contradictions in human nature—qualities that enable us as persons to adapt with a wide range of reactions—but also how an ideal coupling becomes an externalization of one's own deep psychoarchitecture. To put it another way, the fearful symmetry of love is reconstructed from the fearful symmetry of one's own psychoarchitecture. Thus the fated seed of love is sown deeply in the six furrows of our own nature long before love happens. And always remember that this miracle of "discovery" is more or less simultaneously replicated by the loved one. As you now realize, this happening becomes less miraculous when you see that the psychoarchitecture that attracts lovers to each other is an upside down mirror image—lovers are inverted psychological clones. However, there is one fortuitous coincidence that must take place, namely that the features of *one* of the images of the inner self exhibited by a partner must be ranked high in priority and be dominant in the eye—the perception—of the *other* partner and vice versa. So that if you are a woman with a tempestuous persona ranking highly a man under whose calm persona lurks a surprisingly high-spirited and masterful shadow, he must not only possess these qualities, for a good fit, but he must also rank highly in *his* order of priority a woman under whose shrewlike persona lurks a tranquil and loving shadow. In order to help you decide how you rank the personages of the inner self in another, there is a test at the end of this chapter.

I shall return to *Wuthering Heights* to illustrate two coincidental points: first, how this marriage, between what's already inside the psyche and what is discovered outside, works; and second, how a classical novel, or any form of great art, cannot gain everlasting quality without this happening.

At the core of coupling, Heathcliff is Cathy's wild gypsy shadow-cum-anima. Cathy makes the fatal error of marrying a conventional, genteel country squire—Edgar, her social equal. But, as she cries to the keeper of the eternal child within her, her nanny (see Juliet's nanny who had the same function!): "I *am* Heathcliff!" Her error pulls asunder not only what the church had put together, namely Cathy's marriage to Edgar, but also her very being. She is torn by the trifle Heathcliff calls "virtue," the cultural and ethical dictates of the social self. Her persona bids her to remain not only loyal to her husband but also pure in her spiritual vows, while her shadow—which is Heathcliff—and her soul pull her to her lover's cliffs.

In the ideal total love match, with the optimal magical formula in action, all the personages of the inner self of one persona are matched (in contrast) to those in the other person. The pattern in this geometry of coupling is somewhat as follows:

Female	Male
Persona(+)	(−)Persona
Shadow(−)	(+)Shadow
Ideal self(−)	(+)Ideal self
Hominus(+)	(−)Femina
Puella aeterna(+)	(−)Puer aeternus
Anima	Anima

Minus and plus valencies signify opposites.

This fit, this correspondence, occurs alongside the thousand other elements of clicking already described. No wonder, then, that so much must be preselected before encounter and so much must be intuited rapidly following the encounter. No wonder also that the majority of this sifting is left to the calculations of the unconscious, for it is too much for the conscious mind, often misled by emotion and sexual drive, to cope with. No wonder, too, that there might be only two thousand people in the world with whom you'd make a perfect match.

However, there are mitigating factors: These six personages of the inner self have increased overall psychic significance in the later stages of ticking and certainly in sticking together, so that they eventually encompass everything under their umbrella. On the other hand, human imperfections and social restrictions in the choices of mates allow these personages of the inner self to be matched only to a degree, rather than to perfection. Yet for the relationship to work well, the minimal mutual match must be made between the *dominant* personages and welded by a shared anima.

Finally, in order to round off what seems at first perhaps perplexing and complicated, I will remind you that in the reality of the psyche, in the integrity of its architecture at its healthy best, these personages of the inner self, these metaphors shade into one and exist in good alignment. For instance, the pixielike quality of a woman's character may correspond not only to the man's own eternal child (*puer aeternus*) but also spill over into his femina. That is, he is attracted to his childlike self and to an ideal woman who resembles this, at the same time.

Because the need for internal and external balance is universal, the specific need of one person, say for the man to find his shadow externalized in a woman, is *likely* to coincide with that very woman discovering her shadow and/or her eternal child externalized in that very man.

THE PERSONAGES AND TICKING TOGETHER

Now you are in a good position to see how progressive acquaintanceship with these personages in oneself and one's partner takes place in the sequence of love. You will also appreciate the different processes taking place in clicking, when numerous elements are sorted and matched through the screen of sensual perception, and in ticking, when the match is being made, created by fitting the inner personages together emotionally and intuitively.

The persona, the ideal self, and certainly the ideal sex partner (hominus/femina) are first revealed in the clicking because they surface readily. During clicking, the deeper-lying personages are briefly glimpsed or sensed but are not yet experienced or perceived with any clarity. A lot depends on the time interval in courting to allow for the display of these innermost aspects of the self. Clearly, in love at first sight, if it turns out to be a true love, all is sensed and foreshadowed all at once.

The eternal child plays vital psycho-biological roles in coupling. These roles are initiated in the ticking phase and culminate in the sticking phase, during cohabitation or marriage. But they will be fully described at this juncture.

In fact, the two respective eternal children in the couple, together with the two adults (personae) begin to make the love match fit creatively like parts of a jigsaw puzzle.

In fathering the girl child (*puella aeterna*) in his mate, the man reenacts, from *her* point of view, her own relationship with her father, though this time the previously tabooed incest is sexually broken. Indeed, this identification between lover and husband may precipitate the Heavenly Father-versus-the-jock complex, the female equivalent of the madonna-whore in her, and render her frigid to her lover, when he has become her legal husband or later a father to her own children. Yet she may be extraordinarily orgiastic with any jock, in any illicit relationship that is not under this incestuous pall of love; as indeed she may have been orgiastic with her own husband before marriage or before cohabitation—in any case, before he began playing a father role.

On the other hand, from the man's point of view, he is not aware of reenacting the past from his love mate's point of view but he may be aware of anticipating his own future in preenacting fatherliness. This is when an outpouring of tenderness may flow, when he feels overprotective about his "little woman" precast in the image of his future daughter. Now he may well be laying the foundation of a future incestuous (if only in the mind, in the unconscious) relationship with his own daughter, by making love to his woman imagined as child. Thus there is a time-inverted mirror image between the man and the woman; her past sex taboo and his future sex taboo are activated.

If the couple then procreates a boy, the man will reenact with him his own relationship with his father, however consciously modified, having already preenacted the father role with the child, independent of sex, in his woman.

Because what has just been described from the man's point of view may have seemed complicated and complexing, we'll go through its mirror image from the woman's point of view.

As the woman relates to a man's *puer aeternus* (eternal boy) and mothers him, she reactivates *his* past, hence a tabooed incestuous relationship in the unconscious mind with his own mother. This may precipitate in him the madonna-whore complex in that he may then relate to his wife as he did to his mother and become impotent with her and potent only with another woman—although he might well have been potent with "his" woman *before* marriage. In mothering her husband, the woman prepares for motherhood and motherliness, particularly for mothering a boy. This is a continuation of her playing doctor and nurse and playing with dolls and mothering masculine objects. If she has a boy she will replicate her husband's mental situation with his own mother and with herself (as the *puella aeterna*). If she has a girl she will tend to reenact her relationship with her own mother.

Now, back to square one from the man's point of view. If his woman presents no active eternal child to relate to, no *puella aeterna,* then he will have lost this training ground for fatherliness in general and fathering a girl in particular—a distinct deprivation; similarly from the woman's point of view. If then the couple make no children, they will have frustrated their parenthood drive and would tend to fall back (regress) to using each other as children. This accounts for the baby talk and for the mutual spoiling of "my little boy" and "little girl." The couple may also then share sublimating activities in animal love and in creative functions, including their respective work and play. (There are some people, the British for instance, who sublimate their parental love in animal and nature love even when they have their own children, who are, however, denied—"not to be seen or heard.")

If a sublimation of parenthood into the eternal child cannot be had because of the absence of active children within or because of their deep suppression, the couple will be rather grossly deprived—though if the situation is mutual and equal, the fit may still hold.

Now you can work out for yourself, if you're good at geometry, the combinations and permutations of circumstances that arise if one or other lacks an active available eternal child and if a boy or a girl is born to such a coupling. When you add to this the grading and shading in this acted-out relationship, you see what a rich range and fabric you get.

OTHER FACTORS

All through this middle phase of ticking, two more rather global aspects of personality—mood and temperament on the one hand and personality orientation, type, and traits on the other—are added to the magic potion of love. By now, mood and temperament will have declared themselves. Closely similar moods and temperaments are perhaps the most incompatible elements of love. It doesn't do for moodiness in one to drag down the other, or for the highs in one not to be offset by evenness in the other. Balance in this respect counts a great deal in optimal coupling.

Thus both from a genetic and a psychological point of view in simply living together, it is far more beneficial for a couple to have offsetting moods and temperaments, with tolerance between them. On the other hand, extreme opposites, like a person with very high (euphoric) and very low (depressive) moods is hard to blend with a very phlegmatic temperament in the presence of other large differences.

The same reasoning applies to personality orientation and types. Some aspects of personality appear fairly early in a relationship and the differences begin to attract or repel during the clicking phase. Usually extroverts find introverts sexy and vice versa. Thinking types are attracted to emotional types. Sensuous and intuitive types also blend rather well. *Acnophiles* (or small-space lovers) are fascinated by *philobats* (or large-space lovers) and to an extent vice versa.

One of the global factors of personality orientation is the way an individual responds to the physical, natural environment, like indoorsy and out-of-doorsy. It is clear that in this behavioral respect, extreme differences are difficult to accommodate. Yet the difficult only takes a little longer. If such opposites were attracted to each other and if this feature were mutually important (that is to be attracted to environmental opposites) this would indicate an innate attempt at the future approximation of this trend on the part of both people. It is similar with opposite temporal preferences, like the early bird and the night hawk; they can compromise and accommodate each other with mutual benefit.

When we come to a fundamental difference in adaptive maneuvering with respect to the environment, namely the *alloplastic* person (manipulating the environment to suit oneself) as opposed to the *autoplastic* (manipulating oneself in order to adapt to the environment), a compromise is not only possible and probable but it is also highly desirable.

A similar situation exists when we come to a fundamental difference in the preference for social adaptation. In attempting the ideal balance, some people lean toward *individuation* (the rugged individual, the lone wolf), while others lean toward *socialization* (the other-centered, collective-minded or "people-minded"). Once again a blend of moderate opposites is possible, probable, and highly desirable. These compromises will be made under two different circumstances:

1. When these qualities *lack* a high priority in both partners and the differences then are taken in and accepted for processing along with other more important differences, as part of the ratio in the magical formula.

2. When these qualities are given considerable *priority* by both partners who are attracted to each other precisely because of these differences, indicating a perceived need in both people to compromise and change themselves: the night hawk and indoor person works a little more during the day, wakes earlier and enjoys the out-of-doors more, and vice versa.

On the other hand, if the couple is older, if relationships are to be formed between matured, fixed people, too much of a difference in these types of personality is unlikely to attract or blend.

What actually happens in normal cases is that ordinary people do not, by definition, go to extremes. For instance, normals are a mixture of intro- and extroversion. Also, the same person varies with respect to these attributes according to circumstances and especially during the life cycle, so that a young mild extrovert becomes an old mild introvert. However, each person is characterized by a dominance or prevalence of this kind of personality orientation (extro and introversion)-type and trait. And generally, in ticking together, such relative dominances are matched to their opposites. If, however, the dominance of characteristics like being out-of-doorsy, a philobat, highly individualized, and an early bird is decisive, traits cluster together and form a lifestyle. They become assumed as part of the persona. Then they have to have a special appeal to the would-be lover who is usually short of these qualities but wishes to at least live in their presence and make a change toward them.

This then is how the finely tuned quantifiable differences to which I have referred in the previous chapter become graded and measured against a degree of commonality so that they might blend into the magic formula of a love match.

In ticking they are all made to fit together.

Finally, let's turn to the principle of optics quoted at the beginning of this chapter, and which stated the biological need for complementarity. This need, it says, is so strong that the eye *invents* the opposite, or complementary, color if it isn't already there. This is all right for optics but not for coupling. The psyche does the same kind of wishful perceiving. But when it does, when it sees something vital in another person, a highly ranked characteristic standing in opposition to one's own, *which isn't* there, it is making a fatal error.

RANKING THE PERSONAGES OF THE INNER SELF

Please check your answer in the appropriate column to the right. Scoring will be explained at the end of the test.

Here is how I rate or value the following factors when I pay attention to and when I am attracted to (or repelled by) the opposite sex.

	A great deal	Somewhat	Very little
A. Physical appearance, bearing and presence			
Manners, personableness, social conduct			
Intelligence			
Lifestyle			
Personal habits			
B. Moral virtues, such as honesty and faithfulness			
Agressiveness, such as taking the initiative and pushing forward			
Mental or physical energy or drive			
Strength of character or backbone			
Goodness or kindliness			
C. Childlike innocence, impishness or charm			
Spontaneity, freewheeling imagination			

Very little

Somewhat

A great deal

Playfulness, provoking rivalry or competitive gaming

Defenselessness or vulnerability, evoking a feeling of protectiveness

Qualities like stability, evoking a feeling of childlike security in myself

D. The type of person I would consider an ideal male or female in anyone's book

Direct or instant sex appeal

Sensuousness

The type of person whom I would consider to make a constant bed mate

The type of person who arouses my competitive spirit aimed at seduction or exclusive (sexual) possession

E. A capacity to transcend the real world, an element of dreaminess

A quality of earthiness or solid reality

A beautiful soul or a sense of beauty

A quality of tenderness, or capacity for giving and receiving love

A quality of empathy, sympathy or compassion

Scoring and Interpretation
A–Persona
B–Shadow
C–Eternal Child
D–Ideal Mate
E–Anima or Soul Type

1. Add up total score (maximum possible score: 50). Score 2 for A Great Deal, 1 for Somewhat, and 0 for Very Little. If you have scored

   0–10   You lack insight or comprehension.
   11–20 You care too much about superficial characteristics.
   21–30 You may be very well balanced and/or wise in your values, depending on a further calculation you have to make.
   31–40 You may be rich in insight and/or wisdom, again depending on a further calculation to be made.
   41–50 You're greedy!

2. Look at your five scores in each of the categories from A to E. If the difference between your highest score and your lowest score is

   1–2   You are well-balanced/wise.
   3–4   You are over-stressed.
   5–6   You are strained to the limit.
   over 6 You are imbalanced—out of whack!

Examples

1. Suppose your total score is 35, made up like this:

   The greatest gap—between C (eternal child) and D (ideal mate)—is 2. You are rich in insight/wisdom and well-balanced.

   A 7
   B 7
   C 6
   D 8
   E 7
   35

2. Suppose your total score is 41, made up like this:

   The greatest gap—between A-C-D and E—is 7.
   You are greedy and imbalanced.

   A 10
   B 8
   C 10
   D 10
   E 3
   41

3. Suppose your total score is 10, made up like this:

A	3
B	0
C	0
D	7
E	0
	10

The greatest gap—between B-C-E and D—is 7.
You lack insight/comprehension *and* you're imbalanced.

4. Suppose your total score is 25, made up like this:

A	5
B	4
C	5
d	8
E	3
	25

You have a gap of 4 between B and D (the shadow and the ideal mate) and a gap of 5 between D and E (the ideal mate and the anima). You are only moderately well balanced/wise, and you are strained two ways.

4

Sticking

*Natural selection is the pure chance
mating aspects of creating gene pools.*

—DARWIN

This definition of natural selection—one of the cardinal mechanisms of evolution according to Charles Darwin—is demonstrably wrong when it comes to human beings. When the facts laid out in this book become generally applied, very little will be left to pure chance in mating, any more than they would be in genetic engineering. We saw that the ten classes of social-profile variables (like race, social status, environmental factors) are largely geo-socio-politically predetermined, prior to encounter and quite regulated thereafter. These factors are assortatively mated and not randomly mated. That is, the mates are roughly of the same kind and create homogenous cultural and genetic pools. (They are diversified, however, *between* rather than *within* such pools.)

Furthermore, we saw how, as a result of the attraction between opposites, mating is dissortatively matched on purpose and tends to become complementary and heterogenous, thus enriching the gene pool and tending to offset too much likeness and to favor diversity. We also saw that however unsystematic the conscious selection of a mate might be, there is an unconscious overrider that is rigidly systematic. The psyche senses measurable differences and commonalities and makes a match, particularly on the basis of a perceived rank order of important characteristics. Thus there is little room for "pure" chance. However, by chance or by mistake, the psyche and other determinants of human mating (and procreation) do make errors. And this is why I seek to render this entire process of selection controllable and diminish the impacts of its wasteful randomness.

And yet love seems to come by chance, and by chance it also does not come. Furthermore, meeting places for the encounter of the sexes (see Chapter 2) leave far too much to chance, hence to error. If everyone could sample through large numbers of people representing cross sections of the population, then the "natural selection" of coupling might be left to *apparent* randomness—that is, to the wise selectiveness of intuition, to the laws operating unconsciously.

However, there may be a chance factor creeping into the process of coupling and this is due to the sheer number of discrete characteristics available—in excess of one thousand—which are not easily measurable or estimated by intuition, hence they might be carelessly matched.

Let us review them briefly. One order in the elements of love are the ten classes given of the social profile lying in the "background" of coupling. There are perhaps a dozen more groups or classes of characteristics sifted through and selected consciously in a certain preferential and perceptual order ranking: appearance, physical presentation, and body types; health, vitality, and energy; physical, psychological, and social aspects of the persona like voice, eye contact, clothing style and adornments; body language, nonverbal communication; the manifestation of intelligence; manners and ambience (warmth, wisdom, intensity, etc.), lifestyle, taste; sensory preference, personality organization (introversion, alloplasticism, acnophilism, strong individuation, etc.), dominant personality traits; mood and temperament; attitude and opinions, both public and private (like political affiliation); and the personal system of values (universal, instrumental and perceptual). Each of these, as mentioned before, has scores of discrete characteristics, intensities and measures: aggressiveness, gentleness, tallness, sociability, charisma, fashionable taste, risky lifestyle, choleric temperament, and so forth. As a consequence, it is quite possible that not everything is mutually sifted, sorted, and selected in the process of matching. However, if the relationship continues and closes up into intimacy and consorting, once the gating mechanism of cohabitation is reached, I suspect that most if not all of these one thousand or more variables come out in the wash. The wash is the wear-and-tear of a closing relationship past pairing and on the way to bonding by love. Certainly by the time consolidation is reached, let alone breakdown and re-pairing, nearly all is revealed.

Before we plunge into the deeper, metaphysical aspects of sticking, perhaps we should clean up the nitty gritties, the small superficial fellows which, like termites, can by themselves wreck an otherwise perfect coupling.

I am not referring so much to the larger aspects of lifestyle and personality like a really early bird clashing with a night hawk, though that may be strain enough. I am referring to the whole crop of personal habits that only seem to come out by night, as it were, and are worst first thing in the morning when the rosiness of romance has paled somewhat.

Of course, there is a time factor here, too. Clicking and falling in love may have lasted a few months. Ticking and being in love lasts a year or more. But sticking is the biggest step taken—usually toward marriage and ending either in the long walk of separation or in living happily ever after, though ever after may last only an average of five years these days.

In the end, love has taken over—or not. Or else it may have climaxed and already be on the decline. Sex has been transformed, yet persists less prominently, nevertheless vitally, as an amor-meter. Sooner or later habits make their big impact, when couples cohabit and especially when love is on the wane.

Nor am I referring here to the more disgusting habits like nose-picking in front of the TV set and in the presence of neighbors, or belching at the dinner table or getting drunk weekends and propositioning other spouses indiscriminately. After all, anything as gross as those can be banished, in a milieu of love, through trading in other similar habits of the partner—like talking with one's mouth full, farting flatulences on coming to bed, or waving gaily from the bedroom window at passers-by while stark naked. I'm referring to such tiny little habits like always getting up at the dinner table to do something or get something, while the food is getting cold on the table or the guests are politely waiting to start; or showering immediately before and after sex, thus betraying a residual feeling about the foulness of fornication; or forever starting to talk when someone else is and ceasing when they do, or snorting and wracking up mucus—or any similar *contretemps*. Believe me, there are hundreds of these little featurettes. At first they're ignored by starry eyes and rhapsodic ears. Then they penetrate the fringe of awareness, perhaps catalyzed by one's best friend, who will tell.

Then, when the psyche is already stripped naked to the anima (if not the animal) they begin to irk a little; then irritate. In the end, habits could well turn out to be the flea that breaks the elephant's back, though rarely would ex-lovers confess this to the divorce judge. When they do, it always makes unusual news.

Snoring is the most classic of all habits alleged to be capable of breaking up the closest of cohabitations. Snoring is a good little test of love. If you are self-contained, sensitive, and somewhat self-centered and someone's making log-sawing noises in your ears when you're trying to sleep, these could drive you up the pole and straight to a divorce judge—if you're not in love, that is. But if you love the snorer, if he (it's usually a he) is part of you, his noises are reassuring and soothing, whatever their pitch or decibels. In fact, you could learn to miss them and become an insomniac if they're not there to lull you to sleep, because their message is "twelve o'clock midnight and all's well," with the world and with you. If, on the other hand, the snorer makes you feel that his being asleep keeps you wide awake, you're certainly not *in* love and most likely you don't love. You're too preoccupied with yourself to love and likely you're phobic about not sleeping.

How does coupling survive these little *bêtes noires* beyond what has been suggested? After all, I doubt there's a single human being, however aristocratically raised or well self-made, who lacks a couple of bad habits that can crumble some of the cement of love, as proverbial termites crumble other edifices. Can you imagine recapturing the tender emotions of young love in the soft lights of the basement when the man you allegedly still love cracks his knuckles while watching sports on TV, or the woman you love is nervously chewing her eyebrows, which she's plucked while watching a soap opera?

Yet this sort of thing is done daily and nightly. Forebearance. Tolerance. Love goes a long way. *Mirabile dictu,* some of these very little habits like snoring become endearing, rather like the memory of when the bridegroom clumsily spilled soup on the bride's virginal white gown; or when you first made love on the kitchen chair, which collapsed just at the peak.

Once again sex must be reassessed in the sticking phase, for it is here that it plays its noblest role. This time let's put it in this way:

If it is true that modern Western sex is polygamous but that love, by its very exclusive and possessive nature, is monogamous, then the transition between sex and love is one from polygamy to monogamy. Perhaps in the majority of "liberated" Western people this transition from serial and sometimes simultaneous polygamy, bordering on promiscuity (whatever that is today) to strict monogamy or fidelity, is experienced by both sexes. In other words the male, and often the female, has moved from a phase of sexual relationship with a number people, including the loved one, to exclusive lovemaking. This involves a change in lifestyle—from hunting, if you will, to gathering; from active marketing to (more passive) consumption; from uncertainty to certainty. It's a status change based on a mature decision that comes sometime after the due process of clicking and sticking and coincides with cohabitation.

For most people this marital status change is a relief from hunting. It's worth mentioning in passing that this was not always the case in the West and is not the case in other cultures today, in general. For the female the transition may be one from mental polygamy to behavioral monogamy.

In most parts of the world women move from virginity to monosexuality, at least at first (before divorce). Thereafter, sexual liberation and/or a change in life circumstances (like the death of the spouse) may lead to a small series of sexual experiences (through widowhood and/or remarriage). Sometimes even this is forbidden by ancient law. And sometimes the widow is taken under the protection of relatives or in-laws like older brothers and/or the mother-in-law.

For the male, traditionally the transition is one from polygamy to a degree of sexual restriction, depending on the culture, the local mores and the male's status. However, even when there is a degree of polygamy fostered by culture or religion, the male voluntarily restricts sex to the one he loves—as in the case of Akhenaton and Nefertiti or the lovers of Taj Mahal. I dare say even Hollywood has known monogamy!

However, the sexual behavior of the partners has evolved when it comes to sticking. Coupling becomes exclusive, hence a monogamous relationship, and the value of fidelity rises with the quality and intensity of love or bonding.

Even though sexual novelty wears off after a number of years, variety ceases to be the spice of life and chastity becomes love's core.

Sex without love is entirely possible and vastly practiced. In fact the couple about to stick together might well have gone through several episodes of it with others. They might also return to just sex if and when love ceases. But there cannot be love without sex. Without passion perhaps, but not without lovemaking.

Nevertheless and sadly, marital sex, which should be at least a midweek sport, too often turns out to be a weekend bore—on Saturday night brought on by liquor and on Sunday morning occasioned by the kids gaping at goofy TV animations.

In sticking, as mentioned, sex oils the relationship and acts as an amor-meter. This is when love becomes the greatest aphrodisiac. What else keeps contempt away between two increasingly familiar bodies? The two sexes tend to age differentially—the women usually quicker or more critically than the men. This is a problem traditionally solved by an initial age difference when the woman is young enough physically, compared with the man, to prevent his feeling that practicing chastity is heroic. (He gets his comeuppance later when he dies earlier than his female age cohort by about the same number of years that he was older than his spouse. Her compensation then is the luxury of inheritance. But if the match is to be medically timed to cut down the years of widowhood, they must choose between her being some eight years older than him, or else her working throughout their relationship, for this will cut down her longevity in relation to his.)

Sex moves from passion to a "steady state," to its bedrock of deeply satisfying lovemaking. Despite the corroding aspects of familiarity and aging, the gradual decline of sex reaches a steady, nonnegotiable level, jerked up by a variety of surges of love, at whatever advanced age. (I have known at least one couple, married for a quarter of a century, who made love an average of 2.5 times a day, every day! And many others who are less athletic but have a higher output at the end of twenty years than many a younger lover's!)

Yet undeniably the time comes when a nagging curiosity and a wonderment about other bodies and other sexual experiences and fantasizing affairs creep in. Then the cement weathers. How far can monogamy stretch within current and future longevity of men and women and, considering currently high levels of health and vitality, how long can fidelity last? This is something we shall leave to the problematic exposition in a later chapter. Certainly there is something in the fact that with a life to be lived in the here-and-now, rather than as a testing ground for eternity, and with its being long and healthy, there seems to be both the room and a desire for three careers, not just one, and perhaps for three (serial) love relationships, or thereabouts. Much depends on the partner's age, on whether this is the first or a later love, and on their past sexual experience. Certainly, the ex-virgin who's "known" only her husband begins to wonder about other men sometime before the menopause, especially when other things go wrong in the marriage. Certainly physical and biological events can intervene perversely with a rise in female eroticism caused by any threat to her fertility (tubal ligation, hysterectomy, menopause, ill health, etc.). This rise in her passion tends to coincide with a decline in the male's passion due to familiarity. Typical of the perverseness of human nature or else of the conservative tendency, the threat of infidelity and certainly its occurrence, especially when it is only remotely sensed (unconsciously intuited but not allowed to surface), quickens passion even in a sexually tired marriage. It's not so much that what somebody else covets must be good enough for the partner as it is a fight to maintain one's territorial rights over the partner's body. It should be added that it is mostly the *suspicion* rather than the confirmed fact of infidelity that titillates the habitual partner. Also repeated infidelity in the partner has the reverse effect. Resentment kills all passion then. Female and male fluctuations in erotic cycles (together with the spurts of aging) never seem to quite coincide when the couple is of roughly the same age.

To start with, women are generally more precocious than men. They mature earlier, settle into a sticking phase earlier, and experience the biological menopause earlier. So men are not quite psychologically ready for sex at puberty. They're restless and on the hunt when women of the same age are ready to settle. They're ready to settle when women become unsettled usually by their broods growing up. And men get "menopausally" restless again and violently thanatophobic (terrorized by the idea of personal decay and death) and make a bid for rejuvenation with a rise in sex hunting, just when women tend to get tired of it all. Toward the end of coupling the woman's sexuality wanes and is at a low ebb while the man, if he survives and is healthy, remains willing, able, and eager.

Only incarceration in the physical and psychosocial prisons of senescence and lack of opportunity prevent the sexual urges of old age (which also aid longevity) from fulfilling themselves. At the very end, however, to be precise, in the last eight years of life, the woman is still able and often willing, but her man is dead and others are hard to get.

The above is, of course, a wide generalization with enough gaps to drive a bus through. But it is enough to adumbrate some of the troubles raised by the uglier head of sex in the detaching phase of stickiness.

Boredom becomes a threat in an overtranquil, taken-for-granted, sticky love relationship, just as it must have been in the garden of Eden. Consequently if the forbidden "tree of knowledge" were of the sex genus, rather than omniscience or immortality, then sex during boredom would become the sneaky rather than the snaky tempter. A lot depends on opportunity. Traditionally, with the man mobile and the "little woman" held captive and barefoot in the kitchen and chained to cribs, he has all the opportunities. This is why the milkman gets so lucky. But emancipated women have equal opportunities.

As with food, extramarital sex becomes a temptation, especially to those who are overexposed to opportunities. Their infidelity varies from the "zipless fuck" and the "one-night stand," usually held to be free from guilt, to emotional entanglements often filled with guilt.

It follows that the relatively unexposed, whether men in all-male workshops or women immured in their homes, can easily claim the virtue of behavioral if not moral chastity.

It also follows that a society with loose morality renders the monogamy of love virtuous. As for guilt, it goes without saying that if those who are formally bound by love claim that they have no guilt over illicit relationships, either the bond is weakened or they're fooling themselves. Guilt alone will not repair the cement of love, unless it is kept to oneself rather than dumped, especially on the partner. Then this kind of healthy guilt (as opposed to neurotic guilt) in the presence of some residual love has a chance of repairing the bond.

Ultimately monogamy is best served by love alone, whose real virtue is immunity from sexual temptations or at least from acting them out.

In the long haul, sticking is not unlike aging. There are ups and downs, spurts of deterioration and waves of renewal. And there's always wear and tear. More than that, just as human cells seem to have a built-in biological clock determining their longevity and therefore the length of an individual life, so a union seems to have a built-in psychological clock determining its longevity. In other words, the days of a dyad, whether it be marriage or friendship, seem to be numbered from their inception.

Of course, like everything else in coupling, relationships are heavily influenced by culture. In the days and places when divorce was forbidden, marriage was geared to last for the duration—which wasn't long considering maternal mortality and that forty-two years was the average life expectancy (in Britain) at the turn of the century. By no means did this signify that the nature of relationships remained unaltered throughout that period, even if its mental set accepted indissolubility. Unions could well have run a similar pattern of wear and tear with a fixed longevity of passion and love, as they do today.

In the same vein there are people who cannot carry even jobs, much less close relationships, past a certain anniversary date. Indeed some are under periodic compulsion to move on. This wasn't possible, either, a century or more ago when man remained relatively immobile socially and environmentally. And this limitation must have made a difference also to attitude and relationship to work. Yet the cyclical restlessness following a fixed period of contentment might still have been there. Other people (a few and getting fewer), of course, tend to stick for a lifetime to marriage, friendships, and jobs.

To the extent to which sexual drive and satisfaction lead the way to the ups and downs of sticking in heterolove, in terms of weakening or reinforcing it, its average psychobiological time interval seems to be some five years these days—give or take a pregnancy or a couple of years. This is how long it takes bodies and psyches to get overfamiliar with one another. By then the novelty wears thin and psychic integration is done. After that a status quo or steady state seems to settle in. Its fate depends largely on the challenge of external events and the solidity of the coupling in the first place.

One more thing before we plunge into the promised metaphysics at the heart of sticking. We touched upon its edge already when we addressed ourselves to the familiarity aspect of sex. Familiarity may breed contempt in passion but it also brings comfort both to the old shoe and the old coupling. The experience of fitting together all the one thousand pieces of loves jigsaw puzzle, achieving the splendid symmetry of fitting the personages of the inner self into the polar ranges of a union, together with the successive approximation between opposites brought about by bonding—all this is expressed when the lovers say that they "get along well together." By then, the resultant union has a life of its own, a personality of its own, which is the result of the melding of individual characteristics into a common melting pot. To change the metaphor of the shoe fitting comfortably, let us go back to the crucible of love in which the chemistry of caring has wrought its miracle. In this crucible the alchemy of love has now been achieved. It no longer glitters from the sparks of motivations and perceptions and the dynamics of the unconscious. It glitters in its own right, from the gold synthesized through those previous transformations. At this point close relationships possess their own momentum and inertia, like new creations, largely independent of what has gone on before.

On the other hand, coupling may have reached this phase

not because of the right chemistry but because of other circumstances. For instance, a couple may not have quite clicked
into place in the first instance yet they might have gone on
ticking together though out of sync. They may find themselves
now sticking together out of habit because it's too much trouble to let go; because it's even more trouble to start another
relationship all over again; or because of society's prescriptives. This, of course, bodes badly for love.

Certainly marriages of convenience were and are sometimes
desirable. But they usually lasted because couples were fettered by society, not bonded in their hearts and minds—and
the sacrifices were considerable. Sometime, of course, the couple did it all backward; they clicked and ticked after they'd
been stuck together for a period. But today anything that's not
built very well becomes quickly obsolete and deserted. It takes
guts to get out of a relationship of inertia. The sooner the better. All of which brings us to the brink of a definition of the
ultimate desirables in a close love relationship.

THE QUALITIES OF A UNION

If durability is not the only and certainly not the best test
of optimal coupling, particularly since this index can only be
utilized after the passage of considerable time, what is? How
can you tell whether you have a good relationship going? How
can you tell what kind of qualities you are seeking in a love
relationship? There are a number of criteria on which to make
a judgment, apart from the way one feels (remembering the vagaries of emotions) and beyond one's intuition.

1. The structure of a healthy coupling is parallel, like two
upright walls standing together and in touch, rather than the
neurotic lean-to, like a teepee. This enables each person to
stand on his and her own, yet support the other.
2. The mutual benefits from complementarity enable each
partner to do three things they couldn't do without a union:
   a. Rely on the union, on a relationship that is more adaptive and richer than the two individuals separately.

b. Grow, through successive approximations, to resemble the partner, inwardly and outwardly by reaching for the polar opposites presented by him or her.

c. Grow inwardly and outwardly by getting in closer touch with oneself, with one's own inner personages—an action that is catalyzed by the coupling.

This is the essence of the alchemy of love.

3. As a result, the union is stronger, bigger, and better than the coupled individuals. This is synergism. Together they stand; apart they fall. This modifies somewhat my earlier statement as to the apparent truism that the quality of love care can be only as good as that of the lovers. Maybe ultimately the quality is only as good as the elements brought into bond by the lovers. But if they fit well, if the cementing is good, the result transcends the individual quality of the lovers, hence the enormous benefit of a good love match even between humans of rather poor qualities—a fact often recognized by the stage, the screen, and in novels.

4. Also as a result of this alchemy, there is a wondrous blend between the inner and outer aspects of the two personalities; a harmony that raises its chords to the heavens as well as to the ears of other people. This is experienced as compatibility, as getting along marvelously together.

5. What follows from this is a feeling of love, usually experienced in waves of tender emotion, ideally expressed physically as well as verbally—both pre- and postcoitally.

What was a Big Ache and still may be so in the necessary quarrels of conciliation of opposites and in the tensions of uncertainty becomes increasingly a source of happiness, between the bouts of ache and in the troughs of tender love waves.

6. As a derivative of all this, but particularly because of the enhanced strength of the union and its larger range of adaptability, the relationship becomes stabilized and in turn stabilizes whatever turbulence is present in the two individuals. This stabilization, together with the qualities mentioned, accounts for greater endurance, hence the durability or longevity of a good coupling. One of the corollaries of the regularities or laws governing the contribution of the two sexes in a love union is their symmetry, hence their essential equality.

Nowhere can one see how one sex is more important or superior than the other. Even if in the free choice by a woman she prefers a more dominant male, her contribution as a power behind the throne or as the more silent partner or as his mainstay is paramount. For one thing, his dominance can only be exercised by her leave or else the battle of the sexes ensues. But generally dominance is no longer a requisite today except in making a final decision. In this, good partners can and do alternate.

It follows that the only viable relationship in close intimacy or marriage, the only relationship that truly reflects what has happened to bring about a state of love, is one of the full partnership of equals. As we saw, things are never perfectly balanced even in an ideal relationship. Of necessity one partner may be more generous, more giving, for a time while the other is more dependent and more trusting, hence more courageous. One partner may be quicker and better in making some decisions at times than the other. But in the overall, the state of love union calls for equality in partnership. Anything else is a distortion of the mutual processes described and a travesty of love.

We must now elaborate on these criteria of the quality of a love union so that we can better grasp them and also in order to see their dark side. It's a question of cost benefit.

The parallel-walls structure in ideal coupling symbolizes the fact that lovers do not lean upon each other, so that if one collapses (or straightens out in therapy or in a spontaneous flipover) the other will not collapse also. On the contrary, the other remains strong, a source of help. This does not mean that lovers stand apart, with a gap between them. On the contrary they have contact all along their interface. After all this is where the bonding of love occurs, at the interface. The advantages of this structure are triple: Each partner can stand on his own, the union can grow together, and each can grow (upward and downward) independently, to an extent. In other words, the relationship is healthily symbiotic and commensal rather than neurotically saprophytic or parasitic.

Now as to cost, the most obvious sacrifice—if that's the word—is made for the sake of cohabitation or marriage. It is giving up one's lifestyle as a single person. Whatever else one keeps or loses in the bargain, one cannot hold on to single-hood, to its freedom and its loneliness, unless one lives togeth-er, apart; and a common roof does not a love match make. As mentioned, when one is in love, giving up the single swinger life is rarely seen as a sacrifice because the relief of not having to hunt for sex and affection more than compensates for the relative loss of freedom. Moreover, modern couples give each other ample freedom to keep up individual friendships, to work in different walks of life, to enjoy certain pleasures sep-arately. But there is the automatic implicit requisite of report-ing: "How was your day?" is the cue.

The cost of the first three qualities of a union is that a lover may nevertheless learn to rely too heavily on the relationship rather than on the self. Such then are the union dues, that the strength of the relationship may ultimately be at the expense of *individualization*—that is, the dyad may have a strong com-mon identity but insufficient personal identity. Moreover, as mentioned, as the polar charge of contrasting characteristics flows from one lover to the other in the successive approxima-tion between partners, the coupling gains an autonomy through the commonality and likenesses achieved. This cures the imperfections and the incompleteness in the individual lov-ers, maybe at the expense of losing some of the unique char-acteristics originally possessed by each.

In early young love between immature lovers, whose inner cohesion is weak, the benefit may exceed the cost by far and for the longest time because the growth together may exceed in time and quality that which might have occurred separately without love.

However, as the relationship goes on, in the sticking phase there comes a critical time when a close relationship (particu-larly a very close one) may impede some individual growth and certainly a degree of independence. After all, too much in-dependence negates love, as much as a platonic marriage or double or treble love (being in love with two or three people at the same time) negates real love. Too much independence nullifies the Big Ache, including the pangs of absence and con-sequently the joys of reunion.

On the other hand, while coupling may diminish *individual-ization* or the personal mark of identity, it facilitates enormously *individuation,* which is an inner cohesion vital to mental health—getting it together.

Individuation is the ability to be in touch with all the parts of oneself and to have the personages of the inner self flow in confluence rather than be sequestered in their own separate and distant cages.

So a young person who becomes individuated early when catalyzed inwardly by the alchemy of love is ultimately *better able* to grow. Whether or not he does this depends on him and the quality of the relationship.

This is the crux of the timing in this business of love. During the sticking phase there should be enough room to grow upward and downward from the bonded interface. If there isn't, then the couple is bonded improperly in a lean-to or neurotic dependency so that they cannot escape from each other. In this case they must have the guts to break and re-pair, one way or the other. There is an analogy here between the function of such a union and parental love.

Just as parents must let go so that their children may grow and become independent, so such a union must loosen itself or even break up so that the individuals may grow stronger separately. And if this leads to some tension, some sparks and quarrels, so much the better.

Examples of neurotic marriage abound (as we shall see in Chapter 6; Passages) because the patient's consort has a large interest invested in his or her partner's neurosis: For instance, as long as the beautiful but obese wife remains fat (or pregnant), the threat to the husband's masculinity or to his other deficiencies is reduced. Similarly, as long as a married man remains a bisexual, the threat of heterosexual infidelity—a terror that usually haunts the woman who decides to marry such a man—is held off.

The spouse always has a vested interest in a chronically alcoholic patient, if for no other than the scapegoat reason. The alcoholic, the deviant, the fat present obvious shortcomings that cover up the hidden inadequacies and often worse madnesses lurking in the head or even in the secret behavior of the spouse.

In all these cases, in fact, in all lean-tos or teepeelike marriages, the bond in the relationship must slacken considerably or break in order for both partners to be free to grow healthy, for it keeps them both down. This is why people used to quip on the streets of Vienna half a century ago: "Oh, yes, that poor fellow! He's just started his psychoanalysis with Dr. Freud. Six months from now his marriage will break up, you'll see!" Today this need not happen, if the change, even the flipover brought about in one partner (the patient) can pull the other one straight and if the bond can hold. Or else it needn't happen if both partners receive treatment separately, or better if the other spouse sees the *same* therapist once the original patient has finished. But if there was very little virtue or true love in the relationship to begin with and if, as invariably happens, the patient's spouse or consort keeps undoing the therapeutic work and undermining the whole process, a break-up may have to occur eventually for the sake of both people.

Here we come perhaps to the most profoundly paradoxical aspect of love (and of life). If the Big Ache becomes totally assuaged when the couple take each other for granted in blissful tranquility, then an aura of pale blue happiness results and the essence of love and life has ceased. This is the stage of positive entropy. The beginning of the end. Anesthesia. It's the stage described in a cynical Italian saying: "Love makes time pass [it ticks away in the ticking phase] and times makes love pass [if allowed to do so in the sticking phase]."

Life, growth, and love are a throb—conflictual, stressed—a struggle highly charged with entropy and opposition, hence with fear, laughter, acute happiness, and despair. When all this is reduced to near zero, as it tends to be in serene senescence, when nothing matters any more, then death creeps in. This is one of the most powerful reasons why the longevity of coupling by itself is meaningless. This is not like an old comfy shoe but an empty shoe. There is nothing left. Darby and Joan might have gone on for a half century as the walking dead. This is why Romeo and Juliet, and Heathcliff's Cathy had to die young, so that they would not show us the other side of tired love—the empty shell, the nothingness devoid of meaning. This is why Héloïse and Abelard were separated by castration and by God; so that the tension between them—dialectical, sexual, and emotional—would persist until the end, an immortal love. Living happily ever after is a bore. It is literally the end of the story and of love itself. So just merely sticking together is not good enough. Perhaps too many couples stick too short a time because they are improperly bonded, incompletely coupled, defectively attracted, incompetent or insatiably neurotic. But equally too many stick too long because they lack the guts to break, because of habit, because they still rely on the ghost of a crumbled union, or because they've been too long together and fear facing living apart and alone. It is rarely dissension and conflict, especially that between opposites, that exhausts love as much as a false harmony, a soulless inertia.

Most conveniently this brings us into the very heart of the metaphysics of optimal sticking, the final formula for the alchemy of love itself.

THE ANIMA AND STICKING

By now the couple would have made their match. His femina would have fused with her hominus. This would have led to an exchange of ego ideals (one's values embodied in an ideal image of oneself), a mutual adjustment and a compromise with reality. The two shadows would have surfaced and cross-pollinated, as it were, the two personae. The resultant dialectic tension will prevent the couple from spending half a century in immemorable serenity. The eternal child within each person will have begun to enact its triple role in the relationship—fathering and mothering, being children, peers at play. This and having children will keep the couple hopping and alert while holding boredom at bay. The struggle for existence, for family survival, will also do its bit. And coupling will have catalyzed five of the inner personages into a mature self in both partners. Being *in* love will merge into loving and being loved.

There remains but one major personage of the inner self to complete the alchemy. This is the anima. In a way one can say that thus far coupling has had a primary self-serving function in that it has provided the catalytic agent in the mass action of integration of the inner self, with the result that the incomplete man and woman have become more complete both in the union and within themselves. Even the caring for a love object—that is, for each other and for the union itself—has been motivated by psychobiological altruism, that is, by an interest in oneself primarily and in one's gene (in optimal procreation), rather than a purer interest in another human being.

Somewhere halfway through the sticking-together phase, the couple has touched the deepest layer of each other's psyche. They have become soul mates. It is here that his tenderness and her toughness, her wildness and his gentleness, intermingle and blend. This is where they gain such profound knowledge of each other that there is no need for verbal language and little for nonverbal communication, except perhaps through the proximities of their bodies and through pseudo-psychic emanations. This is where the final archetypes of the collective unconscious of two beings meld microcosmically. As Jung had said, "the form of the world into which a person is born is already inborn into him as a virtual image." And the anima is the spiritual archetype governing all collective images.

The symbolisms and myths of archetypes, whether depicted by animals, or by the inanimates of nature, like Mother Earth or the sun, or by geometrical designs like the mandala, generally emerge only in sleep dreams or in the artistic projections of the collective unconscious of mankind. But the anima is felt in the loving. The completion of this entire process is commonly expressed in saying, "I feel part of you . . . we belong together, . . ." which is inaccurate. What is meant is that they feel joined and part of the whole union. But lovers rarely if ever recognize that the field or cement between them, rather than their being is the repository of love. Although they may have said "I couldn't live without you" much earlier in the sequence of love, after clicking, now when their anima has fused they mean it. Absences and bereavement become soul-wrenching.

The following stories exemplify the meeting of the animae.

John was a nomadic, reckless, out-of-doorsy, large-space-loving (philobat), intuitive, virile man in perpetual motion, immersed in cosmic consciousness, always in touch with his surroundings, brimming with energy, seeking objects to whom and to which he wanted to give his endless love and devotion. June, on the other hand, was a timid soul, small-space-loving (acnophile), cautious, pale, soft, feminine, a quiet woman, a sort of earth-seeking lotus flower–like creature, who sat indoors with hands folded in her lap, a thinking introvert with a narrow, focused vision, and a practically burnt-out capacity for love. She sought shelter and security, yet was brave when need be. To him she seemed the perfect love object, into whom he wanted to infuse his energy and loving. To her he seemed the perfect all-embracing heart, by whose flame she could warm her frail frame and thrive. They fell in love and bonded their souls for two decades. Were it not for too large an imbalance between the giving and receiving of love between them, and were it not for his overwhelming exuberance, which smothered rather than infused her timid soul with energy, they might have stuck together longer. But in the crumbling cement of love, her timidity and stunted soul turned to bitter hatred, and his expansive self shrank from hurt, which only goes to show the impermanence of things even if they reach an apotheosis.

Jennifer was one of those women whose straw-colored hair always smelled of newly mown hay and who grew up with horses. Her favorite was a black stallion. She had dreamed repeatedly of riding him to a crowned victory over the world's best jumpers. Peter was a city boy brought up in the rectangular rooms of highrises. He fell in love with Jennifer's wild green eyes and fresh-scented hair, and she with his darkness and stillness. Although she made a perfect hostess for his corporate law practice and he made a perfect contrast to her gypsy-skirted coterie of landscape artists, they woke up one day and pulled up their suburban stakes to live in the Rockies and let their children roam their slopes. They lived happily ever after.

There's no doubt that Eliza Doolittle's anima matched that of Professor Higgins or that the shrewish Kate matched Petruchio's or Scarlett O'Hara's matched Rhett Butler's, or Héloïse's matched Abelard's. In the end, the getting along characteristic of sticking represents not only a match *made* and a blend between all the elements of love inventoried so far, but the fusion of the male and female animae. It is this more than anything else in the symmetrical cementing of lovers that brings their opposites together (in successive approximation) in the union and also catalyzes their coming together within themselves. And when the lover is missed or lost, it is the loss of the soul mate more than anything else that is grieved for and felt to be irreplaceable.

THE FLIPOVER

What else can be said to demystify love? One can be sure of only one thing; that this is not the last word. For one thing, we should note that most people vary from being grossly imperfect to being imperfect. Hence their relationships are imperfect. The magical formula dealing with the thousand elements of love may be missing crucial qualities and quantities in its ingredients. The personages of the inner selves may not be in perfect alignment. All these hazards may undermine the bond of love, which eventually happens perhaps more often than not. This is why a really good love match is so rare.

For another thing, we should remember that sticking is the longest stretch of love. It offers its flanks to buffeting by the blizzards of life. It exposes its edifice of love to the hazards wrought internally not only by the termites of initial and subsequent error but also by the erosions wrought by the passage of time, hence by change.

The one factor more than any other that may founder a relationship in this phase is the always unequal balance between loving and being loved. You saw how this imbalance broke the love in an example given above. And it is this ratio between giving and taking that may cause a relationship to overturn rather suddenly.

Jonathan had been happily married, in the eyes of the world and of his wife, for a decade and a half. They were the ideal couple, with two children; the envy of their neighborhood and of their network of friends, who quarreled, deceived each other, and broke up at a fast clip. One fine Sunday morning Jonathan woke up and said to his wife, "I'm leaving you." She answered, "Where are you going, dear?" and he said, "I dunno! Away." And away he went. It turned out he'd been thinking about it for weeks; but he had long ceased to communicate with his wife anything of importance. They weren't on the same wavelength. He had been telling her only what she wanted to hear for years. She had immersed herself in the house and children, drugged her mind with TV, never read a book or newspaper, never listened to the news, hadn't kept up with her friends, and lived in a pleasant illusory world. She responded to sex and affection, yet never initiated them and was gratified when her constant material demands were met. She knew nothing of her husband's work or whereabouts and generally was not sensitive to him, to his growing older and wiser or to his discontent. "My whole life was wrapped in him!" she exclaimed with the deep hurt of betrayal, when he didn't come back till a year later and then only to ask for a divorce. He said, "I was doing all the giving and she all the asking. When I woke up to this I decided there was not enough in it for me. My business pressures were enough to cope with ... I didn't need hers, the constant criticism of the kids, of me, of others and the demands." He had been an excellent father. The children were the run-of-the-mill spoiled middle-class brats, also good at taking and giving little back. Altogether it didn't compute and he quit. He had been happy the year apart. Peaceful. He'd seen a lot of women but none in particular. He had had an occasional affair before, as she discovered to her utter shock. "I never even suspected it. I thought we were very happy!" Apparently he had given her some cause to suspect. He had hoped she'd pick up the vibes of discontent and of subsequent infidelity by psycho-osmosis. He had heard that such vibes are liable to break up smug, passive indolence. Moreover, all his gentle persuasion to lose her extra fat, to keep up with the news of the world, to take some interest in his business and its problems, had been lost on her. She had ceased growing and relied totally on their union. He had grown apart.

A classic story. What was to happen to them was predictable because this pattern was so clear. She would find somebody only too pleased to make her and her ready-made brood into durable love objects. He, on the other hand, would have far greater difficulty finding somebody new, somebody who would suit him better, now.

There is an inherent conservatism in one's unconscious. The archetypal images adopted by the self are not about to change with the whims of the possessor or even at the behest of a reorientation to life or in style. Jonathan's femina continued to resemble his wife. Yet now he wished for a much more sophisticated spouse, for a more independent woman, but, as you now know, the personages of the inner self are usually in a proportionate and patterned alignment. Consequently Jonathan found it difficult to discover women who matched his wife's physical attractiveness to him, his femina, as well as her background, which he shared, yet who possessed an entirely different eternal child (a more active and playful peer), also a different shadow (more colorful and challenging) and particularly a different anima. So he got burned often. But the pain enlivened him. The quest proved exciting and worthwhile, he felt. She, on the other hand, sank back into her typical semi-oblivion. She took another body to her bed, the body of another Jonathan—as he used to be—and again made a good marriage.

The exact counterpart of this story can and does befall a woman. And the consequences are similar—a sort of natural justice is wrought: The restless and dissatisfied partner tends to get punished for disturbing the status quo and the apparently innocent victim, the sinned-against rather than the active sinner, restores the lost relationship with another body. Yet there is an element of injustice here too. It seems that change through fast growth rather than disloyal and hurtful behavior gets punished for disturbing the equilibrium, while changelessness is treated as a virtue.

All sympathy and sense of rightness go to the changeless wife who had ceased to grow, while rejection, guilt for having hurt her, and failure to find a "better" woman goes to the husband, who dared to grow and flipped over.

Perhaps this is too simplistic a judgment. But it is true that the big spenders of love are also usually more endowed with energy and generosity, while the passive recipients tend to be more anemic or stingy as well as self-seeking. And yet it is far easier to give than to receive. Not only is the bestowing of love a joyful activity that paradoxically pleases the egotism of the donor-hero but it is also by far the safer activity in the equation of love. He who gives also taketh away. He is in command; whereas the receiver relies on being given love and may be able to do little or nothing to prevent its loss, especially when the discrepancy between the two partners is big, as in the example given. The passive receiver often becomes a helpless victim to the vagaries of the emotions of the donor.

In optimal coupling, when the bond is of the finest quality, there is never at one time an exactly equal proportion in the give-and-take because always one or the other is more generous or energetic. But over the weeks, months, and years in the grand scheme of things, considering the many items of exchange in love and care, there is an equitable exchange. When the disparity is great, as indeed it happens with nations no less than with individuals, resentment and rebellion grow, and eventually there is an upset in order to redress the balance. You bite the hand that feeds you and it hits back.

While the magical ratio of loving versus being loved must be in beautiful balance in ideal love, and while its gross imbalance damages the relationship and wrecks it regularly, this is not the essence or nature of what I call the true flipover. This term is more strictly reserved for a personality flip that subsequently overturns the relationship, rather than coupling being upset because of an overloading in the active/passive equation of love. In fact, of course, there is always some change in the personality of the short-changed partner. He often becomes rather suddenly discontent with the imbalanced exchange even if it was what he had originally sought. For one thing, the active, generous, demonstrative lover, in keeping with the principle of attraction of opposites, nearly invariably seeks the more passive receiver, the dependent person. And deep down she/he has a paradoxically selfish motive, or at least a defensive one, for doing so. Often he or she had been a lonely child, accumulating a store of love with no one to give it to. At the same time he or she has learned to distrust the childlike reliance on being loved—after all, this is almost a sacred due of childhood, a reward for being born without being asked. When a child has been let down, one way or another, in the business of being loved, she/he wants to be in control and do the loving. So she/he seeks love objects who will allow themselves to be loved with minimal returns. They are easy to find from among the vast array of grown-up children who haven't been loved enough, or more likely from among those who've been loved only too well and still want to be loved as they had been when they were children. These then are the antecedent dynamics of the happy encounter between the big and little spender of love. The former, described in classic psychological garb, is one who is embarrassed by small signs of being loved that she or he cannot abide, like being praised or even liked too much. She or he would rather be feared or respected than bathed in the glow of warm feelings. His or her psychology is fairly close to the type of neurotic individual we'll encounter later who will not commit to a love relationship, or sometimes to a close relationship of any kind, including friendship, for fear of letdown and usually because they have been burned both as a child and adult. I say fairly close to it because more normal persons with those motivations will commit themselves quite readily if they have found someone safe who will *not* return too much affection.

And so, when a person such as Jonathan decides that he wants a responding, loving partner, one who gives him back more of what he has to give, he changes quite radically. He has then "flipped" his ideal self and becomes more courageous, more certain that he can hold someone's love. Then he is ready to become a love object.

A quite similar dynamic occurs when the passive recipient of love, the love object, becomes independent enough to want to acquire a love object of his or her own, a vessel into which to pour his or her own stuff.

If this kind of flipover occurs more or less simultaneously, if the hitherto giver of love is ready to also receive it while the hitherto receiver is ready to give it (if there's enough left there to give), all may be well and the relationship can stand the earthquakes of the flipover. But if the giver continues to want to dominate in giving and is not prepared to receive, or the hitherto passive recipient has now been activated into initiating or giving love, then one or the other will tend to complain of being smothered and dominated by the other and want out.

Dramatic as this kind of overturn in the giving and receiving of love ratio may be, it is nowhere near so dramatic as the real flipover, which occurs in a person when his or her shadow takes over the persona, lock, stock, and barrel, overnight.

The most sought-after flipover I know is that wished for by an aggressive woman who wants her milquetoast husband to turn into a lion overnight. The usual story begins with the woman being strongly attracted as a child to a soft, cuddly daddy in a matriarchal home that had shrunk him into insignificance. This daddy fixation eventually progresses to a repressed or merely a suppressed despising of weak men or of women-dominated males when the innocently passive acceptance of childhood progresses to the criticalness of adolescence and finds the soft daddy to have been an idol with feet of clay. Unfortunately, despising similar males overlies like a thin veneer an attachment to the very same kind of male. Consequently such a woman becomes caught in the quandary of being about to love somebody whom she will automatically despise for giving in to her and for loving her back, for not fighting her back as her father ought to have fought her mother back. She runs the risk of being hoisted with her own petard.

Now if her intuition were sufficiently astute to gauge the strength and distance of the man's shadow from his persona, she might well succeed in loving a mouse who turns out to have a lion's shadow that he is prepared to let out of its cage. Or else her perception might be sufficiently acute to make her realize that the man's stubborn though pacific determination, his refusal to be sucked into the types of mother-initiated fights and scenes by which she may have gotten brainwashed in her childhood, are abhorrent to him. She might see that this is a real strength.

The ability to detect steely strength beneath milky blandness or violence underneath soft kindness, indeed the perspicacity enabling you to see the diametrical opposites buried inside another person, depends not only upon that person's unguarded moments but also on your observing surprisingly jagged juttings protruding from what should be the smooth roundness of a well-put-together personality, on your divining rather wild contradictions in his or her behavior, or in the subtler aspects of body language. And, of course, it depends on the sharpness of your capacity to observe—interpret, and intuit before this becomes clouded by your perceptions being successively overly impressed, fascinated, infatuated, and fallen-in-love.

Above all, beware of any excesses on the surface: A sugary persona betrays at least a sour shadow; crocodile tears of compassion for the poor butterfly betray at least a streak of cruelty shot through the soul; a passionate dedication to justice points at least to a smudge of inclination to tyranny down below; and a goody two-shoes is liable to carry venom in her heel.

Remember, your own inner psychoarchitecture is built on the same principle of contrasting opposition that governs attraction, like a moth's to light, between humans. A well-integrated, easy-riding person possesses milder contradictions in his character—the personages of his inner self are not too distant from one another, hence they blend well. A loosely integrated, more unstable, awkward person possesses wilder inner contradictions, which he may be at pains to tame—the personages of his inner self are wide apart and may flip over.

But we're not all Scarlet Pimpernels; we cannot easily hide our leopard's spots. So you should have the confidence in your free-wheeling intuition to discern strength beneath apparent (persona) weakness, and evil (shadow) under an angelic mask.

The violent contradiction in a woman's heart when she's loved a mousy man, yet admired the kind of caveman she wished her father had been in order to have tamed her mother, is resolved in the female version of the madonna-whore complex. What happens is that she chooses an exaggerated extremity of each image: She marries a soft, hopeless drip and resents him forevermore. And she takes a beastly, unloving man for a lover, a man who turns her on but whom she cannot love.

Flipovers can be gauged and predicted. But they are not usually taken into account in the coupling or relied upon to occur later, in the sticking part of the relationship. For instance, often hotheaded, fun-loving men will settle down to becoming dull husbands and doting fathers. Or a dazzling and dizzy dame will end up as a domesticated housefrau. In either case, unless the partner unconsciously gauged this kind of flipover and reckoned on it, the couple ends up with what they hadn't bargained for.

Flipovers are caused by a deliberate change of personality in the course of analytical treatment or else occur spontaneously when an interchange occurs between a person's shadow and persona while an identical interchange does not take place in the partner. Then the previous symmetry is out of kilter and may become untenable. For instance, the scrupulously honest, demure demoiselle becomes a mendacious, flamboyant matron. Or the square, meticulous homebody husband, recognized by his dull white-collar work, bursts out by becoming an irresponsible, globe-trotting, itinerant troubador.

In the popular mind, when such sudden reverses occur, they are put down to one "finding oneself," to liberation, or some other such rationalized cause, in the same way that a person's moving from left of Trotsky into true-blue conservatism is ascribed only to age and success. More often than not a flipover does not signify finding oneself or necessarily achieving a healthier integration than before. The flipover is frequently occasioned by the reaching of the halfway mark to death, menopause. It is just an upside-down flip and not necessarily an approximation between polar opposites in oneself, a compromise between persona and shadow.

When this depolarization is dramatic it is due to an excessive opposition between the persona and ideal self on the one hand and the shadow on the other. This inner rebellion is usually precipitated by some external event, some threat to life or psychological limb, or some radical change in circumstances (such as winning a lottery) or due to having chosen the partner unwisely—too close to the persona and ideal self and too far away from one's shadow. A man told he's only got six months to live may flip over from having had an obedient-citizen persona to becoming a late-life bandit. His shadow takes over. In a healthy flipover the transition from shadow toward persona is gradual and may be congruous with the partner—then the individual has "found himself" in the sense of achieving a better relationship with his own shadow. As often as not this is catalyzed by a true love affair.

THE SUCCESSFUL STICK

The overall experience of success in this last phase of love is not only to be sticking together but to continue to be stuck on each other. There must still exist a tension, a sense of mystery, a sense of wonderment and uncertainty about each other, to show that negative entropy, that life, is still there; this against the overwhelming feeling of having settled down, meaning that the tense and active phase of successive approximation, of adapting to each other's differences, is over. And there must be a sense of getting along together, meaning that the blend and bonding of two beings has been achieved. As mentioned, this important feeling indicates that all the personages of the inner self are now in proper alignment and found to be compatible.

By now lifestyles have integrated in a cohabitational or conjugal common style yet left room for individual variations of the partners each doing their own thing, to a degree. Residence of the family unit with a high degree of environmental stability would have been achieved—as a form of nesting and usually in preparation for procreation. For paramarrieds, as I dub them, the interesting question of "What price marriage?" comes up. Marriage, despite changes it has undergone, remains a social contract, a piece of paper often personally embellished with more or less legally viable arrangements. It remains a tradition, a mere convention, a labor-sharing device, a formalization of differing social roles, a male conspiracy to ensure paternity, and a female conspiracy to assure herself property rights. So you'd think modern, liberated couples would despise it. They don't. They marry by the millions. Why? The cynical young men say "to be able to play around like other marrieds—something that's very difficult for cohabitants." Plain women say "for security." But marriage is also the consecration of romance, the legitimization of cohabitation, the solemnization of love, the unique social basis for parenthood and family life, and a social reinforcement of the monogamy of love.

In short, marriage remains the thing to do for settling down lovers, those who are stuck together, just as work remains the thing to do for a settling-down adult—despite the work ethic, women's lib, the sexual and other social revolutions. Not only does marriage symbolize and proclaim to the world the setting of the cement of coupling, but in terms of feeling it adds another dimension to love. The most sophisticated, mature, and even cynical couples, entirely free from other traditional fetters, are regularly surprised by this fact—that marriage makes a difference. Even if the woman does not take the man's name, even if not all documentation is changed accordingly, even if the couple continues to live in the same apartment they had shared for years, even if their friends stay the same, even if they don't actually *believe* in marriage or a social institution,

even if everyone around them seems to be breaking up in bit-
terly contested divorces, marriage remains highly valued. The
dimension marriage adds to love may in fact be no more than
symbolizing the achievement of the principle of love; it marks
a more settled, tranquil phase in loving and it is built in the
sociobiological service of nesting and procreation.

However the feeling is rationalized, the fact is that a couple,
even an elderly couple with no chance of making a bastard
child, feels that a paramarried relationship ends in a cul-de-sac
unless it ends in marriage—which is felt to be the beginning
of a new journey. Certainly marriage consolidates love, whether or not the next milestone is the graveyard of romance. And
curiously enough, or not, if you understand it in these terms,
people are not put off by current statistics indicating that
breakdowns in second-time-arounders are even more frequent,
in America, of course, than breakdowns in the first time
around, if that were possible!

By now, also, child rearing will occur, if it occurs at all. The
old myth was that children strengthen the bond of love and
bring the couple closer together. The new myth is that they do
the opposite. What's the truth? It depends, entirely. Far from
repairing a crumbling coupling, a child accelerates the process,
just as much as buying an emotionally estranged wife a mink
coat may only make her want to break away from what brings
about her shame and guilt. In the same vein, a bombardment
of pregnancies, with three consecutive children within the first
two and a half years of marriage may end the best of romantic
loves. Also, in the same direction, most young parents are relatively unprepared, emotionally, intellectually, and socially,
and unready for parenthood. A child foisted, so to speak, on
a young unsettled couple, with the cement bonding still quite
wet, is not going to help consolidate the relationship and may
actually add enough strain to cause either parent to run from
this added responsibility. And even if they didn't run, even if
they stuck quite well, not handling the infant properly, running into problems and frustrations through immaturity and
ignorance, may well frustrate the marriage beyond endurance
or at least test its limits.

Finally, a lot depends on the type of woman and the economic situation. If she *must* work for the basic family income,

the strain tests her capacity and that of the relationship, even if the husband believes in a sharing partnership and practices it well—though that helps immeasurably. The woman then resents *having* to work and feels guilty about neglecting her infant and young child, particularly in the crucial period of parenting, which occurs between about eighteen months and four to five years. Both overworked parents may also feel sorry for themselves for missing their child's childhood, the little thrills and joys that happen daily in their absence.

So much for the many variables, or the negative side, which, as was said, depend on the age, economic status of the couple, the woman's capacity and aspiration, the level of partnership, the number of children, and so forth, but most of all on the status of love between them.

In my opinion, the positive side, the ayes, have it by far. Let's start with the ideal circumstances: an older, vigorous male, whether or not he has had children by a previous marriage (particularly if not) and a woman ripe for motherhood who has no children and wouldn't miss the experience for the world, a couple in love, highly compatible (well-blended) who have worked out a full partnership in which only different personal (not sex-stereotyped) skills divide their labor. For such a couple a child is a godsend. In fact, if they are a sophisticated couple who have previously cohabitated and stuck together for some years, having a child gives them the same or a bigger surprise than marriage. They would have told you when living together that they couldn't conceive of loving each other more, or more equally, and that they are truly fulfilled. Yet marriage jumps the amor-meter reading by quite a bit. Their first child jumps it again up to the limit. Love is incremented. What's even more convincing objectively is that the social statistics confirm the durability of a parented marriage. The odds against suicide by either partner drop significantly. The marriage becomes more stable. The older couple, grateful for being "blessed" with a child, feels useful and rejuvenated. Moreover, they are usually more able to give their child more attention and care than when they were younger because of their improved economic circumstances. And the chances are that their maturity and wisdom will offset the tendency to dote on the child and spoil it rotten.

One of the drawbacks of this situation, however, is that there may not be time for another child and this child will have to put up with the disadvantages of being the only child of older parents, which brings with it a kind of isolation among adults and a delayed influence of peers. Also there is sometimes a morbid fear of losing an elderly parent prematurely (usually a fear of losing the mother), and/or a feeling of slight embarrassment and of missing something if the parents appear old enough to be grandparents. Once again, this only goes to show that you can never have everything.

Now there are several other factors that strengthen further the idyllic situation of a wanted child in a mature couple. One is the willingness, the strength of the wish for parenthood, and especially the state of informed preparedness of the couple. In ideal circumstances they are able, willing, and ready—they've read all the key books. They are both active participants in parenting. The joys of "working on" fertilization renew the sparks of passion and deepen the sensuality and sexuality of love. The sensuality of child-handling may also enhance love-making. And the pride of parenting may then complete their bliss.

An important factor in parenting is the woman's motivation in regard to the couple's economic status. If a woman does not *have* to work for family income, but if she has a career already and decides to have it minimally interrupted by pregnancy and then by child rearing (for two to three years, when the child is between one-and-a-half and five years), and if she can do that, if the career allows this, then she is better off as a mother and wife doing this rather than sacrificing her career for child and marriage. This is particularly true if the all-important quality baby-sitter or nanny is available and affordable, and if the child is bright and able to benefit from a good day-care center and prekindergarten school.

If, on the other hand, the woman chooses not to work, that's all right too—always providing that such decisions are mutually agreed upon. But if she wants to work, yet is forced by her husband to give up her career, and particularly if she becomes trapped in the home, like the traditional cooped-up agoraphobic housefrau, the whole kit and caboodle comes under strain.

Now if in due course, that is under proper planning, another child is mutually desired and the woman decides to interrupt her career for longer than she would have done for one child, this is all right also, particularly if the second child is equally rewarding in terms of the desired sex, health, and development.

If, on the other hand, the woman and her husband choose that she work and keep in touch with her career, this too is all right, though now a stable live-in or day helper becomes even more important. Naturally problems arise—overattachment to the helper and jealousy by either or both parents or insecurity in the child witnessing forever departing and reappearing parents. Constantly moving around, causing changes in the physical and social environment, is traumatic at this stage and throughout childhood, which demands sameness. And over-busy parents who miss their children's development come to regret this eventually. But all such problems can be overcome by intelligence and love.

Single parenthood, on the other hand, is an entirely different ball game. Some single women (even some men) want children but no spouses—not even a steady mate. This may be all right. It all depends on what's blocking a love relationship, and the chances are that whatever is blocking it will also block healthy maternal or paternal feelings. If economic factors are added to this situation as well and the parent (adoptive or natural) *has* to work, the odds are against success.

If the single parent (usually the woman) was married and is now divorced (or separated) and *has* to work, parenting is much more handicapped than if she didn't have to work but *chooses* to work and if the child or children are old enough. There are so many ifs in this business that we will have to leave it there, particularly since the single situation, by definition, does *not* involve the substance of this book, namely coupled love.

So, on the whole, parenthood is like love—it is better to have had it and missed some of it or even lost it, than not to have had it at all—as all parents must yield their love objects. The alternative is a selfcentered and usually selfish, to the point of narcissism, coupling, which is far more difficult to sustain even if there is no neuroticism. For one thing the link forged by love between its psychology and its biology is then lost. For another thing, one will never know how things might have been, quite apart from being relegated to a minority of childless couples usually regarded as deprived.

There are, of course, many variations of parenthood, in terms of the situation, the motivation of the couple, their ages and socio-economic status, and their cultural demands. They cannot all be discussed in the scope of this book. However, what will be left to another chapter (Chapter 6: Passages) are abnormal variations, such as a narcissistic coupling broken up by a child, or an excessively puerile couple (e.g., overactive eternal children within) becoming jealous of their own child, and psychogenically infertile couples. Suffice it to reiterate in the context of sticking that the actual zygote, the child, in most normal instances, can only symbolize and biologically incarnate the emotional zygote of love in coupling.

And then there are people born to be parents, oozing all the right "instincts" yet unable to commit themselves to the paths leading to parenthood. They are destined to make some lucky child the perfect aunt or uncle.

A TEST OF HEALTHY STICKING TOGETHER

1. Do you feel you can grow psychologically and socially, within the union with your partner?	Yes (definitely)	Somewhat	No
2. Do you feel you would NOT collapse utterly without his support and the strength of your union?	Yes (not collapse)	Partially collapse	No (I'd collapse)
3. Do you feel that on the whole you complement each other so that in your relationship you are better and stronger than you would be alone?	Yes	Somewhat	No
4. Do you feel your relationship has enabled you to grow inwardly and become more in touch with yourself, more secure within yourself and more mature?	Yes	Somewhat	No

5. Are the quarrels between you constructive in that they bring you closer together, toward an appreciation of one another?	Yes	Somewhat	No
6. On the whole, do you feel your relationship to be harmonious, a blend of your different personality gifts?	Yes	Somewhat	No
7. Is your relationship seen by intimates to be close and harmonious?	Yes	Somewhat	No
8. Is your relationship just as alive as it was in its earlier stage in that you still feel the surges of love and the pain of separation?	Yes	Somewhat	No
9. Is your lovemaking as good in quality as it was earlier in the relationship?	Yes	Somewhat	No
10. Is the frequency of your lovemaking on the average not less than half what it was earlier in the relationship and in any case not less than once a week (on the average)?	Yes (not less)	Somewhat less	No (it is less)
11. Do you feel loved about as much as you love, in both quality and quantity?	Yes	Somewhat	No
12. Is there less than one major change and a couple of minor ones (or about four minor ones) you'd wish for in the relationship to make it perfect?	Yes (less)	Somewhat more	No (there are more)
13. Have you been close together and living together for 5 years or more?	Yes	Not quite (3-4 years)	No
14. Do you imagine living together like this forever?	Yes	Somewhat	No
15. Do you feel that even if there were a major change in your life or in your partner's personality (a flipover) the relationship would be able to weather it or even get stronger?	Yes	Somewhat	No

Scoring

Answer each question with one answer only. Score 2 for Yes, 1 for Somewhat, and 0 for No. Add it all up.

Interpretation

30–28	Either you've hit the perfect love or you're living in a fool's paradise.
27–25	You've got a good thing going; stick to it.
24–20	It's promising but see what you can do to make it better.
19–15	It's so-so, but it may be the best you can do, for now.
14–10	You've got a problem worth investigating, perhaps with help.
9–5	Look around for something else.
4–0	Forget it.

5

Late Love

Competitors cannot coexist.

—GAUSS'S LAW

There are at least five varieties of late love: the "late bloomers" and the "second- or third-time-arounders," both winner and loser variants (you can't be a winner if you've been more than three times around); the late lovers afflicted by "autumnal fever" (in praise of either older women or men); the "merry widow and the spider," and the "chronically love-sick."

THE TYPOLOGY

The Late Bloomers

Let us distinguish sharply the late bloomers from the chronically love-sick, who are like horses who keep coming up to the starting gate but are never off and running. Chronic love-sickness is a form of incapacity to love and/or to be loved, totally disguised by the illusion of romanticism, retrievable only by the fake lover. Eventually such people get desperate and so accelerate the succession of love objects that they begin to overlap each other.

In love-sickness three possibilities arise: (1) that you "love" no one but yourself and that eventually you become so taken with yourself (narcissism) that there is no room for anybody else, not even a facsimile of another person. Narcissists, of course, are attracted only to likes. (And giving up on attempts to love is very bad news.) (2) that you've been hurt so much somewhere along the line—let down, rejected, what have you—that you're secretly (unconsciously) determined not to allow yourself to be trapped ever again. This is better news, for all it takes is recognition and courage. (3) that you *imagine* that you've been hurt or would be if you allowed yourself to actually fall in love and stay there. In any case, viewed on the entire spectrum of love gone wrong, to be chronically love-sick is better than to be love-blocked because you have at least loved. On the other hand, the illusion of lovesickness is worse than being chronically sick with its actual hurt. The coverup by illusion is harder to tear off than the healing of actual love wounds.

The late bloomer may, of course, have been a chronic love-sick finally released spontaneously or by therapy, so that he or she becomes psychologically available. But this is rare. More commonly the late bloomer is someone partially delayed along the path, rather than fully blocked. If spontaneous or therapeutic release of the capacity to love comes before rigidity has set in, the cure resembles the case of a postponed young love. In both these instances, the late bloomer should seek contrasting opposition in a partner, despite the fact that his or her tolerance will be somewhat truncated by age.

If release of the capacity to love doesn't happen until rigidity has set in, the case must be treated like one of very late love. Here the reasoning is something like this: In the normal course of late ticking and sticking together, a couple, however far apart or different they were in the beginning, by now resemble one another much more than not, because mutual influence or successive approximation has consolidated them into a unit. This is just as well because by now age and other factors have combined to limit their flexibility and adaptability, hence their tolerance of other people.

Now they no longer need to quarrel in order to reconcile their minimal differences. They've learned to compromise so their energies are spared. Thus in a late love under the circumstances described, when the individual has done his or her growing up and when energy for tolerance has become limited, the would-be lover should be in the same position as that achieved eventually by the young lover. Consequently the mating must be assortative from the beginning—at the clicking stage. This means that the couple must be alike even in their foregrounds and much more still in their backgrounds. Late love then is the apparent exception to the universal law governing close relationship in that likes should match one another. Yet this isn't really an exception because, as you just saw, it's a simple corollary of processing the natural sequel of contrasting opposition to minimal differences.

The most classic example of this sort, bearing out the entire theory pointed out throughout this work, is that of old friends (previously platonic) falling in love at this stage. If you're one of those, I suggest you read the middle part of Chapter, 7: Friendship (where platonic love is denied) in conjunction with the following illustration.

Joan had dated John in desultory fashion in high school. Then she lost sight of him because he was three years her senior, but they kept in touch. They remained good but distant friends yet she was dark, energetic, sanguine, romantic; he fair, languid, phlegmatic, mathematical. They should have made a good contrasting match. John headed straight up the academic ladder and picked himself a wife while still on its lower rungs. John's wife was tawny and seemed energetic and sanguine, but she became drained from the demands of their first two children and from keeping up with the academic Joneses. She needed someone stronger than John to lean on. So she ran away with one of his more mature students, who got a football scholarship elsewhere.

Meanwhile Joan had gone through a protracted relationship with a rather cold, calculating, and distant wealthy potentate who nevertheless steadied her down. At that time Joan and her periodic cohabitant and John and his spouse often went out as couples. Joan discerned that John's wife was overly dependent, and lent her her own increasingly strong shoulder. Joan matured under the influence of her cohabitant, while John had half flipped over to becoming sensuous and romantic, though his wife never noticed this change. She had held too fixed a view of him. It was to Joan that she really turned for strength. And Joan helped her mother John's two children, whose favorite "auntie" she had become. By now Joan had learned to stand on her own two feet and felt she no longer needed to play the concubine to her nawab protector. She finally left him and went through a dark, promiscuous period, which John watched uncomfortably, though from a distance. When John's wife ran off with the football player and left him with the children, he seemed destroyed and listless on the surface. He had loved his wife, he said, and still did. Joan naturally stepped in, took care of the children, pursued her own career successfully, and comforted her old friend. People commented on how alike they were despite their strikingly different looks. For the longest time John held himself aloof, so much so that on making love with Joan he pushed his hands firmly into the bed, refusing to embrace Joan or kiss her for that matter. He hinted strongly about his fear of getting hurt once more. In the end they fell in love—he, graying and balding at the pinnacle of his career, she on top of hers. They felt immense comfort with each other and confessed that this was their very first true love.

The Second-time-arounders

Obviously you realize that humans don't form neat, discrete and exclusive entities, like inanimates. That's why you can't apply pure science to them. Temporary categories are made for the convenience of study. They overlap and merge, sometimes grossly. Second-time-arounders often turn out to be late bloomers; sometimes because they weren't psychologically available for love before, rarely because they were plain unlucky before. At any rate, when they do turn out they thank their lucky stars, saying, "It's better late than never!" Then like all successful late lovers they begin an active campaign to avert the sorry fate of all cowardly nonlovers who're too afraid to take a risk.

But sometimes second-time-arounders are the most fortunate of beings: They were in love before. They loved and lost the first time around—either through death, through some tragic maiming of the loved one, or through a drastic change. And now they're at it again—loving and being loved, picking up where they left off.

The gloomy statistics telling America that the second time around pays even less than the first time (in a staggering number of break-ups) as usual fail to separate the chaff from the wheat. This particular category of second-time-arounders, those who loved before, yields a very different kind of statistic—one of utter and full success. "It was good before but it's incredibly better now" is their motto. The overall reason is simple to grasp: once a champion, always a champion. These are the truly tried people whose instinct never fails, who choose unerringly in the first place—which is the prime secret of success—who tolerate differences well and relish them, being still young at heart. They are born to love and to be loved. Invincible. They become the most militant recruiters to the courageous ranks of those whom they urge, "If at first you don't succeed, try, try, and try again." In this, of course, they're wrong. In the first place that's two tries too many. One is allowed one mistake as "bad luck," maybe two, but never three or more. At that point love is a fiasco. In the second place, like all people who have *it* they're not aware of it—be it charisma, brightness, or loving. So they overestimate those hordes of second-time-arounders who make up the bulk of the bleak statistic—those who haven't made it before, are not making it now, or never will make it unless they change drastically.

Those who made it the first time and are doing it again must realize that they are a small class apart, the aristocrats of lovedom, born virtually with a gift, Cupid's silver arrow in their left hand.

The normative late love, that is, the statistical norm in North America at any rate, is the second-time-arounder who didn't do too badly the first time around but wants to do better now.

Most of the time the old love becomes dormant, like a volcano, but is capable of erupting again, as Mount St. Helens did. This kind of second-time-around heterolove is built on the same lines as the first, provided libido is not all exhausted—so long as there's some molten lava left. It is then that the Gaussian law quoted at the head of this chapter—"competitors cannot coexist"—applies, so that in such cases the members of the couple should still be largely different, and attracted by their preponderant opposites.

But a close second in frequency would be the kind of late

love that follows one that has taken up most of the individual's growth and reproductive period. At this point the corollary of early love applies and likes attract for the reasons mentioned—but even then the couple has to take care so that they won't compete. If they belong to the same walk of life, if they've done their parenting with different sets of children who are still under their new roof, if they share the same personality characteristics and especially the same interests—as is their tendency—they must take great care to excel at different things because one must always subordinate to the other in order to exist. That's the essence of a cooperative relationship.

At the same time, in order to achieve an ideal full partnership, subordination must be compatible with self-esteem and never apply across the board—nor need it conform to traditional sex competences. For example, if she is better at fixing the house, he might be better at fixing the garden; if she's the socialite, he might be the informed reader, and so forth. It can be a thin line to tread, for the tendency toward aggressive competitiveness inside the *same* territory leads to avoidance of sharing that territory in order to preserve the orderliness of a pacific relationship. And yet if that avoidance spreads, the result will be that "never the twain shall meet," under the same roof—a drifting apart, just at a time when the essence of a more tranquil full-time love is the sharing of common interests and companionship. The other bad alternative is to quarrel and fight for domination until one has "won." But such victories turn out to be pyrrhic because the vanquished tend to nurse revenge.

Hence, by far the most successful formula is the natural dividing up of different territories with different leaderships and subordinations, at least at different times. It doesn't matter if in the overall it's not exactly fifty-fifty—it never is—unless one of the partners, the insecure one, keeps a tab.

Now while we're at it, typologizing, let's realize that there are two kinds of second-time-arounders as in any such subspecies. One is when *both* partners are second-time-arounders—an increasingly common phenomenon; the other is when only one is. It makes not too subtle a difference, but sufficient to count significantly on the magical formula of background/foreground ratio of commonality/contrast.

If *both* partners are second-time-arounders, if they've been there before, whether it had been heaven or hell for them, they can afford larger differences in the *foreground* (personality, etc.) than if only one had been there before. The reason is that to have been married (or paramarried) for any significant length of time before, then matched up with a single, counts almost as heavily as a racial, ethnic, or religious difference in the *background*. And this, in turn, as we have learned, leaves less energy for tolerance and adjustments in foreground contrasts.

How much difference there should be when both partners are second-time-arounders depends on their age (especially their *psychological* age), the length of time they've been married before, how happily or otherwise, the nature of their previous failure or loss, and the existence of other background differences.

The foreground differences should be maximized if the new couple is psychologically young, if their previous marital experience was short lived, if the previous error was too much likeness or a wrong order of priorities in foreground contrast, and if their backgrounds are similar. The opposite is equally true: Differences in the foreground should be reduced in proportion to the psychological age of the couple, the longevity and success of their previous marriages, and background differences.

At the risk of insulting some readers' intelligence I shall reiterate the important and perhaps obvious point about why, in the late love of second-time-arounders who've had a long and relatively happy marriage, likes should attract, unless they are a very unusually young-at-heart couple: In the ordinary process of coupling, a previously good relationship would have brought the partners together, brought them to maturity, and eliminated the contrasting opposite factors. Opposition would already have done its genetic, psychological developing, nesting, and rearing work. So by now each partner would have *incorporated* his or her previous partner inside his personality, and new differences would appear strident and stressful and make for invidious comparisons. Likeness makes for a much smoother transition.

If, however, only one of the late new lovers had had a good, long previous marital experience and the other not, then their foreground differences are already substantial and a lot of wise and loving compromise is necessary. In the interest of mental economy little room is allowed for other background differences.

Although the factors of late love matching, herein enumerated, determine a great deal the quantifications of the magical formula to be applied, the single greatest factor is the strength of the pulse of life, the libido one or both lovers possess.

All second (or more)-time-arounders live under the pall of fear of failure; none more than those who belong to the already failed variety—the losers, the compulsive repeaters of previous patterns, and those whose autumnal fever has reached hyper-pyrexic proportions. And with good reason, because the losers stand a good chance of losing again, very much as the same type of gambling sucker does. The autumnal heat-stroked person also has good reason to fear failure if she/he goes ahead with an infatuation, because it has far less chance of succeeding than the marriage that is foolishly abandoned.

We shall come back to the positive-feedback amplifying effect of this fear of failure, whose tendency is to fulfill this self-prophecy when we discuss the problems of passages in the next chapter. This exposition is meant to cover the more normal relationships. In this context one should mention that the aristocrats of lovedom, the ones who've been successful before, rarely are terrified of failure the second time around or rarely fulfill other people's prophecies to that effect. Not because they're fools who rush in where angels (or losers) fear to tread, but because healthy, successful people are generally confident. This doesn't mean that they feel infallible, especially now in later life when the three illusions of youth have waned—those of indestructibility, infallibility, and eternal youth. Sure, they get twinges of doubt—but only enough to separate their quiet confidence from unjustifiable arrogance.

What of the losers, though, apart from those who suffer from an inherent incapacity to love or to be loved or both; apart from the relatively incompetent and chronically love-sick and apart from those too timid to try, and those who justify their avoidance by saying that love isn't the be-all and end-all that it's made out to be and not worth the candle?

What goes wrong with these losers? They're not all neurotics, at least not in terms of their marriages or cohabitative closeness. In fact, lean-to or teepee relationships can last indefinitely if a strong wind doesn't blow them over. So who and what are these losers? Some are neurotics of a kind, described in more detail in Chapter 6: Passages. The great error that losers make is the wrong choice in the very first place. And then, like the children of parents who swear that they'll be different yet become the same as or worse than their parents ever were, these losers repeat their mistakes *ad nauseum.*

Take, for instance, the strong women who attract weak men, then respond positively to them in the false belief that they want to dominate or even domineer men. Ultimately they despise and discard them. Too afraid to tackle stronger or even more average men for fear of being found wanting, they get stuck on this type. And, after a while, they become too tough, bitchy or brittle to be attractive to normal men.

This situation is analogous to intelligent men attracting the classic dumb blondes and falling for them largely because they're reluctant to be challenged by intelligent women. It's as if both their masculinity and their intelligence were simultaneously threatened. The extreme case is that of a strong man attracted to the flower-child bride. Presently he expects her to become a partner and becomes astounded to find nobody there—the flower has metamorphosed into a vacuous fruit.

Then there's the young man raised in the shadow of a plurality of forceful mothers, who looks for yet another one—and when he finds her, both partners are disillusioned with their fixed roles, which are incompatible with romantic love. This same pattern plagues many young women as well. Examples abound.

What losers have in common is that they invariably choose the wrong persona, whose aligned shadow, hominus-femina, eternal child, and anima never fit properly with their own personages. Or else the partner's persona is all right but the rest of the personages of the inner self are not in proper alignment—they are skewed and produce a clash within the partner and in the coupling. Or else they miss on the ultimate magical formula used in the matching because of some overdeterminance of neurotic motivations and/or faulty perceptions. For instance, a couple may strive to overcome an abysmal background difference when they should be looking for commonality. At the same time and as a consequence, they're forced to reduce foreground contrasts when they should seek them.

In this case, some powerful rebellion against parents and cultural norms may have propelled a coupling across religious, ethnic, or racial barriers, where they have to fight bitter battles for themselves and their offspring, whereas they both might possess passive-dependent needs requiring one of them to have been different in this respect.

The tendency is for the loser to obstinately stick to the direction of his neurotic (self-defeating) motivation rather than do an about-face.

If no answer is easily forthcoming, the loser should *ask the shadow,* for the shadow truly knows. It has the key. If his shadow contrasts with hers and resembles her persona, if differences are carefully taken care of, the similarities ought to look after themselves. But the shadow knows.

And by way of motivation, by and large, a woman can't go too wrong looking for a hominus roughly in her father's image, and a man, for a femina in his mother's image. Both can and frequently do go mightily wrong in trying to escape these images and deviate widely from them in a futile act of incomplete rebellion, for underneath it all they're more stuck than they know on these very images.

This rule cannot apply, of course, when these images simply do not exist—because of premature parent death or its equivalent. In this case the fantasy of the parent image will work so long as it fits accurately with the reality of the chosen person.

The other factor breaking this general rule is when the parent of the opposite sex really is hopeless or grossly inadequate. Then a major job of psycho plastic surgery is in order. Even so, the desired rather than the real parent image should then provide the contour of the skeleton while the would-be lover should fill in the flesh of the hominus/femina. But, in order to succeed in really getting away from the parent image or improve on it drastically, the person herself or himself must change. One must be free psychologically to choose—otherwise one's still hung up on an inadequate parent figure, however undesirable this may be, while seeking (and being unlikely to find) a better match than is provided by the parent figure. As you see, this is somewhat of a Catch-22 situation.

Autumnal Fever

This usually involves a psychological, and maybe a biological, age gap going either way in the couple, but it rarely affects two birds of equally aged feather. The problem here is how do you tell the menopausal syndrome (autumnal fever) from a flipover, from a second lease on life, from a late bloomer or from a would-be second-time-arounder, all of which may be better than the first? The reason this diagnosis is such a problem is that the afflicted person never consciously knows to which category he or she belongs but always rationalizes and puts up the best face. What's infinitely worse is that the expert can rarely tell for sure whether a mere menopausal syndrome will turn into a last great love or just fizzle out; or whether the flipover is for real, there to stay, and demanding a change of partners anyhow, or just a flash in the pan. As is usual in such cases, in clinical practice, the truth is revealed in time. But while time may tell, by then so much damage may have been done that there's no going back, if the case turns out to be autumnal fever.

So what clues are there? Several. A bid for sexual rejuvenation leads the menopausal syndrome. Consequently, its accompanying signs and symptoms emphasize physical renovation, like crash slimming diets, increased exercise, new clothes, and attempting the young look. The syndrome is an overcompensatory reaction to the gloom of creeping senescence and the doom of death, once you're over the halfway mark. Directly and exclusively for the woman, it's also a reaction to the certainty that this is the end of her child-bearing capacity—the womb becomes functionless and along with that a good, deep-seated chunk of functional identity is lost.

The leading early sign of autumnal fever is conjugal sexual dissatisfaction and restlessness.

The whole being cries out, "I'm not old and buried yet. There's still life and vitality in me. I'll show you!" And they do, sometimes at the expense of security, throwing caution to the wind and threatening the stability of marriage, seen now as a premature internment. Kick the traces! Live it up! With sexual success comes a "high" and a feeling that indeed anything is possible—again. It's an illusion, of course, because the cruel truth is to the contrary—things that had been possible before, ranging from making children to running the four-minute mile, are no longer possible, and never will be. The elation of achievement offsets the sadness of regrets for what's *not* been done, now that it is too late; for what *has* been done in error, and for what can *no longer* be done.

Well, sex leads this syndrome with its chin, so to speak, and as long as it only leads to concupiscence, it's safe enough, provided the partner doesn't know, turns a blind eye, or can tolerate the hurt.

In the natural history of the syndrome, the black sheep eventually comes back into the fold. But if the person falls into an infatuation, believing that it's the real thing rather than a passing affair, or if the spouse cannot tolerate the hurt and forces the issue of monogamy, with the result that the fevered patient is pushed either way—back into a resented marriage or forward into a fancied love, or if the spouse knows and doesn't care, that's trouble.

It takes the fevered patient fallen into autumnal love much time and skillful persuasion to realize that this might be just a fancy. And it takes a patient spouse with a great deal of love and tolerance to forgive and forget. Sometimes the hurt never heals. If, however, the spouse doesn't really care, then that relationship is probably finished anyway—extinct like the dodo bird. The danger then is that the fevered patient may propel himself (and it's usually a male who does this) precipitously into the first affair that comes along because he realizes that it's all over with the marriage and because he's afraid of being left alone. He's been alone already and didn't know it! Women in such cases are either more circumspect or more courageous. They look before they leap. Or else they lack daring; they hold back so long that they can no longer leap.

The flipover, which we've already described in Chapter 4: Sticking, is a reversal in the self, turning oneself upside down, usually by letting the shadow out and pushing the persona in. At the menopausal stage, however, there's an absolutely normal change that happens to most people. It does favor a flip-over, but it's often merely confused with it. The cardinal change at involution is that however extroverted the person was previously, there is a gradual tendency toward introversion now. However alloplastic one has been, manipulating the world and using power, there is a tendency to use more the autoplastic environmental strategy—that of looking to oneself for inward rewards and adaptations.

Under normal circumstances, at involution there's a restriction of physical activity and a desire for shrinking, for familiar spaces, rather than for new adventures and challenges.

On the other hand, autumnal fever hits headlong against all these "natural" infolding trends, against the composure of the psyche as it were, folding its hands as if in rehearsal of eternal repose. The mood then is expansive, pushing into extroversion, even in a previous introvert; new adventures and physical, mental, and social challenges are sought.

One can diagnose the flipover because it's a dramatic representation of the principle of contrasting opposition determining human psychoarchitecture and the essential contradiction of human nature. The inside person, built in opposition to the outside, flips out. This can only happen in loosely integrated personalities who have repressed big chunks of themselves.

As for sexual direction, in autumnal fever, as part of the rejuvenation bid, there's an insistent search for a much younger mate. In flipover that's not essential. What is sought is a redressed balance—usually more receiving than giving. Thus, although it may be difficult to differentiate, a good knowledge of the person's previous personality ought to help to differentiate autumnal fever from flipover.

The late bloomer is usually not so late that she or he has hit the autumn of her/his days. It is a retraceably (analytically) more gradual process than either the sudden flipover—at least sudden in the end spurt—or the explosive menopausal syndrome, precipitated by such things as newly found gray hair, balding, wrinkled face, sagging skin, extra tires, fatigue, joint ache, and all the indignities of involution, including memory slippage. Something has finally unblocked in a previously emotionally constipated late bloomer.

This all sounds pretty clearly definitive, but in real life nothing ever is. The *approach* of "autumn" may precipitate a whole sequence of events. Noticeably, in modern times with their vast hiatus in traditional and absolute values and the expectation of a long life, when rewards are sought in the here-and-now and not the hereafter, the psychological menopause, primarily in men but also in women, comes earlier and earlier. So now this syndrome is outdistancing physical menopause by a decade or more. Both sexes may be hit in their mid thirties, while their bodies may last well into their fifties, until the final hormonal change of involution comes about. The threat of the mid years of life could precipitate a flipover and part of this could bring into bloom a hitherto hidden bud of love. And a break in previously close relationships could bring about a second, and conceivably a third and best, heterolove. Thus these discrete phases could interact and merge and emerge as a "syndrome" with undeterminable consequences, at one point in development. In such a case only a skilled expert could help the person disentangle the knots and undo them. But even then, because of the relative unpredictability of the outcome— in a case that's *not* clear-cut—all the expert can do in the end is to outline alternative futures and allow the person to choose the course. Furthermore, here, as in many instances in life, it's a question of "nothing ventured, nothing gained." If one doesn't take a risk consciously, one will have to risk something nevertheless—namely, going to the grave without ever finding out what might have happened if one had had the courage to follow one's feelings, however much in error they might have turned out to be. One last word, though, about therapeutic intervention at this difficult juncture of a differential diagnosis. A late bloomer would or should be young enough at heart, by definition, to be attracted and attractive to a person standing in fair contrast to the self. Certainly a "flipped-over" condition demands a drastic rematching—unless, as mentioned before, the existing partner has the capacity to flip or change significantly also. Whereas a "menopausal" case or the compulsive second- or third-time-arounder perpetuating an error will not necessarily be motivated to seek her or his opposite. At the most the menopausal case will be sexually directed to someone quite a bit younger, but not necessarily different. If, for instance, the person merely wants a *younger* edition of a formerly loved someone and therefore like their own daughter or son (e.g. opposite in sex to the person), then that person is likely to be merely menopausally driven—a dirty old man or woman. If, however, the person seeks a real change in the partner's looks and personality, and if a real change has happened inwardly, then the situation is likely to be much more serious—and resemble a late bloomer or a flipover.

The Merry Widow and the Spider

To clarify these metaphors, the "widow" is merry when she feels released from her husband by his death (or equivalent) and takes a second lease on life. The "spider" is the "widower" (or elderly equivalent) enticing new flies into his web. In other words, they are the two sexes in the situation of release in late life—free to start again, more or less *tabula rasa*.

Here fate takes a hand to encourage a late bloomer—and if we're to believe the papers, this can happen to anyone all the way from the septuagenarian to those congratulated by the Queen or President for reaching a century. The late death of a spouse *could* cause a flipover, but this is likely to be temporary and more part of a psychological dislocation than a real personality change. And most certainly widowhood presents, at least psychologically if not physically, the opportunity for taking the big step the second or third time around.

Certainly widowhood offers the chance of renewed romance. Yet both the merry widow and the spider, especially if over the midlife milestone, tend to go more for security and ultimately for nursing and/or economic care than merely for sex or even romance. The important consideration in this context is to allow enough time to absorb both the grief and the merriment or elation of widowhood—or for the discovery that an old spider can indeed catch nice juicy young flies—before drastic decisions are made.

Time is required in order to make sure that you're beyond the dangerous grasp of a belated infatuation and that the right choice of mate is made.

For one thing the romantic elations of late life in the wake of release from a long marriage make fertile soil for unscrupulous defrauding crooks, whether gigolos or courtesans, working both sides of the law; the detectably illicit and the nondetectable. The reasons that "there's no fool like an old fool" in these matters are many. Among them is a feeling of guilt due to such things as: previous death wishes toward the spouse, or simply that one has survived while the other is being eaten by worms, or for whatever real or imagined sins of omission or commission, or previous ambivalence. The net result is, of course, that guilt calls tacitly for punishment, hence for becoming a more than ordinary dupe. Another reason is that a long marriage, especially if happy or tranquil, insulates a person from appreciating the sharper changes in the psychosocial mores of the outside world. Consequently, one's not aware and tends to become gullible. Also, such a previous marriage blunts one's antennae, already battered by age.

So the first rule for both the merry widow and the elated spider is to fall in love, by all means, but don't sign anything till you've consulted an independent and skillful lawyer, and don't do anything else foolish until you've sorted yourself out in the manner that follows.

If the widows or spiders are old enough at heart as well as in age, and if, as is likely, they have lived a long life in the companionship of someone else and are well entrenched in their habits and expectations as well as in a conservative, rigid personality, then they should obey the law of late love—the mutual attraction of likes. This is when likes are not competitors. They're companions who extend and supplement each other's needs. In this, more than any other situation, you will have done all your growing before. You'll have changed *in relation* to a previous partner during a long time and arrived at a *modus vivendi,* a settled if not rutted life that cannot and must not be changed. In these circumstances one must not allow the first flush of elation or escape—however exciting or apparently rejuvenating—to obfuscate the need for replacement with one similar to oneself, perhaps a somewhat improved but not radically different love object from the dead spouse.

The devil of it, however, is that all too often the widow or the spider finally released from a prolonged marriage, with considerable ambivalence to the previous partner, fancies that all along she/he wanted somebody else. If that somebody else stands in great contrast to the merry escapee, and to the dead spouse, the question becomes "Isn't it too late now for such shenanigans?"

The Chronically Love-sick

We have met them before in these pages, the people who see themselves as "incurably romantic." They become infatuated time after time. They even fall in love, but they never quite manage to actually stay in love for any significant length of time. They deceive themselves more than others, who can see through them and realize that a strong attachment to themselves prevents them from committing themselves to others. Sometimes their addiction to romance, requited or not, resembles that to food ending in obesity, or to drink ending in alcoholism.

The only reason for their inclusion in this category of late love is that, pathetically, the passage of time does nothing to cure them but finds them still on love's threshold, too late to step over it.

Unlike late bloomers, second-time-arounders, and merry widows and widowers, and more like those afflicted with autumnal fever, the chronically love-sick know little or nothing of real love. Theirs is an ingenuous illusion.

Having issued all these warnings and counsels, having urged you to differentially diagnose yourself in terms of the taxonomy offered here, let me tell you that there's nothing wrong whatsoever with genuine late love. Late love, like late studentship or late parenthood, makes for serious and highly valued achievement. In many ways, even with respect to love, G. B. Shaw might have been right when he asserted that "youth is wasted on the young."

One last thing: In late love a vital question that arises is whether or not to have children. For the younger woman, around forty, this question is usually asked in connection with the fear of breeding a mongoloid or Downe's Syndrome (intellectually retarded or mentally defective) child. It is resolved by three factors:

1. The couple's need, motivation, and determination to have a child in order to complete their coupling as an act of love.
2. The woman's continued ability to ovulate (and the man's spermatogenetic capacity), the couple's sexual drive, and fertility.
3. Whether the woman has previously had normal children, which increases the likelihood of a normal child, perhaps as late as age forty-seven.

If they are lukewarm and want a child for other than the best reasons, if they can't afford to give that child the best care possible and if the woman hasn't had any children before, or not been pregnant before or has already had an abnormal child—or if the man has had an abnormal child, or if there's a hereditary contraindication on either side, having a child is most undesirable. Of course, infertility or spontaneous abortion settles the issue of want. But if a child is on the way, amniocentesis becomes a must. If either parent is against this procedure on whatever grounds, or if either is against therapeutic abortion (should it be required because of a damaged fetus) on whatever grounds, there really should be no conception in the first place.

Perhaps the question of having a child occurs much more commonly at a much later time for a male, a second-time-arounder (in his fifties)—that is, well after the normal time for a man's "menopause." It arises when he couples with a younger, fertile, healthy woman, particularly if she hasn't had a child by a previous marriage.

The answer depends first of all on the kind of late love this is. Clearly, in the abnormal and undesirable varieties of coupling—like autumnal fever and chronic love-sickness or compulsory and repetitive neurotic relationships—people can hardly cope with themselves and their union, let alone with the challenge of a child in their late years. So we're only considering the best of late love.

If the couple is capable and willing to have a *complementary* relationship; that is, if the attraction is by opposites still, as in late bloomers or in second-time-arounders who were not losers the first time, and if they really desire a child as the apotheosis of their love, then the situation deserves serious consideration. The chief disadvantages are:

1. To the child, having a father old enough to be his or her grandfather and certain to be mistaken by strangers for a grandparent. To say the least this stresses the sensitivities of the child.

2. To the surviving parent, the mother in this case, having to raise a child single-handedly if the husband dies in the course of rearing the child or children.

Much depends on the man in question and the strength of the relationship. If the man is young for his age, if he's able and willing, fit and competent, if he can do with his growing child what he did or ought to have done with his previous children (or what other fathers of a more appropriate age do or should do)—and this means physically no less than socially—that's very positive. If in addition he has adequate means to ensure that the mother (albeit she could work *and* do the job of rearing) has a cushion to fall back on, that's another positive factor.

But if the couple is really in love, if it takes a child to top that relationship, if they thought it all through much more carefully than a younger couple might have done and they still want a child, they should probably go ahead. In such cases, representing the aristocracy of lovedom, the parenting is a far better one than is usual with younger parents because the cradling with love is there, because the child is seen as a blessing and feels that much more precious. Also the competitiveness that is so much of an intrinsic feature of younger parent-child relationships is replaced by a deeply satisfying adoration, when everything else is well and good.

Then here comes a paradox. Imagine a couple really in love, who've known each other a good five years, lived together happily, and are well into the sticking phase. They've got the energy for a contrasting-opposite complementary coupling. They've made a child successfully and are happier than ever.

Say he's over fifty-five by now and she thirty-five or so. The thing to do, if they can cope, is to have two children. No, the reason isn't that children are cheaper by the half dozen or because you might as well be hung for a sheep as for a lamb! The reason is the future of the first child. The chances are that there are probably no grandparents on the man's side and that whatever close relationships and blood ties he's had would not be available during his young child's lifetime. If the mother's parents are elderly or ailing; if she on her own side hasn't much more to offer her young child than herself—with whatever normal risks there might be to her age and sex—then the child would have few, if anyone, as close blood ties. A sibling would then be like a godsend. It's a question of there being strength in that number. Those who feel badly about bringing a child into our world with its dim future may feel very badly about this suggestion. It's like a bigger sin—the second child— to cover up a big enough one; bringing a child into the world who's sure to be deprived. I won't go into the arguments why the world mustn't stop because its future looks dim; or why the best stock shouldn't weaken the genetic pool by withholding below the zero-population growth rate, or that having children may be unfashionable today but it has been healthy and fashionable before and will be again. I will only point out that the primary justification for having a child at all is as an act of love, its acme; that parenting strengthens the bond of heterolove and makes it unselfish and even more worthwhile. And that in this exceptional case—the only one I know of and for the reasons already mentioned—having two children is better than having only one. They rejuvenate and generate more love to go around and they'll need each other later in maturity.

A TEST OF COMPATIBILITY IN LATE HETEROLOVE

Please answer each question once only with a check, and score later according to the instructions.

Part A. The Status of Late Heterolove

A. TEST 1

	True	*Somewhat*	*No*
1. I feel I've never really loved and been loved before now, in my middle years or past them.			
2. I've only had one close-enough relationship before this one that could have given me the chance to love.		Two	Three or more
3. I'm attracted to a person quite a bit different from myself.			
4. Sexual attraction is important but not the most important part of my feelings of love.			
5. I am currently satisfied sexually but it is not enough to make me happy unless I can love and be loved.			
6. I could feel the capacity for love and the yearning to discharge it for some time before now.			
7. I do not feel threatened by age or menopause directly.			
8. I have not been widowed or suddenly become single by an act of fate.			
9. I haven't actually found yet a last love object but I'm actively looking for such a person.			

	True	*Somewhat*	*No*

10. Though there has been a change in me (my heart) it is not a major change in my personality.

Scoring
Score 2 for Yes, 1 for Somewhat (middle) and 0 for No.

Interpretation

17–20   You're likely to be a late bloomer though you might be a second-time-arounder or widowed or somewhat flipped.

10–17   You're not likely to be a late bloomer so you belong to one of the categories found in test 2 and 3 below.

0–9   You might be in no category of late love at all.

TEST 2

	More than two	*More than one*	*One only*

1. I've had more than one hetero-love relationship.

2. Most of them haven't worked out well.   Yes   Somewhat   No

3. I'm in my middle years or past them.

4. I feel I lack sexual fulfillment.

5. I feel I lack affection fulfillment (love itself).

Scoring
Same as in Test 1

Interpretation
Assuming you scored no more than 15 on Test 1:

7–10   You're likely to be chronically love-sick or a compulsive repeater (third or more time around) making poor choices and/or poor relationships.

3–7   You don't belong to either of these two categories thus far.

0–3 There's some mistake you might have made in these tests—try again.

TEST 3

	Yes	*Somewhat*	*No*

1. I feel threatened by age or "menopause." (involution)

2. I feel driven to seek greater sexual satisfaction.

3. I feel I am missing something big in love now though I have had something like it before.

4. I'm afraid of death and dying.

5. I wish to start life, sex, love all over again as if I had a second chance.

6. I want to feel young again though I know I'm well past actual youth.

7. My behavior has changed quite a bit though I know I'm basically the same person.

Scoring
Same as in Test 1

Interpretation
Assuming you scored no higher than 15 in Test 1 and no higher than 7 in Test 2:

10–14 You're likely to suffer from autumnal fever only, and it will pass.

5–9 You may also have flipped over somewhat or have been widowed (or equivalent).

0–4 You don't belong to the above categories—therefore you may be a second- or third-time-arounder but not a loser (necessarily). You might be just a "released" widow or spider.

Note

If you fall in between in all three tests you're a mixed-up difficult case, as described in the test.

Part B. Test of Compatibility

This test is for a high scorer in Test 1 (late bloomer) only if she/he has found a potential or actual mate, and for the flipover and widow/spider with a high score in Test 3.

	Yes	Somewhat	No
1. I feel young at heart and my partner is quite different from myself. or I'm set in my ways and my partner is similar to myself.			
2. Our quarrels are constructive and quite easily reconciled			or we don't quarrel
3. We are sexually compatible.			
4. I have taken the test in Chapter 1 and scored and ranked high.			
5. I have taken the test in Chapter 4 and scored and ranked high.			

Scoring

Same as in Test 1

Interpretation

8–10   You're highly compatible.

5–8   You should be satisfied.

0–4   Either you don't belong in the late bloomer, winning second-time-arounder or flipover category *or* you've got the wrong mate.

If you're in Test 2 status of late love—chronic love-sick or compulsive loser—or in Test 3 status of autumnal fever, it's no use looking for a stable mate or compatibility because you suffer from a chronic or temporary aberration that precludes a compatible mate until you correct the error in yourself.

Back to the drawing board!

6

Passages

Jack Spratt would eat no fat
his wife would eat no lean.

So far we have looked at normal or ideal love between man and woman. But in real life the "normal" in love is probably rather rare. Heterolove is a veritable mine field of problems and pitfalls.

I have learned much of what I know about coupling from my patients, who presented these problems to me in order to help them solve them. The abnormal or faulty relationship is far simpler to observe and far easier to project than the normal. Moreover, it does present itself to expert scrutiny infinitely more often than does the normal, the silent majority of lovers. Hence science generally, and certainly mental science, must progress from an understanding of the unusual and abnormal to that of the normal and from prediction of extreme events to prediction of usual events.

Thus, partly because the inspiration of this book comes largely from patients and mostly because in these respects of love we are all liable to become patients for a while, I intend to conclude the chapters on heterolove with this one on passages. My use of this title—passages—includes the more normative but problematic circumstances created by the passage of time, as well as the transient and transitory aspects of heterolove brought about by faulty personalities like narcissists and by faulty relationships like neurotic coupling.

SEX AND MARRIAGE GAMES

It's not easy to predict how it will be for the rising generation. But for the ones now in full bloom or fading, marriage is a game. The paths of bride and groom intersect at least once, around the ceremony; then, several more times, if they are lucky. But the paths never really coincide. Hide-and-go-seek doesn't quite describe the situation because early in the game no one is seeking anymore and pretty soon no one bothers to hide properly. Perhaps seven successive games are being acted out:

1. *Post office.* This is, or was, a period of innocence. At least, the boy is innocent. The girl, more mature in body and in social interest, focused on sex and loving, is shifting chairs rapidly. Occasionally the boy sits in her lap, like a puppy. They kiss, she full of carnal knowledge, with a keen sense of sin lightly mixed with a maternal premonition. More often she looks for someone much older, not so clumsy, more dominating. He is bashful, romantic, full of self-consciousness.

Yet, it's a happy period for her. She knows what she is doing. In later years, she'll come back to these days in her memory and replay the game. For him it is too confused a phase, too painful to recollect.

2. *Fish.* His glands are now fully developed. He thinks he knows exactly what he wants. But it's only the one thing, which is never "romantic" enough for her. Of course, he can't help but pull the right card sometimes. There are only so many in the pack and this is a game of chance. Their bodies meet.

As for their minds, she sees in him what she wants to see and he does much the same. At this time, she's worldly-wise, fully matured intellectually, still leading the class, full of expectancy, still optimistic. He is fumbling, in every way but one, with a fond, lingering narcissism, admiring the splendor of his own body in full flexure and extension, reaching for trophies.

For her, sex is already a part of an existing scenery. For him, it is life itself. His moments of diary-inscribed introversion are brief, though they may be poignant and sometimes enduring. Her homo crushes are over with the Post Office mistress, unless she lacks a benign mother figure.

3. *Crazy Hearts.* Usually Fish goes on until they both seem to win. Of course, by the rules of the game, this is impossible. There's only one pack of cards. It's decided, for a long spell of the game, who's to be the principal giver and who the principal taker. They are married. She's bursting full of motherhood and motherliness.

He is not at all ready, except for the full attention and indulgence given him by his mother. He doesn't want to share. And he doesn't. They kiss, still significantly, in bed at night. The kiss in the morning becomes ritualized, the signal for the formalization of the relationship, and for the clear transfer or division of power.

For him, the nest is a first distinctive social achievement. For her, it may be the last. And she clings to this game of Crazy Hearts forever.

4. *Monopoly.* This is the property phase. His are the Park Places and Boardwalks, the big hotels and the macro world that he has discovered and in which he has secured a niche, at the cost of a decade of life. In the end she collects the rent for eight years after his demise.

He looks from without, inward, valuing his nest and his own family abstractly as "property," giving as his public opinion that he is ready to die solely for them. She looks from within, outwards. He has made these rules, the game, not she. Though it wasn't part of the arrangement, it is she who hangs on for dear life to her physical property, because there's nothing else left to possess.

Always idealistic and abstract, he philosophizes forever. They speak a different language now over the breakfast newspaper. Sometimes the language is so idiosyncratic that there's nothing but the silence of misunderstanding or of a complete gulf between them.

He is evolving and finally maturing, even sexually. Never satisfied, he wants more. But for her, his body is her sacred preserve. This game doesn't last forever, especially because, with his vestigial hunter drive, he won't allow it.

5. *Poker.* As he evolves, she involutes prematurely. He goes out farther and farther but protests he wants in. She goes in deeper and deeper but wants out. The threat of pregnancy gone, she opens up more widely than ever, sexually. But he

isn't there to be received. He's some other place, either staking his fortune (and theirs) on a "full house," in order to get the pot at one stroke, or staking it all on a bluff, or playing for different stakes in flesh and blood rather than a metal heap, bricks, or land deals.

By now, he is a social lion and a private ham. She has remained a social deer though she has grown into a private tigress.

This is a turning point. She's compelled to play, win or lose. But because she has become increasingly conservative she doesn't want to take the risk. Occasionally the tigress breaks out in her and forces the game with a "flush" or a bluff. He rarely shows his hand. Rarely does he want to play Crazy Hearts again, not with her. She'd like nothing better.

6. *Double Solitaire.* Poker was strenuous, but at least it was played together. She plays this game alone and wins every time. If he had died much earlier, suddenly and saintly, this would become a different game. He would go to heaven as a dying god and she would play a game with candles lit in his memory. He'd be some kind of winner then.

But if he survived the strenuous game of Poker, he'd be playing Solitaire too, but alas, they would be apart, one in each corner of the room, under separate lamps. Yet they are playing the same game of uncovering the aces that weren't there in the first place and making it all follow smoothly and come out on the table as it never really did in life. The kids come in and mess up a hand or two. Pretty soon the grandchildren come and play underfoot.

This Double Solitaire is a long game, played deep into the night. Even now, their energies don't coincide. He tires early, and his arthritic joints have to be helped to bed. She has just discovered the macro world. Unweighted by the burden of motherhood, she is ready to lift against gravity. He can't make it, poor soul! And the game remains unfinished, as he goes out with the early morning light.

7. *Single Solitaire.* She plays this for many years, sometimes under her own lamp, smiling whimsically, sometimes while on ever such a nice cruise in the Mediterranean. She smiles bittersweetly, at the unfolding sequences that others are now playing; Post Office and Fish. Will the games be more fun for

them? Will anybody really win? She notices that the rules have changed quite a bit. Poker is being played earlier. Fish and Crazy Hearts are played all the time, between the same or with different couples and with few penalties.

Everybody seems to be winning. But, of course, the pot is a great deal smaller. There's always a detached, mechanical, invisible hand that keeps pinching all the money, or most of it. On it are tattooed the letters t-a-x. Monopoly has gone out of vogue, except in the top social circles. But then in those circles the games have always been much faster, with quicker changes of players and much more at stake.

These, of course, were seven chronological stages marking the passage of time in normal coupling. But as stated, the pristine inspiration for this book came from problems presented by patients. Thus what follows are the passages of imperfect couplings. I suspect that they represent not that unusual an aspect of the human condition.

NARCISSISTIC COUPLING

Having been a beautiful prize-winning baby, a handsome child, and a venerated Adonis teenager, raven-haired, crystal clear blue-eyed, alabaster complexioned, and classically proportioned, Phillip could hardly escape being in love with himself. And like all physically self-preoccupied narcissists, deep down he despised himself for lack of masculinity—meaning guts. He couldn't have it both ways. Either he was to guard from marring his beauty at all costs, or else he'd respond aggressively to escalating charges of his being sissy. He paid the price. And indeed his sexual orientation became deviant—not so much toward his own sex (homo) except for envying ruggedness, but strictly toward himself (auto sex). His quick but modest mental abilities weren't sufficient to get him out of the hold of dissatisfied wandering in search of himself. He never did find himself again. That is he never again found the lovely little boy everyone adored or the man he might have grown into. But incredibly he found Phillipa. Either it was a chance in a million or the mysterious magnetism of beautiful people that brought them together. There she was, riding a bicycle on a beach, taking a glance at him and skidding off to come to a heap at his feet—just as Adonis might have ordained. He looked at her alabaster skin, raven-black hair, crystal clear blue eyes, perfect figure and laughed. She laughed too—but for the sex difference they might have been clones, psyches and all. Even if they hadn't fallen "in love"—if that's the right word, for they were already in love—others would have driven them into an official union. "Meant for each other," the chorus chanted. That they were not. They competed for the admiration of both sexes equally (without being in any sensible meaning of the word bisexual). They also competed for any other kind of dominance possible. They knew each other's weaknesses and they hurt each other without hesitation. Predictably they lived unhappily with each other, breeding two beautiful and narcissistic children—a boy and a girl. Then their hair began to turn gray, their skin wrinkled and, with the help of alcohol, they turned into the embodiment of the picture of Dorian Gray.

One need hardly elaborate this case by analyzing it in terms of the theoretical structure advanced in these pages, except to add that no amount of skillful analysis and intellectual insight proved sufficient to save them. One more illustration of the disillusionment in the wake of Freud about man's essential lack of rationality. They knew better, but they couldn't do better. At best, insight saved them from probable greater hurt, if this were possible.

THE LEAN-TO

Ideally, coupling should be forged between intimates who stand up on their own though they become closely cemented together.

In real life, however, people lean on each other. When they lean hard and are stuck together while thusly coupled, I call this a lean-to. Such close relationships are unfortunately fundamentally faulty, as you shall see from what follows.

Once you realize that neurotic couplings, whether in heterolove or in friendship, are made between people who appear to have contrasting personae but are really minted in the same coin, you realize that the personages of the inner self are aligned in the *same* antagonistic symmetry of likes as they are in the purer narcissists. The lean-to is a parasitic coupling of need, not of ideal want. Given the handicap of a prominent neurosis, there may be little choice than to attract and be attracted by an essentially similar person who is *bound* to have a corresponding order of priorities—the sadist who couples with the masochist, the fat with the thin, the effeminate with the masculine, the domineering with the passive. Once the coupling is made, each partner develops a vested interest in the other's hang-up.

The one whose need is greater is the patient *consort,* the more silent partner, the one trying harder to hide behind the scapegoat—the alcoholic's mate, the compulsive gambler's wife, the gangster's moll. The one whose need is *less* becomes the declared patient. Of course, these positions are taken in relative unawareness and held on to with as much despair as there is a feeling of hopelessness about self-change. The scapegoat, the manifest patient, is usually well aware of his or her dependency on the partner but not consciously aware of being held back into the bondage of that sickness or being made a scapegoat by the spouse (or friend).

Once the patient's consort becomes aware of her or his vested interest, guilt ensues and begins to erode the lean-to's abutment or interface. This and an insight-directed change busting up the joint are the only ways out. Even then, the strong tendency to re-create the same kind of relationship persists, unless the change in personality is radical—specifically unless the neurosis has abated so that the order of priorities of preferred characteristics is broken down: The shadow and the persona must approximate or interchange (the flipover). The hominus/femina must change radically, thus inducing a direct change in the sex ideal. Clearly this amounts to a basic structural change following a major shake-up, in fact, following a cataclysmic collapse.

This explains several things: Why neurotics make the same mistakes over and over again in the choice of partners and in the type of relationships they make and why effective therapy or spontaneous change (flipover) threatens the foundation of both marriage and friendship. Also, why it's necessary to be worse before one can get better; and why one must break the resistance exhibited by the patient trying to maintain the status quo, and why one must fend off the subtle (sometimes gross) undermining carried out by the consort. Also, it is clear why the conscious determination to change, to do better in love and consortings, provides an insufficient motive so long as the inner change is not radical enough to produce different vibes, to induce different attractions, both to and from. The real opposite to any neurotic deviance is a "normal" person. But it is unlikely that the chemistry, attracting a neurotic to a normal, can work. For one thing priorities are bound to be very different, hence contrasts will exist all right, but they'll be out of whack. The personages of the inner self will be out of alignment. However, by chance or by good fortune, the neurotic may land a normal.

The only way this can happen is for the normal to be attracted to highly prized qualities the neurotic possesses, despite the handicap, and for the neurotic to set priorities that do *not* involve significant interaction with one's neuroticism and which are fulfilled by the normal. It is this latter correspondence that renders such couplings rare. It means, for instance, that the agoraphobic woman would be much more attracted to strength and determination in a man than to the usual weakness she seeks, whereby she could lead him by the nose with her agoraphobia.

In such a case, healing may result or else a bitter conflict ensues between the forces of equilibrium and normalcy, and the forces of instability and aberration. This conflict can make or break the coupling. Theoretically the bond should snap before the "normal" partner is torn asunder by "love." Also, theoretically, love can't be mutual or of the same quality because neuroticism, with its ballast of narcissism, is relatively short of love.

Typical examples of this are the man married to a woman whose morbid jealousy reaches a paranoid limit; or a woman married to an alcoholic, who must break the bond for the sake of her sanity at some point after everything else has been tried. For one thing, loving must be balanced eventually, and chronic emotional sickness renders it progressively unrequited. Even in relatively normal people, if the give and take is not balanced, the bond breaks—or should break.

The parasitic relationship described in terms of heterolove

and marriage, that is in elective relationship, also occurs in compulsory ones. This is when one person—say an obese girl or a black sheep (sociopathic boy) or a sex deviant—is the scapegoat (the patient). Then the other members of his family are no less "sick" in their own way but derive some support or protection, at any rate some gain, from the behavior of the scapegoat. The lucky members of a family who escape this kind of snare, usually escape the house physically as soon as possible, as well as become psychologically emancipated or liberated.

So strong is the cage of psychic illness in some families that if one is absolutely mad, two or three others may become almost as crazy. They then erect a protective screen around themselves—a condition known as *folie-à-deux, trois,* or *quatre*. A similar condition is environmentally induced by isolation—cabin fever or arctic hysteria—in which the weakest link in the family chain breaks down and usually becomes paranoid about the nearest neighbors (or the rest of the family), and they all join in. This psychic infection may affect a group or a whole culture who'll then close the circle around its more insane members, thus preventing the outside ozonized air of sanity from penetrating its sickly core. The dynamics are analogous whether in Trobriand islanders or in Nazism. So what goes wrong between two in a coupling can be duplicated in a group or a whole society and spread like brush fire.

As mentioned in Chapter 1, on choosing one's mate, there's usually enough time and opportunity to find out not only what she/he is really like, but what she/he is going to become. However accelerated the stages of clicking, ticking, and sticking might have been, prior to marriage, however premature the marriage, the psyche senses intuitively what is and what's to come. There are exceptions, of course. But they usually occur in an abnormal social context, such as in a war or in a fulminating romance or other very unusual circumstances. Whenever I have taken individuals, especially the patient's consort or a couple, back to the "scene of the crime," as it were, to when the decision to marry was made before all the evidence was in, I was always able to get the confession that they had more than an inkling of the truth; that in fact, they had reckoned with the spouse's weakness. So strong were these patterns that in the years since their initial uncovering, I learned to predict the typical personalities my patients would be attracted to and by, both in love and in friendships. I could predict such personalities on a range from the "halfway house," the spouse who might take the patient halfway on the road to normalcy but no further, to the lucky coupling that would take him or her all the way.

The personality of the patient's existing consort, whether perfectionist or masochist, fat or lean, domineering or passive, becomes eminently predictable. More than that, the likely psychological *background* of the consort becomes predictable because there are only so many variables that conspire to create the "halfway house" female, for instance, for the bisexual male. So I could now describe what the patient's family relationships might have been.

The following example provides the main points for predictability.

Miriam was the headstrong eldest daughter of a rough-and-tough self-made man, the apple of his eye, though they had clashed since she was two years old, since she was able to say *NO* to him. They were Orthodox Jews and there were no boys in the family. Miriam resented being a girl, at a time when a girl's place was not favored under the sun. She fought her father for dominance and despised her weak, submissive mother. Miriam poured out her forced charm in order to conquer a Christian called George who had sufficient social and professional standing to satisfy at least that family requirement. He accepted the fact that in the Jewish tradition their children would be raised Jewish. This placated the father—but barely. Besides, the fiancé was pleasant, giving, generous, peaceful, and passive enough to be manipulated. As soon as she married him Miriam revealed the shrew barely disguised inside her. She was a failed rebel (against Father and his tradition), hostile, mean, and raucous. And she hated George for being a doormat like her mother. She accused him of being his mama's boy (which he was) and insinuated that he was "less than a man . . . a sissy or worse" (which he wasn't). She said he only had "one ball" and proceeded to bust it.

When asked, years later, "Why did you marry him?" she replied at first "I never dreamed he'd turn out that way." Yet she knew of his attachment to his mother, his father having died in his early childhood. When asked how she thought he'd turn out, she replied "Gentler, kind, polite but a real man." When cornered, she finally confessed "He'd be easy to deal with and I'd be the man about the house ... so long as he brings home the bacon." On further pressuring about her motivations she admitted that "Father would be furious ... real hurt that I'd run away with a goy!" Now that Father and George were in cahoots to keep Miriam down, she proceeded to test them both by going out with a progressive succession of undesirable men, first with George's younger and more aggressive brother, whom she seduced out of hand, then with others.

Each time Miriam went off, she left a clear trail for her father's detective to find her and bring her home. Miriam wanted a big scandal and her husband's humiliation, but her powerful father shielded George, smothered potential scandals, and acted as if he knew that George was merely a tool, an outsider, and that the real battle was being fought between him and his daughter. Father bought off her lovers and kept Miriam's affairs "within the family" while threatening to dispossess her if she told George and if she failed to cease and desist in her "hussy behavior." She told George all, then went out and picked up a derelict. What brought her back this time, however, was not her father's henchmen but curiosity. She was dying to know what George would do to her. George forgave her magnanimously, without even being asked. Miriam then announced that she had another lover—"a black man, a jailbird, waiting in the wings"—whereupon George fell on bended knees and begged her to stay with him and raise their family. Her father, in constant touch, uncovered the scene, got out his whip, lashed her a couple, summoned his lawyer, and arranged for a divorce, which was Miriam's price for behaving herself in the future. For a while, Miriam stopped her forays because she feared that her father really would disinherit her and cast her out. As it was, he browbeat and bribed her ex-husband and obtained custody of the two children, having proved in court that Miriam was an unfit mother. He settled a considerable part of his fortune on them—the only grandchildren.

There were two other interesting and classic features to this case: First, the "real men" Miriam scooped up were far from Peking cavemen or arboreal gorillas, though they looked like them and she had them trained to behave that way. They were, in fact, hand-fed pigeons. As soon as they cared for her, even a little, she threw them over. She dare not actually choose a man really like her own father, though she ought to have done—because this would have healed her inner split between wanting to ball-bust men and wishing they'd make her submit. She got trapped in the middle.

Second, Miriam, like all chronic discontents, never found the right mate; her error perpetuated itself, while George, the victim, was an example of a "natural justice" of sorts, for he found himself a less bossy and more tolerable wife of his own kind and lived peacefully ever after.

EXPENDED LOVE

One of the most critical aspects of the passage of time, even in ideal, let alone in defective, coupling, is the waning of sexual arousal; yet familiarity must not lead to frigidity or impotence.

Can fidelity last a lifetime? Can sexual familiarity with the same body breed any other than a take-it-or-leave-it feeling in the long run? Can love spring eternal? Obviously the answer to all of these questions is a resounding *YES* from all those people who've experienced a high quality of sex, love, and monogamy and are willing to testify accordingly. The answer is also *NO* from the modern middle-class Western heterosexual majority.

Specifically, fidelity is surest and lasts longest with a practicing bisexual—whose "behind-the-counter" outlet is invariably homosexual. However, it can last longer than usual in the normal heterosexual if there's a lot to lose like money and a lot to fear like a Mafia-type vendetta for illicit intercourse. Fidelity tends to last as long as love itself—which we argued was monogamous in the sense of being exclusive. It *may* last as long as the sexual drive itself, which wanes in octogenarians but is not extinguished totally except by death.

However, one of these answers, namely fidelity forced by "love," begs the question of the existence of love in the first place. In this case love brings in a negative quantity in that sexual transgression would bring the threat of its withdrawal. Moreover, the cement even of a well-built union may weather and deteriorate. Even parental love, obligatory and automatically owed though it is, can wear thin and wear out if its recipient tries hard and long enough to become unlovable.

So the question becomes: What sorts of things can expend the store of love, the psychic energy invested in the bond, thus allowing inevitable sexual familiarity to raise Eros' curious head, to tempt and finally to seduce? In the sticking phase, as we pointed out, the answer lies very much with the balance of love—its give and take and its positive qualities. This is measured by the threat of its loss. An ideal match between bodies, in terms of age spread and physical preservation, aids the sustaining of sexuality.

Having children works both ways. On the one hand, they tend to strengthen the bond of love, if they were thusly conceived and wanted. On the other hand, they tend to take their toll on the female body. Childlessness also works both ways. It increases selfishness, hence the desire not to miss anything, to get the most; but also, in the long run, it narrows one's basis of security vested in the coupling.

Probably the single biggest cause of breakdown in a relatively normal or successful coupling is a sexual turn-off by a partner, for whatever reason. This leaves the normally sexed and desirous partner in a Catch-22 situation. If that partner gives in after a conjugal fight for sex (one of the commonest causes) and he or she remains faithful indefinitely by turning to masturbation and such like, the winner's a dunderhead, to say the least, and ends up a loser. On the other hand, if the partner insisting on sex wins, the other one, the one that "gives in," does it resentfully. Then sex becomes passive, a gift soon resented by the sexual aggressor as well, for he or she is placed in the role of violator. And if the conjugal battle for sex is lost, the deprived partner goes out seeking the oblivion of liquor with or without sex on the side, yet feels that he or she has betrayed a near-sacred trust.

Finally, if the deprived partner is given permission to go for sex elsewhere because it cannot be got at home, although the spouse is physically intact (that is, not mutilated or degenerated but only sexually turned off, yet still attractive) something's very rotten in the marital state. Whether the permit for illicit sex is meant as a test of fidelity or given in defiance of the norm matters relatively little. Sooner or later the invitation will be accepted by the "normal" individual. If the invitation is rejected, that partner will be back in the position of dammed-up sex and unfair deprivation. Thus all roads lead to a loss, to an unraveling of love by the thread of sex, because no one can love a member of the other sex while encouraging him or her to find an outlet somewhere else, no one, that is, except a physically crippled saint.

It may be too obvious to point out that when one spouse invites the other to have extramarital affairs, the usual or normal motive is that he or she already has another lover or wants to be free to have one.

Moving right along to the abnormal extremity of a no-win marital or paramarital situation, there is the paranoia of infidelity, where the partner, often in the involutional (menopausal) phase, accuses the other, usually a perfectly innocent and loving mate, of conjugal infidelity. One must remember that underlying this sickness is also an extreme feeling of unworthiness and despicableness on the part of the accuser. This projection defense symptom says: "If I were married to me or living with me, I'd run around like mad. So obviously you are." Your denial only leads to an escalation of paranoia and of accusation. This means: "How can you be such a dummy and not run around? Nobody I'd respect would fail to do so!" This is very much like Groucho Marx saying, "I wouldn't belong to any club that would have me." The thing to do, of course, is not to deny or to wait too long. You've got a losing situation anyway. A skilled therapist may help. But it will help the therapist and the situation more if the partner lets on that sure he or she is "running around like mad" and will carry on unless the accusations cease. Intuition may tell the sickly person that this is a false admission, so far. Then you might as well make it true and thus save yourself from lying. At this point anything might happen—it's a remake-or-break situation. As mentioned before, no one but a masochist stays in that sort of situation till his or her sanity is lost.

Unfortunately the usual story is that the partner is virtually incapable psychologically of betrayal or of being "cruel in order to be kind," even if he or she understands the psychopathology. It's very like the husband or wife who will not stoop to mental or physical abuse of the "loved one" even if the latter asks, indeed begs, for it. In both these situations the victim or scapegoat is similar in personality and temperament and invariably rationalizes his or her dour and civilized response on moral arguments. "Two wrongs don't make a right," they say. Rarely, very rarely, is the patient's consort a strong, healthy person who has the freedom of choice. Commonly, the incapacity of the patient's consort to act appropriately is not a virtue but a weakness. It's due to timidity, passivity, and fear of failure. To paraphrase Boileau, *"Rien comprendre c'est rien risquer"* (If you understand nothing you risk nothing). Moreover, the reason for not hitting back is not really kindness to another human being, but basically self-concern, a rationalized incapacity backed by an unwillingness to put oneself so far out from one's "norm." And that norm is one of readily assuming and relishing the victim role.

The only time that the patient consort is not weakly and sickly, as described before, is when the patient's paranoia comes out of the blue, in late middle age. But mostly the tendency to project has announced itself by fits of unwarranted jealousy and distrust, decades before the menopause. The consort's psyche should have sensed that the storm would break presently.

The wonder of it is how long such a lean-to can sustain the ravages of this particular storm. A slight shift in the direction of the winds, a slightly different kind of breeze, and the paranoid structure will collapse—for it is constructed to withstand the onslaught of protestations of innocence and purity, not the strain of rugged reality.

Probably the single biggest *threat* to a normal coupling is autumnal fever, indulged with the rationalization that "what you don't know doesn't hurt you" and that "flings" don't count where emotional fidelity is maintained. Usually the extramarital excursions of autumnal fever, in the presence of the loving spouse, are miserable affairs. They're guilt-riddled one-night stands, hardly worthwhile hit-and-runs. At best they're lost weekends. Such affairs, however, are mighty costly to conscience, especially in the long run when the idyllic illusion of the menopausal syndrome fades.

Specific threats to the foundation of fidelity and love come from a defective selection of materials and construction—the teepee or lean-to—from an imbalance between giving and taking, and from the flipover. These situations have all been discussed already in their different contexts.

But perhaps the most usual challenge to love occurs when one of the couple has "outgrown" the other, independently. This is usually the man and the couple have usually been teenage lovers whose marathon marriage may have lasted twenty years and they will not have hit their forties yet. Individual growth has brought about a change in the alignment of the personages of the inner self so that they are no longer in symmetrical juxtaposition (see Sticking: Chapter 4).

Let us now review systematically the problems of passages by looking at the most frequent problems encountered in clicking, ticking, and sticking.

"I NEVER CLICKED!"

Or "the right person hasn't come along yet." And if they're over the hump, in their forties, and possess the usual number of eyes, ears, organs, points of I.Q., etc., you know that the "right persons" have been and gone by, because they were ignored, rejected, or automatically repelled. Why? Usually because unconsciously the person doesn't have it (love) to give or is too afraid to trust (being loved) or is sexually blocked, or is afraid of the obligations of marriage and the burdens of parenthood—or a combination of these.

Rarely is such an individual exceptionally self-sufficient or independent and consequently in no need to love in order to grow because such people go a little further into ticking before they want out. Much more usually, nonstarters are utterly narcissistic.

Max was forty and a confirmed bachelor, except that he kept on trying. He had a different "lady" every fortnight.

He was handsome, debonair, of impeccable descent, scion of a rich family, and women fell over him as the most eligible bachelor of the decade. And he sifted through them carefully, playing a "psychological game" of how quickly he could take them to bed. He'd work on the girl's "funny bone" or whatever "made her tick," with the facade of a modern gentleman but the underside of an M.C.P. You'd have little sympathy for him unless you knew a few more things about him, such as the fact that he couldn't stick with any girl for any length of time (weeks) no matter how glamorous she was, because he'd get "bored." Actually he'd quit before getting impotent. He was terrified of being trapped into a relationship and deeply concerned that he'd be found shallow and empty. (He was.) Attached to his mother and sister emotionally, but actually stuck on his whole extended family, he had never quite made it in the world on his own and was afraid to try it even in a marriage. He had broken away from home many times, but always returned with his tail between his legs—another in the band of failed rebels. He couldn't stand anybody telling him what to do, yet realized (unconsciously) that his dependency needs would put him in a position where a woman with any strength or interest in taking him over would tell him what to do all the time. (One did and he took nine months to shake her off.) Furthermore, his sleep dreams had occasional homosexual undercurrents in the form of a mixed-up love object. (He had never been homosexually orientated or ever performed a homosexual act.)

His shopping list of desirable female traits was a mile long and full of incompatible elements. Though he wasn't exceptionally bright, he could be penetratingly critical and it took him about a fortnight to destroy the image of any female, whether he took her to bed or not. Needless to add, the best of them wouldn't touch him with a barge pole, but I suspect that if one did, even for fun, his consummate skill in emitting negative vibes and fending off would defeat the stoutest of souls. They'd wake one morning saying to themselves, "What am I doing wasting my time with this numbskull!"

Similarly, fear of sex, of proving to be sexually inadequate, of subsequent infidelity, fear of marriage, of being committed, of being found wanting, of discovery of one's interior shadow, fear of pregnancy, of the pain of delivery, of disfigurement; fear of mothering, of impaired health, of responsibility; fear of rearing children, of being trapped, an inadequate parent, exploited, and deserted, all on an escalated range of magnitude, have prevented many a woman from clicking. Once one diagnoses the cause, it is easy to go on to recognizing the defensive pattern employed in order to avoid clicking with close relationships. Rarely have I found the patient who became cured and *psychologically available* but who nonetheless failed to click with somebody subsequently. When this happened it was usually because by that time (aged forty and over) meeting places, introduction opportunities, and general encounters pared down the chances considerably, and because of sheer bad luck. I've already pointed out how many elements have to click into place before a couple can make it and this reduces the chances and funnels them down to rarities, over time.

CLICKING BUT NOT YET TICKING.

The underlying motivations for this pattern are the same as in people who never click, but the *quantity,* the strength of motive, is less, so these people go a little along the way of love. When and how they stop, however, quickly reveals the pattern of defense. The nonclickers are forever not only barking up the wrong tree but also know for sure that their relationship is going nowhere. Yet they cling to it for years after this has become obvious, in the unconscious hope that one of these days it will be too late to walk away from it.

This is the woman who's forever attracting fatherly "safe" men who are married—unavailable—yet never manages to catch them single, even if she *knew* them while they were single! It's the woman who gets herself loved and left, or abused; the man who's forever cuckolded or hen-pecked until he shakes off the hen. Sometimes when the original click is good, the person has to try hard to dislodge the natural links formed.

TICKING BUT NOT STICKING

So near and yet so far! The man who makes it is also motivated by the factors described in the last section, but his power is too weak to be stopped earlier. Sometimes the man is of an entirely different makeup from the nonclicker: These are people who cannot sustain things, jobs or relationships. Sooner or later they become dissatisfied or exhausted—unable to give anymore. Or else they feel themselves trapped or smothered and actively want out. There are a bunch of factors—motives—accounting for lack of staying power, tolerance or backbone. Among them are (1) a restlessness due to a drive for varied experience, (2) a desire for greatness. (Hence they are unable to sustain their end in a relationship—especially when they're chasing a wisp of immortality.) (3) a sudden attack of introversion, a strong wish to "be alone," which may do it and snap the long stretch of accommodation that sticking requires, (4) a restless mental state due to having been raised as a gypsy or a globe-trotter by parents in the diplomatic corps or in the jet set, or by itinerant mercenaries, for instance. But in the main, particularly if a breakdown occurs at this stage (as it often does in youth when many relationships are tried on a hit-or-miss basis), the cause is (5) a mismatch. And the breakdown is natural.

These victims who become repeatedly unstuck should "to their own selves be true." So when they complain, "why do I get such lemons?" the answer is, you only get what you deserve.

There are a kind of people, namely the misogynist and his female equivalent, the female castrator, who, depending on the *strength* or intensity of their psychopathology, either never make it, or click without ticking or get pretty far before they strike out, hurt and unstuck. Then they coil up like snakes and bide their time before they mesmerize and again strike a (relatively) innocent victim. These people are far more vicious (sick) than other varieties of nonstickers. They are destroyers.

What makes for either of these types of people is easier to see than is their behavior easy to detect by a member of the opposite sex who is the current victim, "in love" with them. The woman-hater is a man who has been badly hurt while young and swears revenge on the opposite sex. A mother has betrayed her son (in his eyes), or a father his daughter, that's how the hatred of the opposite sex begins. The betrayal, like all *traumata* that leave their mark, is never a single act. It's always either a series of actions deemed to be a betrayal or a series of different hurts. By far the commonest is for a child of tender years to see or hear a parent commit adultery or to know that she/he did it, and for that to result in the loss, or in the repeated hurt, of the other parent. This leads to an early rejection of sex. The usual enemy, later to be punished, is the prurient parent of the opposite sex—so the son hates his adulterous mother (and womanhood through her) and the daughter hates her adulterous father. He or she vows revenge on the opposite sex.

This hatred is complicated by the fact that such a child is usually at a critical period of psychosexual development—the Oedipal or Electra period around eight years of age or so. This means that the child imagines deep down that he or she would have liked to do the same thing with the betraying parent, that is commit incest, hence incite adultery. So the son would have liked to have made love to his mother (Oedipus) or the daughter to her father (Electra). This compounds the guilt and ultimately the hatred for the parent who couldn't be possessed because of an interloper who took the incestuous love object away from the child. The child feels too immature and weak at that age to cope with a *rival* and to hate him, like the boy hating the "other man" or the girl hating the "other woman." At a later age, this competitive hatred might happen instead of hating the parent. Or it might happen in addition. In this case, the boy hates other men and the girl other women. But at all times the parent of the opposite sex is hard to forgive.

There are other hurts or cruelties that would turn a child into an avenger of his own sex, or turn him or her away from his/her own sex altogether—but parental sexual betrayal is the commonest.

Given these antecedents, the pattern of subsequent behavior is easy to diagnose with a rear-view mirror held high up so that one can see the whole thing. It's especially easy to see when an impartial observer (like a psychiatrist) uses the mirror. But, as I said, it is difficult for the victim to spot his or her own pattern because he (or she) stands too close to himself to gain perspective.

The pattern consists of the misogynist or castrator turning on maximal charm, giving sexuality a full throttle. If she or he has physical talents or other powers like money, this thrust becomes irresistible, especially with practice making perfect. He or she lures the victims, finds their Achilles' heel and at the right moment, when the victim least expects it, the heel is pierced. For the castrator, a mild version of this pattern is mere "prick teasing"; for the misogynist, it is cold seduction, "love and leave." This pathological person wants to see the victim of the opposite sex sweating and squirming, as it were. Sometimes satisfaction is only achieved by a total sexual deviance—namely bondage. But the real zenith is to see the victim squirm with humiliation, plead for mercy, fire up with reciprocated hatred, and end up in utter defeat and despair, perhaps suicidal. If, however, the intended victim laughs off the bully, a catastrophic reaction shatters the misogynist or castrator.

Like all neurotic behavior, this one feeds on itself and is insatiable, so the behavior becomes habitual and cyclical. Rarely, and then usually only with males, does misogynism turn into murder. The murderer has seen his mother carry on with other men, brands her as a trollop and goes on years later cutting the throats of young women whom he perceives to be immoral prostitutes.

Don Juan and Casanova, latent homosexuals though they might have been, were misogynists, like all male homosexuals whose main basis is hatred of feminine sexuality. In their many different forms the misogynist/castrator is much commoner than you might think. This pattern may be acted out anytime from clicking right through to sticking. But the longer a relationship lasts the more deeply diseased the person is and the more he/she hates the victim of the opposite sex, because the hurt increases with trust and time.

However, there's a kind of natural justice here, as there is in all deviances, in that the punisher gets punished in the long run—long before he or she loses the power to inflict pain—because such people can never love anyone. Too much libido is taken up by their pathological pattern.

One difficulty in undoing this knot is that the hating person rarely has the wisdom to see that he or she is a patient—particularly if the kicks come in thick and fast and provide pleasure. Even more rarely does such a person have the wisdom to come to a therapist of the *opposite* sex for cure, even though this has a far better chance to work than with a therapist of the same sex. When they do come, however, the transference is stormy, therapy is dangerously protracted, and the therapist has much sweating to do: The therapist takes on the victim role and then throws it off.

GETTING UNSTUCK

One of the things that never ceases to amaze me about couples ending in divorce after sticking together for decades is their acrimony. Surely people who've grown old with each other should realize that whatever aspersions they cast upon their spouses, blow back into their faces like the proverbial spit (or worse) ejected against the wind. Short of a catacylsmic change in the spouse, the deterioration and certainly the simple erosion in the relationship could have been a mutual affair. And anyone who chose to live so long with a schmuck, however much this is rationalized in terms of the children, is a shmuck himself or herself, if indeed the accuser isn't the principal offender. In fact, I find that just as the patient's consort, who uses the partner's patienthood as a scapegoat, is usually tougher to tackle and to cure, so is the acrimonious principal accuser in the bitterness of divorce. The accuser is the main culprit. If the accusations are equally bitter and vicious and both parents foist their hatred upon the children, then both are equally ignorant and responsible for the breakdown. But whoever is the defender, the greater gentleman or gentlewoman, the more generous, whether openly guilty of the breakdown or not, is the *less* responsible—unless he or she is a congenital drip.

Having gotten that off one's chest, let's turn to the question of when it's too late to repair and what's worth repairing.

The only case in which it's worthwhile working on a relationship, to "repair" it, is when the break is due to more contrasting opposition than a couple can bear inside a teepee structure. If one of the dyad has snapped or strained the connections between their excessively opposite personages of the inner self while genuinely trying to connect them, it's worth getting out the psychological repair kit.

Also, whenever serious and successful psychotherapeutic

work starts on a patient, it's worth mending the inevitable rent that occurs in the coupling in order to see if the consort can be pulled along and the union can be salvaged.

By and large in other cases where the malaise is deeper than a transient autumnal fever, and especially when the rift is natural as is the "last straw" in a mismatch, and when strain is actually beneficial in that it would lead to a liberation of two souls, it is better to stand back and let it happen. The things that are worth doing are salvaging dignity, and preventing unnecessary hurt to others, particularly to the innocents—children.

In summary, while this book is largely an almanac for love containing diagnoses and recipes for close relationships, this chapter has looked at the quite frequent if not entirely usual problems and crises in heterolove.

One set of such problems is caused by the simple passage of time, the *contretemps* in the development of romance crisscrossing between the two sexes. Another quite different problem is caused by the tendency for love to run out after a while, to be expended in the course of time. Two major factors accounting for a lot of unsatisfactory close relationships have been singled out, and follow.

Narcissism blocks a person from loving another because of excessive and improper attachment to oneself. This condition actually reverses the laws of attraction between young couples in that narcissists, like the Hollywood types of beautiful people, are attracted to the same kind, not to opposites.

The lean-to neurotic relationship found so frequently in patients (almost anyone) *appears* to follow the law of attraction of opposites but actually doesn't, because couples who lean on each other too hard are attracted in the first place by the opposite side of the *same* coin (the excessively fat to the excessively lean, the obsessively erotic to the deviants). Thus they resemble narcissists more than normals. Moreover, they select one another and they stick to each other because of a very narrow cluster of (neurotic) mutual characteristics.

The rest of the chapter takes a systematic look at the special problems in the passage or succession of heterolove from clicking to ticking and sticking.

A TEST OF LOVE'S CRISES

It is assumed that the responder is around 30 years of age or more and that there have been opportunities for love. Answer only the questions that apply, by checking the appropriate response column. The scoring is weighted, as you'll see.

	Yes	*Somewhat Sometime*	*No*
1. I have never met a person of the opposite sex whom I could care for.		perhaps once or twice	A few times
2. I've met such a person or persons but never clicked.		' ' ' '	I clicked
3. I've related to such a person (or persons) only to find hatred, revulsion or dislike, or a desire to hurt (in myself or the other person) in the end.		to a degree	I never experienced this
4. I've related closely heterosexually but gotten hurt by jealousy and false accusations of infidelity.			
5. I've clicked but never quite ticked together (in the sense of Chapter 3).			I have ticked
6. I've ticked but never stuck for any length of time or to any depth (in the sense of Chapter 4).			I have stuck
7. I would describe my hetero relationship as a match of likes, when both of us have been chiefly interested in ourselves.			
8. I would describe my heterolove as a lean-to (or teepee) relationship of mutual need or dependency rather than want.			

	Yes	Somewhat Sometime	No

9. I would describe my hetero relationship(s) as repeated mistakes (mismatches and lack of blending).

10. I would describe my heterolove as a major mismatch (too much alike where we should have differed).

11. I would describe my heterolove as a minor mismatch (too different and not quite able to bridge the gap).

12. I've had a good experience (or more) in heterolove but we've become unstuck because of an infatuation or the "menopausal syndrome."

13. I've had a good experience (or more) in heterolove but we've become unstuck because of a sexual turn off.

14. I've had a good experience (or more) in heterolove but we've become unstuck because we are drifting or growing apart, or have quietly exhausted our love.

15. I've had a good experience (or more) in heterolove but we've become unstuck because of minor illicit affair(s) (without emotional attachments).

Scoring

Questions		score	
1–4,	score	5 for Yes	
		3 for Somewhat (middle)	
		0 for No	
5,	score	4 for Yes	
		3 for Somewhat	
		0 for No	
6–12,	score	3 for Yes	
		2 for Somewhat	
		0 for No	
13–15,	score	2 for Yes	
		1 for Somewhat	
		0 for No	

Interpretation

30–50 You're either incapable of love or severely blocked and in need of "psychosurgery" to remove the block and get cleaned out, if possible. You may have to forego love.

20–29 You're neurotically motivated to make the wrong choices or to make neurotic relationships. You need much help to undo the pattern and much help to become psychologically available (with proper vibes).

10–19 If your score comes mainly from the first seven questions rather than the next eight you're in deeper trouble than it would appear from this score and fall in one of the above two categories. If the score comes from questions 8–15 you still need help but your case is less critical—unless you're 40 years or over.

4–9 Reread this book and try again.

Under 4 Either you're fibbing or what the heck are you doing testing yourself here?!

7

Friendship

Birds of a feather do not always flock together.

A friend of mine did so well in business in one boom year that he was able to choose where in the world he wanted to live. He had just turned forty years of age and was single. He chose to stay in the city where he had spent half of his life—the city that made his fortune—simply because "this is where my friends are." He could imagine making new friends but he felt that both his age and his newly acquired wealth bore the odds against their ever coming up to the standards of his old friends. He could imagine traveling frequently to keep up his valuable friendships but saw no point in that. Years later he was glad of this choice.

More than once I met women whose best friends had said to them "Don't ever leave me . . . I couldn't live without you!" They weren't lesbians; no hint of it, even. They were quite happily married adult women, around forty, with grown-up children.

I have come across women who lived with a certain amount of trepidation lest their husbands or families separated them from their best friends either by distance or by a rift. Some of them confessed that if it came to a clear choice between husband and best friend they would be hard put to choose. These, too, were quite happily married, well-matched women and successful mothers. Such is the new bond of sisterhood!

I have never heard a man say of another "I couldn't live without you"—unless they were homosexual—nor have I ever heard of one even remotely considering it a threat being separated by wife or family from an old friend. This isn't to say that men couldn't or haven't felt this way. They might have expressed this sentiment but probably so discreetly that my long antennae haven't picked it up. More likely, they haven't thought it "manly" to avow such feelings aloud because stoicism—the "grin and bear it" attitude—has been fostered in male children since time immemorial.

All this goes to show, among other things, that men and women appear to form somewhat different kinds of friendships, at least in the public eye. And they may exhibit a different value system in relation to their elective loves, both hetero and in friendship. This comes as no surprise to me, at any rate, since I discovered that there is an apparently astonishing difference between the sexes with respect to the value they place upon the physical home. When the spirit of one's home is broken, in the course of separation and divorce I find that women can walk away from it serenely—they *can* but in fact they rarely *do,* because they often have children still to raise there. Men, however, are heartbroken by the loss of their physical home. This is understandable upon reflection. Women are genuinely keener on relationships than on physical environments. Moreover, the physical home is in most cases her workplace, whereas it is the man's castle—the symbol for which he works.

When it comes to friendships, however, the differences are harder to explain. In fact, the whole modern trend of friendship among women set me thinking and studying this phenomenon. For one thing, several times in my twenty years' practice of analytical psychotherapy women patients have referred a whole coterie of friends or a camaraderie of workmates to me. I've never had the equivalent experience with a man patient. Once again this is a somewhat obfuscated reflection on friendship because it also involves the male attitude to therapy, which may be more tainted with false pride or shame, because of "not being able to do it by myself," than in the case of women.

For another thing, the whole history of the friendship of

men and of women, such as it is recorded, seems to point to intriguing differences. We shall come back to these substantive behavioral and attitudinal differences between the sexes presently. Just now let us sketch a taxonomy of friendship for the sake of a systematic approach to the subject and attempt a definition so that we can be as precise as possible.

A TAXONOMY OF FRIENDSHIP

There seem to be a number of factors that make a considerable difference to friendship—perhaps even determining its type. They are the place where the bond was made, its onset in the life cycle, sex, marital status, number or grouping and, of course, the historical and cultural context. For example, an old school chum seems to be an entirely different beastie from a war buddy or a friend made in time of acute stress. An old or lifelong friend appears to have a different connotation from a new friend and neighbor. The sexes present three quite different facets of friendship: (1) separate friends made independently of sex coupling or marriage, whether of the same sex or not; (2) friends made as a couple, usually new friends; and (3) cross-sexual friendship, so-called platonic or otherwise.

Marital status makes a fundamental difference in the valuation of friends. For instance, little girls can get quite desperate about being accepted by one another. Generally the single status enhances the love of friendship.

On the other hand, in the trauma of divorce, one searches for friends in the woodwork, and in widowhood, friendship may make a difference to life itself.

There is a difference between a group or circle of friends and single friendships, especially one's best friend.

Historically and in many cultures still, friendships, at least publicly and heroically, were reserved for men. Women, if they were granted the ability to make friends, were supposed to make them quietly, and preferably invisibly or behind curtains, from among family members. Certainly they weren't supposed to make sacrifices for friendship's sake either in war or in peace. They were too busy with the family and with chores and unlikely to stray too far away from home. Their vanity, allegedly, was too great to make room for love of their own sex. Besides, their energy when young was engaged in competitiveness among themselves, in capturing the most coveted men. But then, as we noted before, history was written by men and for men until very recently, and women were treated like British children, not to be heard and preferably not to be seen either—for they were held to be wicked temptresses ever since they had truck with the Devil and the serpent up in Eden. In fact, they wore veils and purdahs to cover their faces, and shapeless long dresses to hide their figures, for that reason; unless their virtue was easy or they were poor.

A DEFINITION OF FRIENDSHIP

But then what *is* friendship? It's a close elective relationship, a highly altruistic, sexless love bond, even if the friend is chosen from among the given members of one's family, and even if its ultimate biological source proves to be no less an example of biological altruism than heterolove. By this I mean even if the herd instinct were as ancient as heterolove and its purpose were to preserve one's genes through "fine feathered friends" whose flock bond is stronger even than one's own family bond. Although deeper analysis may show that a friend is for need, that one of the motivations is for personal gain, in all appearances friendship is selfless, or as selfless as humans can be with other humans. Hierarchically one can place friendship a step below agape, the zenith of selfless love. The bond is often more durable if not more valuable than that of heterolove and may transcend even love of one's family, which may be forsaken or dispensed with, while close friendship may end only with death itself.

Although a friendship may be a very rugged bond between people, it contains a very delicate balance of functions and roles. Thus friendship between the sexes may balance on a pivot of sexual attraction but cannot turn them into lovers without losing what was a friendship. Similarly friendship is confiding without becoming a confessor or therapist. It is showing without becoming a teacher. And it is helping without becoming a business partner. As soon as pure and pristine friendship tips over into such different special roles it loses its significance, its place, and its unique power, as we shall see.

In terms of its own hierarchy, one may classify friendship's steps as follows:

1. Acquaintances in various degrees, from casual to close.
2. Friendships varying not only qualitatively from fair to good but also in terms of the taxonomy herein presented, such as old and new, lifelong and special.

Insofar as friendship is an elective close relationship and modeled, as we shall elaborate, on heterolove, as far as its psychoarchitecture and dynamics are concerned, it can be tested along the lines presented in the very first test given (in Chapter 1) without adding the sexual element to it. And the goodness of the bond itself may also be tested along the lines of a heterolove union (given in Chapter 4: Sticking), leaving out again the sexual element.

Let us see now whether the rough-and-ready taxonomy offered yields useful qualities and distinctions, descriptively if not also functionally.

THE DETERMINANTS OF FRIENDSHIP

It is rather natural that the school be a primary place for the early bonds of friendship because it is the first place we go to away from home. And some of the best and oldest of friends are formed in public school or in the neighborhood and very likely in both because the chances are that school chums live in the same neighborhood. These friendships almost invariably are between members of the same sex because as soon as sexual differentiations are made, in the first five years of life, there's a strong tendency toward sexual segregation, at least in terms of more direct and personal pals if not in terms of the gangs or crowds one travels with. The extraordinary thing about such friendships is that their loyalty and durability often exceed the length and strength of love and marriage. The question is, Why? Why should such bonds become so precious? The answer inevitably is in the way these friends are chosen, the best of them that is, the ones that make a love bond. It doesn't take profound observations to see that the principle of contrasting opposition is at work, building complementary relationships in their purest form. I say purest because in the absence of sexual complementarity it is the psychological characteristics that are sought with the express though unconscious purpose of trading one's strengths for the sake of offsetting one's weaknesses within the relationship. You'll see brawn, even at the polar range of a bully, team up with brains in whatever scrawny encasing; shyness attracted to brashness, dominance matched with submissiveness, sweetness and charm go for dourness, the whole thing wrought out of a mutual admiration society. A curious intuition seems to associate physical with psychological characteristics at a very early age, long before body imagery has matured—that is before the beautiful blue-eyed blonde with big bones can appreciate her own physique well enough to know that in matching herself to the delicate-boned brunette she is also offsetting some of her mental characteristics in the friendship. It is almost as though the biological instinct for sexual matching of opposites were at work here, relying on the fact that physical differences are concordant with mental ones. The impulse certainly is the same as in heterolove only more so since these humans are tangibly immature—in fact children. It is an instinct for completion, for balancing one's characteristics. What children do seem to perceive closely in each other is the thing they admire most. They're not aware that what they do admire most is what they intuit that they lack in themselves, but that is how the ranking of priorities is carried out then, and later in heterolove. This is the perceptual basis for the fearful symmetry that seems so necessary in a state of immaturity, with the feeling of incompleteness raw inside oneself, particularly when some strength is lost through detachment from mother, parents, and immediate family. To go fearlessly forward into the brave new world, one needs a buddy, an alter ego, a friend.

Yet parents and other observers forever astonish me by their statements of surprise when they say of two little girls sitting close together and giggling, or two little boys obviously devoted to one another, "They're inseparable . . . and yet they're so different!" I really cannot comprehend why the children's intuitive process isn't recognized by parents; why it has been lost to conscious intelligence. But it is obvious to me why such old and good friendships work so well, why they can be picked up again, after years of little or no contact, and why they're so devoted. It is because they were built by pure intuition, before reasoning and language could mislead. And yet there's another element in school friendships—the common enemy or challenge, namely the teacher and schooling itself. This introduces a certain element of competitiveness, which is perhaps inevitable when both the age and the sex group are the same, but this rivalry tends to be denied and buried. Some kids almost feel guilty if they outstrip their pals.

Schools, as they go on to higher grades, colleges, and universities, are the places where a large cross-section of peers congregate in increasing numbers, offering increasing choices for friendships and for heterolove. They are the waiting rooms and playrooms prepaiatory for life and probably the best marriage bureaus. Schools, with their playing fields and arenas and neighborhoods, are, after all, the chief environments beyond the home—the place of compulsory relationships—where important events occur in the first couple of decades that determine much of what's to happen later.

This is where you're either in or out or sitting on the fence, as far as the central peer group goes. If in, you find your natural place as a leader, at the center, or as the first lieutenant, or as one of the crowd in midstream, or at the periphery, or with one foot in and one out. If out, you're either self-sufficient, a loner content to observe, or else deprived and desperate, wanting in and feeling miserable as an outsider. The social pattern adopted early, along with the friends, tends to be imprinted and continued unless a valiant, usually conscious attempt is made to make oneself over, or unless there's some big break environmentally, or unless you're lucky enough—more likely manipulative enough—to have been an outsider brought in from the cold by a friend. Your relationship with the crowd, the peer group, determines to a large extent both the number and the type and depth of friendships made. Although friends, certainly close or best friends, are essentially dyads like love pairs, an in-group or a clique tends to form multiple nuclei of friendships, albeit with strong preferences still between certain pairs. A marginal fence-sitter or an outsider usually latches on to one friend more tightly and singly than does a popular insider.

We should attempt to analyze at this juncture a question that has most certainly arisen in your mind before. What's in it for the *insider*, the extrovert, the dominant personality in associating with an opposite, especially an outsider? The synergism between brain and brawn is obvious and that between leader and acolyte is too, but what can the popular brazen type admire—if that's the key sentiment leading to priority setting, hence to the matching of opposites—in the shy, delicate wallflower or hanger-on? No doubt his psyche sees, as in a crystal ball, into the shadow of the apparently inferior creature, even into the outcast the shape of things to come in the future, the profitable liaison. Perhaps it is a certain personal strength the introvert has in not requiring the limelight for reassurance. Perhaps the "inferior" fellow possesses some stubborn streak of perseverance, or the plotting cunning that often goes with someone who was disenfranchised early in life. Who knows? But there is something there that's needed, for if it's just the passivity and worship of the acolyte, the ardor of an admirer, the king and his footman, the princess and her chambermaid, this is not enough for friendship, which, like heterolove, is a two-way street. Like heterolove, it cannot survive unrequited. To the extent to which friendship may resemble a "crush," or infatuation, to that extent, like its sexual correlate, it is just a baby friendship—more a figment of wishful thinking than a burgeoning relationship. However much rejection hurts in unrequited friendship, that's not evidence of its validity. So the other guy must have something positive to offer, though its nature may not yet be revealed. It may be that the accomplished leader has to play father or mother to the eternal child that the chum represents, or it may be that he enters into that child's lively imagination or warms at the luminous glow of the chum's anima. In consequence of this deep-fitting and dovetailing of personalities that occurs in friendship, a deep trust develops that may well transcend that of heterolove, where trust plays a relatively minor role. And if adventure is shared with a friend and a risk is taken together, a blood brotherhood or sisterhood develops, which may and often does transcend that forged by the sharing of real blood—by genes actually.

This brings us to another very interesting place for forging friendship; in war or under similarly stressful circumstances, where the enemy makes human holding to human a matter of life and death. Again and again these types of brotherhoods of the trenches, as it were, seem to have a unique texture. At the height of danger, when braving death itself or persecution or some natural or man-made catastrophe, the chosen friend begins to become the repository of all that's dear in life—parent, sibling, heterolove object, one's own being, and the future. No sacrifice, not even life itself, is big enough. No grief can surpass that felt at the loss of such a friend. But when the emergency is over, when everybody goes home, this kind of friendship gets locked away. Its door can always be opened again, in a legionnaires' hall, in a veterans' hospital, at a ladies' reunion—but not for long. The reason for this transitory relationship, yet permanently imprinted friendship, is at least threefold. The powerful external situation of danger, rather than free-wheeling volition, has had an overwhelming hand in making the choice. And the bond is made in a hurry, rather as in love at first sight. Consequently the war buddy isn't as well and carefully, albeit unconsciously and intuitively, considered as a normal peacetime friend. Nor has the usual time gone by for the stages equivalent to those of heterolove, from first encounter to going together, to unfold in order to consolidate the relationship. And third, the magic formula of love is rarely fully used in such cases. Especially lacking is the commonality of the givens in the background. The chances are high that the friends of the trenches would walk different highways and byways in civilian life and become separated by them. In ordinary times they wouldn't have liked each other or bonded, or even met in the first place.

All that happened dynamically was a rough matching of opposites or of differences, not regularly ordered on a priority basis to last a lifetime but expediently motivated, again however unconsciously, in order to complement oneself "for the duration." If you like, war-buddying is a jerry-built affair made for the moment, notwithstanding its unique significance and its everlasting value in the mainstream of memory. And it's for similar reasons that war brides or bridegrooms don't last.

A variation of this kind of friendship was experienced by Gerda when she was a young girl and lucky enough to be able to flee the Hun and come to friendly Britain for shelter and safety. There she met a slightly older woman, also a refugee, who taught her the ways of the adopted country. Gerda, an intelligent, aggressive woman, proved a fast learner for which Myra, a slow, deliberate, and profoundly shy woman, admired her. Both chose their mates from the local population, Myra first. Both married outside their faith and cared little at the time for a religion that had brought them nothing but grief. But when they settled down they bought adjacent houses, revived the religion they shared, and lived happily in each other's kitchens for what seemed like ever after. After they had brought up their children—with love and grief—Gerda's girl emigrated to the New World. Then her husband insisted that they join them. Gerda demurred, but not because she feared pining for her only son, who was to be left behind (he had been a lot of trouble and she wanted to forget him). It was because neither woman could see herself living without the other, even though they had their separate friends as well as a common clique of couples. After Gerda left, her separation anxiety was so deep that it precipitated a severe reactive depression. However, she survived it psychologically. A few years later she survived her husband as well.

She ruptured, then reunited tentatively, her relationship with her daughter. By now, although she had dreamed for many years of retiring next to Myra on the edge of a British common, she found she couldn't forsake her new life and set of latter-day friends. To-and-fro visits helped to put the Gerda–Myra friendship in perspective. Both husbands had been acutely jealous of their wives' intimacy. Now Myra's husband had nothing further to fear from Gerda. And Gerda never went back to live next to Myra. And poor Gerda's husband will never know how, in a sense, his death and his grave in the New World reduced his wife's friendship, which had been the major black cloud hanging over his life. He had said sadly, practically with his last breath, "Now you'll be able to go back to your beloved Myra!"

There is another parallel to be found between trench friendship and the effect of the demographic drift that occurs in marriage. When husbands, propelled by social mobility, drift up and away from their homes and their children-fettered wives, they lose their basis of commonality and loosen their bonds of marriage no less than when friends, as a result of the same kind of mobility, drift apart and move in different social and cultural circles. The magical formula is then broken not only because the newly acquired background shears them apart but also because the foreground no longer presents a challenge resulting in an integrity of opposites fitting together. By then, in the course of time, because of mutual influence or what we have called before successive approximation, the couple—of friends and lovers—have become more like one another. Therefore, paradoxically they no longer have anything in common. And, indeed, that's the constant complaint in all such cases, no longer having anything in common.

Holiday friendships in a curious way resemble their trench cousins because of their transience, despite their deeply felt significance at the time. You can easily work out why, given the highly emotionally charged situation that brought people together during vacations or exciting festive occasions, the romantic (the equivalent of the dramatic wartime) atmosphere, and the shortness of time in development, all of which obscure the algorithms of the heart.

ONSET IN THE LIFE CYCLE

Clearly, the most disinterested friendships, if that's the accurate term, occur earlier in life, before there is sufficient awareness of the self and of one's life circumstances; therefore before there can be a clear perception of gain. Early-life friendship works much better than very young heterolove because at that time intuition is unimpeded by sex drive or by thinking that a beautiful balance between two young people is built to last.

As time goes on, needs and motivations make themselves felt and tend to adulterate the pure symmetry of the dyad of both friendship and heterolove.

Perhaps the main reason intuition and clear perception are in perfect alignment in earlier childhood, and that they can do their best work of contrasting complementarity in the foreground is that the background is well sorted out on a homogeneous basis, so the magical formula has its best chance. That background is based on location of home and school. It's a question of taking care of the differences because the likenesses are well taken care of by the fact that both the neighborhood and the school strongly favor similar backgrounds. In fact, the only time this works the same way in heterolove is in the case of childhood sweethearts—which rarely works out in the end because of the rapid and differential changes in the two sexes. Moreover, early sexual familiarity is a handicap whereas vintage friendship is an enormous advantage. But perhaps the most important factor favoring the longevity of friendship against that of marriage is that friends do not normally cohabitate. They can get away from one another. And they're not normally accountable to one another so that there's much more breathing space.

Although friendship is commonly tested by need, which then brings out caring, sheer need is not a good motivator of friendship because it is circumstantial and tends to shoulder out the all-important aspect of matchmaking. Loneliness, divorce, widowhood, and losses of any kind are the usual needs motivating friendship in later years, and tolerance must then be stretched to the limit for fear of losing contact. On the other hand, a friendship born out of love rather than need withstands quarrels, criticisms, and hurts almost as well as does heterolove.

Apart from onset as a factor in life cycle, age gap also plays an important part. This is the classic friendship between an older and a younger woman and the even more classic bond between an older man, a mentor, a protector, a *loco parentis* figure, and a younger one. Rarely does this occur between the sexes because the sexual element, at least from the older person's perspective, however suppressed, tends to interfere. The nurse in Shakespearean plays, or the old nanny in Russian drama, is the classic keeper of the eternal child, usually represented by a girl about to fall upon grief in love, but sometimes represented by a boy as well. In the latter case the relationship is indeed platonic because the nurse's sexual impulses are blocked by incestlike taboos as well as by the fact that the old nurse is often a spinster who sees her ward as a child (substitute) rather than a lover. Sexuality for the nurse is sublimated in her vicarious pleasure in helping young lovers.

The older mentor and the younger man usually have an unequal friendship in the sense that one gives much more overtly than the other, and it is usually a thing of the mind—unless it is a classic platonic relationship, that is homosexual, which is both outside the scope of this work and outside friendship. Heterosexuality spoils friendship, a sexual deviance makes it impossible.

The same factors that cause heterolove to be on the shrink yet magnify its contemporary importance also cause friendships to become relatively rare but highly valued relationships. Some of these are: high physical and social mobility, putting distance between old friends and requiring us to make later and late friendships; the pace and fragmentation of lifestyles, leaving little time and energy for the spontaneity of contact and demanding that we make a constant effort to keep up old friendships or to make new ones; and the apparent self-sufficiency, more likely the self-centeredness and relative isolation, of urban life rendering us less capable of giving though we always stand in need of receiving the benefit of close relationships.

Marriages, break-ups, new jobs; all these things demand that we make new friends all along the way. In fact, one of the saddest conditions of old age is that old friends die off and one has long lost the capacity to make new ones.

For these reasons we shall discuss in this chapter, among other things, the impediments and requirements of late friendships and how to test their goodness of fit.

SEX

Several quite different relationships occur in this context. First there are the separate friendships made before sexual coupling and brought into or else excluded from marriage later, as opposed to friendships made *as* a couple with individuals and again as opposed to those made with a couple. And then there are the man-to-man and woman-to-woman friendships, as well as the problematic ones made across the sexual barrier. Let me hurry on here to explain why sexual fidelity is automatically protected in what must be the commonest of friendships in the middle years. This is one of the many fascinating permutations of love that occurs as a consequence of the principle of contrasting opposition. Usually both a man and a woman in a sexual coupling bring in one or two special friends—by definition there can be only one best friend and one is indeed rich to have a couple of them. And usually they are of the same sex—man to man and woman to woman—and they are each usually coupled themselves. So you have, say, three pairs. Let's take it first from the man's, the husband's, point of view: The woman's special women friends will be her opposites in aspects important to her. They will tend to *resemble* her husband. Therefore his wife's women friends will *not* be his type. They're not likely to bear the image of his femina, exemplified by his wife and the daughter most resembling her. In fact, because likes tend to repel one another, these women friends will be somewhat antagonistic to him and vice versa. They will be tolerated by him for the sake of his wife, though they may also be resented because she shares intimacy and confidences with them before and perhaps since the marriage. On the other hand, the husbands of these women friends will resemble the wife and present a contrast to himself. Therefore they'll make natural friends for the husband. This explains why it happens so often that well-matched couples who have well-matched friends produce new friends of the *same sex* for the spouses.

An identical picture is made, of course, by the husband's male friends, who will be disagreeable or even slightly repulsive to the wife because they are too much like her, while their wives will be compatible with the man's wife. So everything works out in splendid and safe symmetry.

Now obviously this foolproof formula sometimes breaks down for one of three main reasons. The commonest is an error, a mismatch either in the original couple or in the friendship or in the friend's marriage. Insufficient repulsion of likes will facilitate *sexual* attraction.

The second likelihood is a change in the original couple or along the line of friendship in further coupling when, through successive approximation (mutual influence), the sex couple or the friends have become too much like each other. Then they become open to attraction to what now *becomes* the opposite in the opposite sex, again allowing sex to raise its "ugly head."

And the third is perhaps the most usual. This occurs when

the members of the various couplings have matured and aged to the point of fixity. Now the attraction becomes one of *likes*—they fit like an old shoe. If anything happens to break down any of the coupling, like continuous and unreconciled opposition, or a death, there is a tendency for the "old friends" of the opposite sex to pair up. In fact, in my experience, this is how "platonic" friendship across the sexual barrier breaks down in all cases. Where the age gap renders sexual attraction possible, sex is shelved for the sake of friendship until something radical happens, like a divorce, a death, or some other sudden change, and a need arises. Then the hetero undercover sex object vested in the friend is taken off the shelf as it were, carefully dusted off, and put into bed.

The friends made as a couple, as opposed to the ones brought into marriage, are a much bigger threat sexually, partly because there is less libido (psychic energy) invested in the relationship over far less time, and partly because they are more rapidly, more casually, and more situation-and need-motivated than other friendships. Hence the matching is rarely good enough and certainly not likely to be ideally symmetrical. Often these friendships tend to have less depth and loyalty unless they have time to mature. Incidentally, you can see for yourselves how much more threatening friendships *between* the sexes are when brought into a marriage and especially if acquired subsequently. For one thing, they must be based on exactly the same model as heterolove, only with sexuality consciously or semiconsciously inhibited. This means that the wife's *male* friend will be incompatible with the husband, because they'll be likes, highly competitive with each other, and likely to be jealous of each other. To make matters worse, the man's wife will then be normally attractive to the husband. And if the husband also has a female friend, we'll have an explosive situation with quadruple jeopardy. No wonder so many married couples play musical chairs under these unwise circumstances. Actually this kind of situation is even more dangerous, both to heterolove and friendship, than "Hollywood" or "open" marriages and promiscuous multiple couplings. The worst that they do is to attempt group sex. If there's any love left in the end, group sex induces enormous and often irreparable hurt and usually impotence resulting in the defeat of the male who first promoted the idea. (If his wife promotes the idea, her husband still gets ball-busted!)

One of the many penalties of the lean-to, of faulty marital matching, is that such a couple's friendships are far from safe. This is perhaps the reason one hears so often that so-and-so has run off or taken up with her husband's best friend. For example:

The only striking difference between Josephine and Mark was a quarter-century in age spread. Otherwise he was just as immature as she was, perhaps even more impulsive, "penny-wise and pound foolish," obsessive in many ways, and self-centered. Both were WASPs of slightly upper middle class and shared the same profession as well as the same sexual fantasies and quirks.

Peter had been Mark's lifelong friend, as stable, quiet, and introverted as the latter was irresponsible and extroverted. Mary, his wife, was much like Peter. So naturally when they met, Josephine and Mary fell over each other; so much so that they suspected, wrongly as it happened, that their strong attachment had homosexual overtones. On the other hand, Josephine, an appealing young woman, also became sexually attracted to Peter who promptly proposed a threesome or foursome orgy. It didn't come off because the older citizens, Mary and Mark, stood little to gain from it. Nor did they want sex to break up their beautiful friendship. But the subsequent fantasies released chiefly by Josephine played havoc with her marital relationship.

Let us now reiterate and look at all the possible permutations resulting in so-called platonic friendships between the sexes.

You are "protected" from the electromagnetism of sexual attraction and the basic chemistry of deep affection from both sides in the situation of couples if your basic friend is of the same sex. In other words, as a woman normally you're not going to be attracted to your best friend's husband or to your husband's best friend because they'd be too much like you. This, of course, is provided your friend's coupling and your husband's friendship were healthy (not neurotic) and therefore built on the principle of contrasting opposition; also provided the order ranking of characteristics in your coupling, that of your female friend and in your husband's friendship, was roughly the same and accurately perceived all around. In other words, the elements of contrast must have been given roughly equal top ranking all around and perceived as such. For instance, you're a lively extrovert, your female best friend is a quiet introvert, and her husband is a lively extrovert like you; then your husband is a quiet introvert and his best friend is a lively extrovert like you. So if the matching is done well and all elements are in good alignment, you're safe here.

However, if any friendship, yours *or* your husband's, is across the sexes, not only may you come into trouble but you may bring it upon yourself. The reason is that you're then breaking the entire symmetry of coupling and friendship. To be specific, the man who becomes your good friend should be much like your husband, give or take a few characteristics ranked highly (in the first half-dozen). This means that he'll be sitting in the wings for you if anything goes wrong with your marriage, and you'll be sitting in the wings for him. But more than that, his wife will tend to be like you, give or take a few things. In fact she might present a better mix than you in your husband's eye and your husband will be as naturally attracted to her as he is to you and as he will be to your daughter, if she resembles you physically and/or in personality (which is the basis of the Elektra attraction between father and daughter). Surely this means and often is trouble. The very same rules apply to your husband. Such are the hetero relationships that are safe and unsafe from sexually illicit temptation presented by friends.

The moral of this story is that in the old days when friendships were initiated only with one's own sex, all was relatively safe in the natural way of things, as explained. But nowadays, when this whole can of worms is opened up by "sexual liberation," the risks are that much greater and the actual social consequences (statistics) are a witness to this fact.

It is well and good to trust yourself in defiance of these natural rules, especially if you are aware of them (which helps greatly), aware of unconscious processes beyond your control, and courageous enough to take the consequences of your risky actions. But there is another serious consequence to running across "natural" boundaries and temporarily turning sexuality into "platonic" relationships, during the current social forces of discontent, over which you have little control, and in defiance of the unconscious forces of temptation. Some of the forces of discontent come from a massive breakdown of traditional values and from social and biological changes resulting from a longer, healthier life. The consequence is a desire to live life to the full because there is nothing hereafter to aspire to. Hence there arise extraordinary expectations of self-fulfillment—aided and abetted by the illusion of equality. These forces interact with basic sexual temptations, the perception of "greener fields," and reinforce the desire to experience excitement and "fulfillment" at all costs. Hence trouble.

This crossing of sexual barriers is similar to crossing other "traditional" or natural barriers in heterolove. The risk is calculably increased in view of the arithmetic and geometry presented in these equations.

A friend still cannot break up a home without compunction because this act threatens the foundations of both friendship and home. I suspect that when the pendulum of moral values swings, with the coming of a neo-puritan generation, all such barriers will no longer be easily breached.

The moral of this objective explanation of why barriers were erected in revered old traditions is not to forbid breaking them at this time. Changes must always come about or be induced. The purpose is merely to be aware of the "natural" bases for such traditions and to know that the payment for upsetting human ecology is mental and social upset. The dictates of mental economy and wisdom are such that when one takes risks of this order in one psychosocial direction, one should offset them by reducing other risks in other spheres. Or else one should offset stresses and tip back the scale in the other direction. In other words, compensatory conservatism is a necessary correlate of all adventurous advances.

Another fascinating difference between men and women pertains to the apparently different nature of the friendship they establish with their own sex. Characteristically, at least in Anglo-Saxon cultures, the men are more closed-in and undemonstrative, and talk of little that is personal or deep, while women classically confide in each other. Both sexes gossip, of course, and often descend to pettiness. The apparent differences in these respects are both historical and cultural.

Historically men bonded themselves in friendship for war and war games or sports with unquestioned devotion. In fact, some types of bonds were as strong as that between the males in the family—father and son and brothers. They were, and in some parts of the world still are, halfway between blood ties and friendship, so they were hardly elective. For example, the "milk brothers" of a Highland clan: When the chieftain's son was fed at the breast of a foster mother along with her own sons, they were pledged for life because of both the milk tie and the blood tie of the clan. This kind of barbaric brotherhood, whether among the bedouins of the desert or the Indians of the plains (a somewhat more elective affair, especially if it was sworn between Indian and white blood), was a matter of life and death. Indeed all such friendships among men were fierce and stoic, leaving little room for unseemly emotional displays or soul searching. When emotions broke out, though, they tended to be dramatic, especially between near peers like Thomas à Becket and Henry II, or even between an older man and a younger one, such as when poor Falstaff was rejected by Henry V when the latter came to the throne.

The long history of friendship between males and its implicit "manly" purposes amount to what E. T. Hall calls a "high contextual culture," when there is little need for words and understanding is achieved unspokenly.

Women, on the other hand, having a very short history of elective and noncompetitive friendship, form a "low contextual culture" requiring a great deal of talking in order to inform one another of all pertinent things. So while men have secured tribal friends since time immemorial and their collective unconscious is well in tune, women need to make things explicit in order to be in harmony with each other.

Perhaps the newest pattern of friendship is that being created by married urban women. The most numerous shut-ins in the world, the urban housewives rearing a couple of children under the age of five have discovered two things: First is that heterolove is not enough to keep their sanity. They cannot use the husband, especially if he is regarded as the jailer, as a stand-in for everyone else they need—counselor, friend, acquaintance, playmate, parent, and therapist. Second is the realization that friends are especially important in these transient times. Husbands come and go but friends stick; good ones last a whole lifetime. For this reason alone, there's a considerable struggle to keep one's friends, especially those made in childhood—against all constraints of distance, physical mobility, and competitive tensions with home love ties. It also follows that urban friends ought to be carefully chosen or, better still, intuitively well matched so that they will last well.

Now that women have had their overdue revolution, now that they have largely liberated themselves from the aftermath of the agrarian revolution of ten thousand years ago, when they had become the "inside" workers in enclosures shared with goods and chattels, they've also found out that it's cold and unpleasant "out there." In fact, it's lethal, as their numbers who have entered the work force (some 40 percent in North America) have found. I would predict that women will voluntarily return to the homestead. Indeed they'll be eager to do that most delicate and vital job of child-raising and home-making, at least for a decade or so in their younger and middle years. But the job will be done under very different attitudes, both their own and society's.

One of the differences will be a better social structuring whereby existing female friendships will be maintained and valued, at least as highly as heterolove, and new ones will be continuously cultivated. The shut-in feeling must and will go. It must go for the aged, let alone the young and vigorous. Hence the new importance of friendship among women; also the importance of a new style of friendship. In the harem days of kept women, wives, and mistresses, in the days of headhunting and captivating men, it was only natural that the contrasting opposite of the settled agrarian in the woman's collective unconscious, the frustrated *hunter shadow,* should be suppressed and eventually repressed deep down. Therefore it was equally natural that that style of female friendship should be covert yet highly competitive. The rivalries extended from those between sisters to those between neighbors. Women were stereotyped, at least in the middle classes, as the incarnation of "the vanity of vanities" and of envy—usually because of the superficialities of skin-deep beauty and for the sake of material possessions. Later, during motherhood and motherliness, there were—and still are—the endless comparisons of those extensions of the self, the children, exhibited again with an underlying vein of vanity. No doubt much of this will continue. Men have also gotten into the latter act with their protestations of fatherhood. The whole child-raising thing has lost its factory-goods ethos and has become a preciously creative endeavor.

But the feminine style of friendship is changing. Competitiveness is giving way to cooperation, and social mating is sought and achieved between women in the same way in which social history recorded its achievements among men.

Friendships run into lean and sticky times before marriage occurs. When the phone isn't ringing often enough for dates and jumpiness increases, even the best of friends are often put off for the sake of a "lousy date." Of course this shouldn't happen and is much regretted in retrospect—it becomes a matter of shame—but at the time, the pressure is so great that friendships are risked and foresaken until the sanctuary of marriage or permanent cohabitation is achieved.

Nonetheless, steadfastness and loyalty are being rapidly acquired. Somehow, to achieve this, the image of the woman predator, the woman on the loose and on the make—whether separated, divorced, widowed, or otherwise dislocated—must vanish or else suspicion may continue to divide friends. And the cattiness or the impression of cattiness must also go.

As for one who insists that his lover is also his friend, unless this is a *façon-de-parler,* just a misunderstanding of what heterolove is, or a word reserved for just some of its ten commandments (whereas friendship is virtually all of *them* minus sex), he is making a grievous error. For the lover shouldn't be the best friend any more than she or he should be the therapist, mentor, or anything else. One such job is big enough. More is expecting too much and courting severe problems. Also I noticed that it's usually only one of the partners who makes this claim of heterolove and friendship, while the other is silent on the matter. That won't do either, because friendship is a two-way street, like heterolove. The partner's silence is no doubt due to superior knowledge and the realization that there is or should be too much of a mutual sex objective involved in heterolove to allow room for friendship.

MARITAL STATUS

Friends normally precede heterolove by quite a number of years, so they are made in childhood and youth while the person lives in a pristine single state. This is when the knot of friendship is firmly tied. But it is really appreciated, like everything else, much later, during or after the first marriage and, of course, in retirement and old age.

You usually go through a number of crowds, or else you pass outside them, before you're married, while you keep your special friends.

Depending on when and where marriage or cohabitation occurs, the lasting friends are then brought into the conjugal or semiconjugal relationship singly or as couples. Previous coteries or crowds are usually not brought into the heterolove and family relationships in that the man (especially if he's a "man's man," whatever that is) goes out "with the boys" once or twice a week rather than bringing them in, while the woman goes out "with the girls." Not infrequently this is resented, not so much out of jealousy, which is only aroused when there's a real threat to love, but because of the time it takes. Here again there is a traditional difference between the "working man" and the "domesticated woman" in that the "boys" take away from her time, whereas the "girls" do not take away from his time because they usually meet during the day. Evenings are usually taken up by coupled friends—and we've considered their relationship already.

The lonely urban crowd, especially the singles crowd, is very hard put to find new friends in order to offset their aloneness and loneliness. Not that they aren't there, just as much as the opposite sex is there, but because they're hard to find—the social and environmental structure of the modern city is not designed for encounter.

NUMBERS

There is a tendency for some people, generally the introverts, to stick hard to one or two major friendships, while others, generally the extroverts, go for coteries or cliques. But even the latter, as mentioned, choose their favorites from among their circle. Yet there is an inevitable qualitative difference in that the introvert makes his fewer shots count more just as she/he tends to be more careful with her/his psychosocial investments than the more extravagant extrovert, who goes with and for the crowd. Though both kinds of people experience difficulties in keeping up with their friends in our current mobile society, the extroverts have a harder time because of the likelihood that their crowd will break up and because of the increasing difficulty presented by marriage, family, and age in striking up with a new group of friends.

Once again the sexes present different tendencies inasmuch as women are more tenacious in holding on both to special friends and their circle. In this conservative attitude women are being supported by their children, for once they enter the peer-linked teens, they also become reluctant to dig up their roots. Moreover, as mentioned, women also tend to form close and confiding relationships, which means that rupture is extremely traumatic.

Men, on the other hand, choose their pals or at least their circles from among co-workers, club members, and the like and they cannot afford to plant their roots too deeply, in this respect, because they know that they must move to where their work takes them. And they are apt therefore to make new friends from among the same sort of crowd, though these are then not special friends, more locker-room buddies.

There is also, traditionally, a division of "social labor," whereby the wife, especially if she is home-bound, is charged with making new friends after the family has moved. As time goes on, the family presents an ever-mounting resistance to a man's career requirement to move so that his toil becomes truly accompanied by his sweat in the face of bloody battles with the wife and kids. Eventually he must choose between the calls of his career and his family; their friends and his own. When he stops the plunge to power or fortune, it isn't always because he has reached his natural level of incompetence (Peter's Principle). Sometimes it's because the conservative forces win. This is one of the reasons that we so often read in the papers that a public figure has decided to give up his or her perch or status in order "to retire" from public life. His motive may also be reinforced by the need to replenish the family coffers and by the modern ability to take several different paths in one's walks of life.

If we were rational beings, we would not leave the greatest emotional investments made in life—heterolove, friendship, child-rearing, one's life work—to even apparent chance and certainly not to a large chunk of luck. Nor would we leave to chance the number and quality of friends made over a lifetime. With respect to the latter, for one thing, we should reckon with natural attrition, with distances that do not "make the heart grow fonder" but rather follow the adage "out of sight out of mind," and with loss through disease or death. If we were rational, we would not crowd out this tiny planet with our numbers while having only a few friends, if any, against the times of solitude and stress. And one should use friends up with the trepidation of a person using his water supply while trekking across a desert. Yet even if we wanted to lay in supplies of friends against hard times, as we do with other things, it can hardly be done in the present lifestyle.

For instance, the happy crowds one meets in the carefree days of vacation vanish even faster than those blood-sworn friends in times of acute stress or war, despite all protestations to keep up. Daily chores, energy-sapping secondary relationships push us on until it's too late in the day to follow up with visits, letters, or even Christmas cards. As to the unusual experience of "close" friendships springing up mainly in the no-man's-land of vacations, a subsequent reunion in real life is as disappointing as revisiting the romance-impregnated places of one's honeymoon.

And the same sort of thing can be said about the neighborhood crowd when a cohesive community gives way to fragmentation into an inchoate vicinity. It seems that the group, the clique, has a life and place of its own so that once it breaks up, once the key people who make up its heart and soul move away, the whole thing disappears forever.

Then there's another phenomeon testifying to the essential unfairness of the real world. As with everything else, those most in need of whatever it may be, like love, friendship, or success, usually get the short end of the stick and vice versa. It's not only that if you "laugh and the world laughs with you, cry and you cry alone," and because "misery loves its own company," but because those in need are necessarily those up-tight about whatever they require—which gives off bad vibes—while those with a surfeit can afford to be cavalier, pleasant, and generous. So people most in need of a friend rarely have one.

Consequently what happens with the numbers and perhaps with the quality of friendship—as indeed with life altogether—has a sort of inverted trumpet shape. You have a surfeit in early life, when the world is your oyster. Then you tend to narrow down to a few friends while creating a family. You keep them if you're lucky and in the end you're reduced to people-watching, to contemplating relationships and to regrets in ever-dwindling space and time.

You might ask, Why the American preoccupation with quantity? What does the quantity of friendships matter? Surely it's quality that matters, however practical it may be to have many different and lasting friendships, with many different interests. And you're right. Quality matters, especially to the introvert, though quantity also matters, especially to the extrovert. It also matters as a stock laid against total attrition.

Although comparisons may be odious, science could not function without them and truth could never be fully revealed. It is said with some degree of truth (sometimes by people on both sides of the Atlantic) that friendship as well as heterolove thrives deeper and more lastingly in Europe than in North America. To the extent to which this may be true there must be several explanations. One is that Europeans have an older, more stable, or at least static, culture. They also have to be more conservative environmentally and socially; otherwise they could not survive. Consequently they build everything more carefully, conscientiously, and for longer than the expansive, mobile, and carefree North Americans. But another reason might also be that North Americans, with their faster tempo of living, more intense lifestyle, and desire to achieve more (whatever that is) in record time, have less energy left—given similar endowments—than the Europeans. Consequently they cannot endure the tests and vicissitudes of heterolove and friendship, so they break off or drift much more easily than Europeans.

If this is so then to that extent the quality of life must be better in Europe than in North America, except perhaps in respect to material things—and even that's changing fast now. This would explain why so many immigrants come to North America to make their pile, only to return to Europe in order to savor it; and why many native North Americans (meaning, of course, immigrants a few generations ago) prefer to live in Europe as part-exiles, if they can do so comfortably.

LATE FRIENDSHIP

The rule of attraction in late heterolove also applies to friendship made in the mature years of the life cycle; namely that likes tend to attract one another once the personality has ripened and rigidified. When we no longer possess the flexibility and tolerance of youth, we cannot accommodate vast contrasts in friendship. If we cannot have the old-shoe comfort of a relationship fashioned in youth, then we must seek the compatibility of common interests, endeavors, and values. This doesn't mean that once child bearing is over, once the competitiveness in careers has given way to the rut of security, compatible friendship should be sought at the hairstyling parlors where gray hair is shaded with blue, or at knitting bees for grandchildren, or in the tired sofas of musty clubs, or in the parks where old codgers meet. But it does mean that we can no longer rush into relationships when our tread is cautious and uncertain. For one thing, part of the diffidence in making new friends in middle and older age is due to the feeling, real or unwarranted, that social circles are closed and self-sufficient; that you are unwanted. This is a feeling that increases pathetically with age. For another thing, one's sensitivities become far from blunted by age. On the contrary, they sharpen. And the search for compatibility becomes cautious and veers more than ever on similarities. And yet some need for differences remains; if not in the background, when distances in social profiles now become impossible to bridge, then at least in the foreground, in terms of a milder yet still complementary blend in personalities.

For instance, as in all close relationships, there is never a perfect balance between giving and taking, between initiating and responding. One person may do more of the calling, making the contact—without counting how much more often she/he did this than the friend—and the other person may have a greater need to be wanted. But, as in cohabitational consortings short of marriage, tolerance toward the little things, petty idiosyncrasies and habits, tends to diminish and irritation rises to tax burgeoning late friendships.

Would-be late friends in urban life, like second (or more)-time-arounders, share with them the difficulty of finding a location for new encounters. Our society has simply not caught up with the social technology to absorb the adverse effects of the physical technology that has broken down traditional patterns. The "Michelin Guide" for meeting would-be lovers offered in this book must be modified for late friendship in that the neighborhood and work place should be ranked higher in this case.

Finally, what constitutes a good friend? Longevity, despite the last few words to be read in this chapter, is not the only or even the main test of a good fit in friendship any more than it is in heterolove. Moreover, one can make a good friend later in life. Neither is sharing one's misery, like divorce, boredom, bereavement, or sciatica, an optimal quality of friendship. What is then? What's the single most important characteristic? It's a feeling that the friend is always there, that the friend will help in need, no matter what, with few or no questions asked and that she/he will not adulterate the many facets of this omnibus relationship by adopting a special role or attitude—whether parental, romantic, professional, or what have you.

At any rate, in late life when friends really matter the most, when they are appreciated as never before, time has distilled the best of friendships just as it does a vintage wine. Well, let's see if you've distilled some friends by testing yourself against the criteria provided in the following test.

A TEST OF FRIENDSHIP

Answer by checking off one of the responses to each question.

	Yes	Maybe or Somewhat	No

1. Provided he/she didn't change substantially toward you, would you still feel the same way toward your friend if he fell into a great fortune (of any kind) or into great misery?

2. Do you think he/she would also feel the same toward you if one of the above extreme fates befell you?

3. Would you be prepared to risk your life almost as readily for your friend as for another loved one?

4. Do you think he or she would risk life for you?

5. If you haven't seen or spoken to your friend for a while, do you experience an increasing longing to do so, which must finally be satisfied?

6. Is contact between you and your friend initiated by either of you and in roughly equal measure?

7. Are you always and fully open to each other?

8. If your marriage or family life threatened your continued friendship, would you go to any length to save it?

9. Would he or she do the same do you think?

10. Do you feel that your devotion to your friend is selfless, that is not motivated by a conscious gain?

11. Is his or her motivation the same do you think?

12. If the circumstances of your friend legitimately demanded that you overcome your greatest fear or revulsion, would you do so without question?

13. Do you think the same applies to your friend?

14. If the circumstances of your friend demanded that you assume a blame, would you be prepared to do it?

15. Would he or she do the same do you think?

16. Would you risk your friendship by telling your friend something you know will hurt if you were convinced that this action would also help immeasurably?

17. If he or she said or did the same sort of thing to you in the same spirit of "only your best friend would tell you," would you be able to take it and accept the deed without loss of feeling for your friend?

18. Would you allow your sexual satisfaction to threaten your friendship?

19. Would you hesitate significantly to betray your friend for the sake of your country or justice?

20. Do you think he or she would do the same?

21. Would you lend your friend anything that you know would be beneficial?

22. Would he or she do the same do you think?

23. Does your friend know everything about you (no major secrets)?

24. Do you believe you are in the same position?

25. Do you feel you set each other off in a complementary balance of virtues and weaknesses?

Scoring
Score 2 for Yes, 1 for Maybe or Somewhat, 0 for No

Interpretation

48–50	Too good to be true! Maybe you're kidding yourself.
40–47	You've got a good thing going. Hold on to it for dear life.
35–39	It's iffy, but maybe it'll grow from fair friendship to better.
30–34	Unless you've been overly pessimistic or overly cautious in your answers, it's doubtful whether you've got something better than a good acquaintance.
25–29	An acquaintance and that's all.
Under 25	Look elsewhere.

NOTES

1. As in all these tests, this one is set up in such a way that you can easily see what's intended, but if you cheat it's nobody but yourself.

2. If you've accumulated most of the points from the questions inquiring about *your* feelings rather than equally from these and those reflecting your *friend's,* either your giving-and-receiving equation is out of whack or you're excessively cautious about your friend's feeling for you—which also goes against the relationship.

3. You might be inclined to weight the last question by as much as two or even three times more—I would. And if this brings up your total to a more respectable level, bully for you!

8

Other Consortings

Tell me who your associates are
and I'll tell you who you are.

—ANONYMOUS

Although the personages of the inner self manifest themselves, however subtly, at all times, it's only in the closeness of intimate consorting that they normally yield themselves to discovery by others. So when it comes to consortings that fall short of the closeness of heterolove or friendship, matching people can only be roughly carried out on the principle of contrasting opposition of personae, unless a future well-programmed computer or personnel consultant can penetrate beyond.

It is important not to mismatch people in elective consortings that fall short of closeness because a great deal of the success of their purpose depends on such associations, and a great deal of energy and time is devoted to such relationships. Moveover, often some of these consortings provide more intense and more prolonged physical proximity—like room and travel mating—than friendship, or even than the noncohabitative phases of heterolove. So it is important for consorts of all kinds to click, tick, and stick with you, as anyone with a mismatched roommate, travel, or work mate will tell you. Especially as a single person you can easily get trapped in a badly chosen consorting and room-mating situation, which becomes stressful enough to drive you up the pole. In fact, one of the simpler reasons friendships may last longer than heterolove is that you don't usually live with your friends, or at least not for long. If you don't live together with a consort of any kind, you avoid the abrasions of the lavatory, bathroom, breakfast time, and quarrels about budgeting, slovenliness or compulsive cleanliness, hoarding, noise, lousy TV shows, and on and on, as well as the frustrations of cohabitant sex. Yet consortings short of friendship or heterolove often involve living together at close quarters. While traveling or rooming together, you cannot avoid those kinds of stress-provoking situations so you had better click well enough and tick along for the sake of your sanity; or else avoid cohabitant situations.

Also, as every young homebody wife knows, a husband is liable to spend more waking hours cheek by jowl with his secretary or business partner than with her. Consequently, even such consortings must be well-matched if the work is to go well and smoothly.

Finally, a proper matching of groups and personnel can make the difference between high morale and achievement on the one hand and unhappiness and failure on the other in an institution, in a business, or even in the running of a country. And some of these activities not only transcend in overall importance the affairs of the home, but they also determine them to an astonishing extent.

Some of the insights to be imparted in this context conform to popular, well-tried, and intuitive knowledge. They are no more than common sense. For instance, everybody knows or should know that a successful private business depends on the melding of two opposites—the somewhat disorganized entrepreneur with a touch of genius who takes the risks of a gambler, working with a highly organized, careful, methodical, rational right-hand man or woman. Experience teaches that one cannot do without the other. While the obsessive executive cannot and should not rise too high in responsibility, because he'll break at the top, if she/he works in close association with a flexible free-wheeling type of person, both will thrive and so will their enterprise. For one thing, obsessive people tend to miss the forest for the trees while high-flying entrepreneurs hardly ever see a tree.

Similarly, if a small group, a committee, a bunch of academics, a top bureaucracy, a President's cabinet, or a scientific team is to create and produce top-quality stuff, it must contain clashing elements—the odd and angular in proportion to the square, the shit disturber, and the traditionalist. And yet again and again grave errors are made when the boss has the power to appoint his successor, his co-workers, and underlings. In the first place, he or she tends to create a hiatus of quality between his top perch and those underneath because he or she fears their ascent and assault. And in the second place, the boss chooses people of his own ilk with whom she/he is more comfortable and who can be more easily bossed into yes-persons. He should choose contrasting opposites to himself and between them and blend them into a team.

Boss-choosing by common consent, the current democratic process, is even worse than the autocratic one because it is random and favors mediocrity and popularity rather than excellence. Also it always excludes the lone wolf, the outsider, the person without a constituency or power base, the independent introvert, and the aggressive extrovert, who are so essential to the chemistry of a successful enterprise. Also, the democratic process presents no opportunity whatsoever for a carefully balanced and selective choice of individuals melded into a production group: While autocracy does present such an opportunity, even it is rarely taken. To digress for a moment, it's quite amazing that this chance is so rarely taken. The reason must be that the boss cannot truly believe in his own strength, or is afraid of his or her failing powers and that toward the end (of his life or of the established enterprise) he takes the unconscious attitude *"après moi le deluge,"* (after the flood) or that of Samson pulling down the pillars of the temple, rather than wanting to preserve his (institutionalized) creation. Declining institutions particularly need this rejuvenating and re-creative element that comes from the right chemistry of people-matching (see the argument in the last pages of Chapter 1 on love) if they are to survive or develop themselves.

THE TAXONOMY

Having established the importance of these nearly close relationships, let's taxonomize them and see how people can be "chemically" matched for the clicking and subsequent phases. And let's do it backwards, from some of the least to the most important groups, then from some of the least to the most important coupled consortings, thus from the necessarily superficial to the deeper selections. There are a number of transitory groups gathered mostly for pleasure and recreation like (1) dinner party and conversation groups, and others gathered for higher purposes like (2) decision-making, research, and brainstorming (synectics). Then, coming down in numbers from small groups to couples there are a number of matings varying in importance of purpose like (3) partnerships, mostly in business, (4) elective or chosen work-mating, (5) roommating, (6) playmating, for both children and adults, and (7) travel-mating.

Let's say the obvious at the outset. The more important the purpose and the more likely a prolonged physical proximity, the closer and better or fuller should the matching be. Consequently, decision-making groups, partners, and workmates (the noncohabitational) on the one hand and room and travel mates (temporarily cohabitational) on the other should be more closely matched than the rest—although the better the match the better the result, whatever the purpose.

As far as private pleasure groups are concerned, often much of the matching *to oneself* has already been carried out because the persons involved are already friends. There are two things about that.

One is that they may be friends of yours, as in a dinner party or in a partnership, but they're not necessarily friends of other people involved. Moreover, many of these consorting situations involve a *product*—and not just the relationship between you and another—like scientific discoveries, decisions, business success, traveling, and even fun at a party. So that makes a difference to the goal of the relationship, hence the selection of the members of a group.

The other thing has to do with a perverseness of Anglo-Saxons, who bend backwards for the sake of fairness to favor the other guy, who is neither one's blood (compulsive closeness) nor one's friend (elective closeness). They're wrong. Clearly, from what we've said already about the importance of the work and product of these relationships, it's objectively essential to produce a well-matched group. And, all other things being equal, like qualification for the job, it is far better to use one's own than others. A surgical team of brothers who get along or a partnership or standing committee of friends will work far better than one of strangers. In this sense patronage and nepotism pay objectively—that is in terms of the ultimate benefit to others.

However, the same argument does not apply as uncomplicatedly to heterolove.

Despite the successful matches of Dr. and Madame Curie, or even Simone de Beauvoir and Sartre, and many others, for many reasons it is not always a good thing to mix work and love—the way some professionals do (lawyers, doctors, artists, writers). The paramount reason is that competitors cannot coexist. If their personalities are not alike and their strengths and specialties are different, this obstacle is surmounted. Not otherwise. Other reasons have to do with living too close together at work, play, and privately to the point of claustrophobia—too many opportunities for boredom, for criticism, for the familiarity that may bring contempt. Always there's the interfering factor of sex, which is best sublimated (rather than discharged) for the sake of the product of the consortings we're considering. If we lived in a paradise of plenty it's doubtful whether we'd create anything or work to any useful extent. But since scarcity has always been with us and will continue to be as far as human eye can see, productivity is paramount.

Many people fear mixing friendship with work or partnership. They're afraid of losing out on friendship. True, as already pointed out, as you move from friendship to a collegial cluster, the goal changes from personal relationship to a product, so that allowances must be made in the chemistry of matching, and a shift in the nature of previous relationships like friendship is inevitable. For one thing, a chain of command must be established. On the other hand, the utility of a prior friendship (or blood relationship) has already been pointed out and those kinds of relationships should stand up to the challenge.

Finally, in terms of using the principle of contrasting opposition or rather its magical formula for the selection of these consortings, the more transient and unimportant they are the more one must build up the commonality of background so as to enhance quick familiarity. The opposite is also true—the more intimate and prolonged the relationship and the more important, the more vital it is that the mixing of actively contrasting ingredients works its chemistry.

In order to simplify and generalize the descriptions of selection that follow we shall assume that the people involved are vital, young at heart, and capable of growing in these relationships, rather than fixed or spent. Clearly, if we're considering the latter type, the mating and grouping of mental and emotional octogenarians (or of narcissists), then the accommodation comes largely from a matching of likes, with minimal variations in order to offset competitiveness.

PRINCIPLES OF SELECTION

Small Groups

By definition a small group is much more dynamic, active, and functional than a larger group. It gives every personality a chance to display itself as fully as is compatible with its purpose, time, and place. And it provides a chance for personalities to gel so as to consolidate and form a unit where two or more heads and hearts are better than one. The ideal group consists of no fewer than four and no more than eight members in all. A group of ten to twelve requires much more contact time and tends to break down into cliques. Also a larger group tends to call for relatively fixed leadership and the quick establishment of a hierarchy or at least of verbal dominance. This threatens the quality of its work and achievement. Too often a large group is used by leaders as a gallery for posturing or an electorate for power-gathering or as minions for ego stroking. Whereas a small, integrated group does not call for a fixed leadership but only for transient initiators. This also favors the emergence of high-quality contributions from the more silent members. Trust and consolidation are more easily established in a smaller group.

Selection of a group for dinner or conversation or for other similar purposes should follow certain specific rules, beyond the absolute limitation of its number. Yet in this very context let's add that if the group exceeds six or eight, it is physically impossible to spontaneously rotate speaking members in order to achieve Socratic dialogues around a dinner table, so everyone can listen to everyone else in turn and respond. Sometimes it's difficult enough even with smaller numbers because of the tendency for the thread of conversation to break up into two or three shoulder-to-shoulder or opposite-sitting people talking to each other. In this respect the study of *proxemics* is relevant, because it deals with private space and the significance of seating arrangements.

The first rule of matching dinner parties is that the majority of invited guests should be fairly close acquaintances or friends of the host so as to establish a solid commonality of backgrounds. This diminishes tension because it relaxes the host, who has at least a treble task: catering, introducing, and leading the proceedings. This overload makes it desirable for hosts to reduce their own tension by not having to absorb more than a couple of relative strangers at one party.

The second rule, however, is "nothing ventured nothing gained" or, to paraphrase Boileau again, wildly, *"rien comprendre c'est rien risquer."* A certain risk must be taken by the hosts with at least one couple or two persons who are less well known to the hosts than the rest, or about whose behavior there might be some uncertainty. This is one way of introducing two necessary elements in to the dynamics: (1) injecting people who are relative strangers in to the majority (of friends) and (2) introducing the element of difference—of heterogeneity—which is so essential to the chemistry of interest in relationships.

The third rule is to ensure a large degree of familiarity right off the bat—so as to minimize the general tension that comes from too much unfamiliarity—through the dual activities of meeting strangers, which too often elicits defensiveness, and participating in discussions and proceedings. The guests must feel that their primary task is to bring themselves to the party and participate—nothing much more. Yet they should know that the ultimate success of a social event rests not solely upon the shoulders of the hosts, but is up to everybody equally.

Far too frequently in unsophisticated societies or generally in socially gauche and uptight middle classes, both hosts and guests become so tense and self-concerned before a party that they have to liquor up for the occasion. Ideally such people should be kept to a minimum at a successful dinner party or conversation group, for they perform badly—at cocktail parties it matters far less. But the syndrome of narcissistic uncertainty is so widespread that to eliminate its sufferers from such gatherings might mean not being able to hold them at all.

Wise hosts build up a reputation for their relaxed parties and may influence their uptight guests, especially if they're close friends, to partake only of the alcohol offered after arrival and to use it for the sake of conviviality, not as medicine.

(I wouldn't want the reader to take the above prescriptives as those of a snobbish puritan, for they apply solely to a very particular group dynamic whose output is joyful socializing and/or intellectual stimulation. For instance, luncheons are the worst news—teas and orgies, among others, are entirely different occasions usually not requiring or allowing for careful selection or relative abstinence.)

In order to facilitate a relaxed milieu, both the physical surroundings or environment and the guests must be quickly recognized and acceptable to those invited—otherwise these factors distract and take energy away from the main task.

The fourth and last rule is to introduce an element of surprise in judicious proportion. This requirement enables us to modify, for group dynamics purposes, two cardinal rules that apply to the dynamics of dyadic relationships.

In coupling the rule is to make sure of the difference, for the similarities will look after themselves. In group dynamics it is just the opposite: Make sure of background homogeneity, for the differences in personality will look after themselves.

In coupling, the spark is supplied by contrasts *within* the person, which display themselves in time in the milieu of intimacy and cohabitation.

In groups the spark must be supplied by representing the typically contrasting personages of the inner self via the personae selected, using the leader or host as the prime model. In other words the personages stacked up longitudinally, as it were, or in depth inside the hosts should be represented, as it were, horizontally by the personae selected for the group party.

This means, of course, that the hosts must be whizzes at self-analysis and extremely honest to boot; for they are asked to select for such creative gatherings people representing their ideal self, their femina/hominus (who might be best represented by each other if they are ideally matched husband and wife), their eternal children, shadows, and their animae—more or less.

"But that's ridiculous!" I hear you exclaim. Not really, though it is perhaps an extreme, as all perfection is. You see, in doing this, in displaying the longitudinal psychoarchitecture of two hosts horizontally through representative personae at a dinner party, they create a human network sure to interact magnificently. This would be a work of art. Even its approximation would be an achievement.

The guests, most of whom are already part of the hosts' networks, are bound to have a psychic connection with them—built in a pattern of contrasts and similarities—so that they are also bound to interact significantly with one another.

In a quarter of a century of private analytical group psychotherapy I've always selected group members on the basis of their sharing not only the same problem but also the same causes and backgrounds. The differences in age, sometimes in sex, in aspects of social profile, physique, lifestyle, intelligence, and personalities always took care of themselves. It was the purpose of the group to solve the problem they shared. Similarly in these sorts of groups, whether for a dinner party or a President's cabinet, one must ensure maximal familiarity with the environment and a sharing of purpose and interest. One must also allow differences to emerge. The objective here is the obverse of *de pluribus unum,* as that wonderful gas bag the Wizard of Oz insisted. That is, in order to achieve a quick consolidation of a group on common ground, a musketeer feeling of "all for one and one for all" without offering an opportunity for grandstanding, *initial* commonality is needed to forge the right spirit.

At a party one cannot rely on sufficient time and intimacy for the revelation of inner contrasts, so one must cause what would have been revealed in time by each person to appear all at once, in the personae of the members of the party. Because there are some six personages of the inner self, and the ideal group is limited to six, it is necessary to use only one principal model—the host or leader who does the selecting. The objective here is to achieve the same kind of "chemical" unity in the group as that occurring within a person and to achieve the same kind of union of opposites that exists in the alchemy of coupling. The hosts act as the self, the integrating function.

The primary purpose of a group should determine the amount and quality of commonality and contrasts, that is the proportion in the magical formula. At a dinner party or conversation group the prime purpose is exchange of wit and conversation, so the majority should have these skills. But one couple at least must have a different kind and style of wit—perhaps quieter and more profound or more caustic and sharp. For conversation, the majority of members should be verbal and interested in whatever theme will take up the exchange, but a couple of people should supply other tangential, surprising, and irreverent qualities—be the devil's advocates.

You can see how the priority or rank order of qualities and skills differs with the purpose and longevity of a group by contrasting these (limited) *desiderata* of a dinner party with those of heteroloves, friendship, war buddies, or sports partners.

It also follows that an intelligent manager of a sports team, like hockey or football, would direct his psychological or phys ed consultants to cooperate in bringing about the magical formula for success.

How then does one select the back-room boys that win a war or an election? How shall you put together a President's cabinet to successfully govern a country? How do you choose the personnel and talent in a company in order to achieve a meteoric rise? What ingredients do you mix in a team of scientists in order to uncover the secret of cancer or of eternal life? In order to maximize the inventive and the creative so as to expend human energy wisely, you must:

1. Keep the effective group to within the number that can relate intimately and fully (four to twelve, average seven).

2. Ensure homogeneity in purpose, like devotion to country or to scientific discovery.

3. Ensure homogeneity in background, like social profile, plus scientific qualification or political experience, but also:

4. Introduce variety like including members with different ultimate purposes, devotions, and value systems.

5. Try to have a minority with different social profiles (social class, age, sex, ethnicity, even race); certainly different training, expertise, viewpoints, and most certainly different personalities.

Yet these differences must be fully absorbable within the lifetime of the group and integrated by "host" or leader through achieving rewards in the pursuit of goals. Furthermore, in this as in any group, one must typify the personages of at least one individual's private psyche, the leader's, again representing his or her ideal self, eternal child and particularly the shadow and the anima in the working group. This means, in effect, that if the leader is square, scrupulously honest, earnest, methodical, serious, introverted, a stickler for formality, for evidence, truth, and logic, at least one or perhaps two of the group must be differently shaped: cavalier, looser morally, childlike, extroverted, fun-loving, irreverent, intuitive, somewhat illogical, and keener on beauty or ethics than on truth. The representation of the archetypes of the hominus/femina is somewhat more contentious in groups whose explicit purpose excludes sexuality—as in decision-making or science—but its inclusion is all right at parties. And yet the judicious introduction of sexuality might be profitable in that its energy will be necessarily inhibited in its aim (no sex among the membership unless it includes ready-made couples), so this inhibited energy may be usefully sublimated into the purpose of the exercise.

Just as any modern, self-respecting sports team manager should take note of these "chemical" prescriptives, so should any writer for a successful, lasting television show. Indeed, if you examined the shows with highest ratings that have survived longest, you will see the characters blend in contrasting opposition against the commonality of background and dedication to purpose. Try your hand at dissecting Mary Tyler Moore's show or Lou Grant's or "Bonanza." We've already done a partial job in this respect on "All in the Family" (see Chapter 3).

Close Consortings
This includes partnerships, the work mates whom we can select, some playmates and roommates sharing for a reasonably long time, possibly travel mates. We've already dealt with the question of sex and marriage in these relationships, so we will take the typical situation as being sexless and probably existing between people of the same sex, short of friendship or overlapping with it.

The main division within this category then is that of cohabitation. We shall take it that partners and playmates generally do not cohabit, whereas travel mates and especially roommates do. So we'll treat them somewhat differently.

Partners are geared to a product, whether it be money-making in business or the apprehension of criminals in police work. Commonality is ensured by their joint purpose, to which there must be roughly equal devotion though the ultimate value systems—at their perceptual, pragmatic or operational and absolute levels—do not need to coincide. However, too great a difference in this respect, like opposite political persuasions or too great a difference in social profile, must not be allowed to absorb so much energy and time as to prevent crucial differences in personality. These latter differences should be between persona and shadow or at least persona and eternal child. We've already mentioned the essential mix between the risk-taking dreamer—the entrepreneur—an often disorganized person who must lead because he shouldn't be fettered, and his steady, plodding, cautious, realistic sidekick—similar to the joker and the straight man, the muscle man and the brains in shows.

If work depended on the quality of productivity instead of on the Peter Principle, or Murphy's or Parkinson's laws, work-mating would be carried out carefully and according to the principles of selection herein described.

Much the same rules apply to playmating—the adventuresome initiator and the more thoughtful responder; the jack-of-all-trades, experientially oriented, and the master of one skill, a burgeoning perfectionist; the bookworm and the out-of-doors explorer. This is the quintessence of the chemistry of such consortings.

On the other hand, impermanent cohabitation calls for less strident differences, particularly in the realm of daily habits. If there is no prior love to absorb differences and render them tolerable, they must be reduced, especially in areas of likely friction—which, in this case, are habit and lifestyle rather than intelligence, personality, or ultimate values.

Some examples:

Rick was a perfectionist, the president of a branch of the companies Joe owned. Joe was your typical dreamer-entrepreneur, with no stomach for detail or analytical abilities. He was all intuition while Rick had none—just the power of inexorable logic. Rick ran his company like clockwork while Joe ran his consortium by the seat of his pants. This is how he made the millions Rick hadn't made. But Joe made the mistake of despising Rick's womanish worries, egging him on to taking greater risks for greater rewards, and teasing him mercilessly. What's worse, he never took Rick into his confidence or closer into the leadership of the consortium because he was afraid of being held "down to earth by that mole." Rick feared Joe, his laughter, and his unpredictability. The two men thoroughly disliked one another, although Rick ran the only part of the business that made Joe a profit and Joe had given Rick his best opportunity to show what he could do.

Presently Rick recognized that the business was being so badly run and so disorganized that it might collapse. He warned Joe, who dismissed him as a "chronic doomsday worrier." He even sacked him and took over the management of his company, while offering Rick a much less familiar perch—that of a foreign sales representative. Rick plodded away and brought back fat foreign bacon. But it was too late. Joe had meanwhile messed up his only profitable company and lost its top echelon. Moreover, he had run the whole show into the ground, or rather into the hands of the receiver.

Emily was a chubby, blue-eyed blonde, an overactive little girl, pushy, aggressive, and bright. She got into everything.

One day she found Jean, a dark little thing, quietly crying on a rock, chin into her small thin hands. "What's the matter, baby?" asked Emily, putting her pudgy pink arms around the scrawny shoulders. There was nothing but a brown baleful look back. But Emily ignored this in her customary busy way, directed Jean to her private playground, and coaxed her to escalate her slide, which the latter hadn't done before. Jean's tears were soon forgotten. The two played happily ever after. Sometimes Emily would do all her athletic antics while Jean just sat and watched amusedly. But sometimes Jean drew Emily into the story books the scrawny dark girl loved and elaborated them with tales from her own imagination. Both mothers were pleased because Emily had quieted down and become more socialized while Jean had perked up and become more socialized, too. Yet these playmates puzzled both the other children and their mothers. Emily's many acolytes, including those she frightened and bowled over with her energy, couldn't understand what she saw in the shy little thing Jean. Nor could Emily's mother. And Jean's bigger brothers, who were greatly amused by Emily, couldn't see why she bothered with their dull little sister. Nor could Jean's mother, though she was thankful for it.

The fact was that the two girls preferred to play and spend time with each other, than to play with the noisier group or withdraw respectively.

Michael and Gabriel should have known not to share rooms at the university because they were both archangels and somewhat frightened virgins. Gabriel spent a lot of time swatting and criticising Michael. Michael spent a lot of time swatting and defending himself from Gabriel's criticisms. Gabriel played daddy and analyzed Michael's dependency and old-womanish ways while Michael couldn't help noticing that Gabriel was always grumpier when Michael had been away and spent his time cleaning up the place, tidying up, then chastising Michael for his slovenliness. They had been pals but came to a parting of the ways when Michael finally exploded and told Gabriel where he could go—to the gates of the other place. And the latter broke up in tears and promised to be a good boy. This so disgusted Michael that he went and got deflowered and promised himself never again to share rooms with a "friend."

The rules of successful cohabitation in roommating are very much based on the principle of contrasting opposition described in heterolove. The durability, even the existence of the odd couple, not to speak of the success of the movie and the long run and fun of the television series, is owed to the comical contrasts between Oscar and his roommate, Felix.

However, one must scale down and modify the tolerance for opposites or even for wide differences, as one goes down the scale of love in consortings from heterolove and friendship to roommating and traveling together. The most important aspect of this necessary modification is that, much more than in cohabitational heterolove, the little things—habits—in roommating matter a lot. And close proximity in living together makes it mandatory to clear *beforehand* the highlights of these little habits that may lead to violent incompatibility. The early bird does not mix well with the nighthawk, particularly if they chirrup and screech respectively and loudly. And the promiscuous mixes badly with the virginal. In fact, at this low love level of consorting the magical formula for affection, which dictates that the *background* should coincide while the *foreground* may contrast, becomes partly reversed. In roommating, many background features may differ, such as the age, social status, and ethnic subgroupings of the social profile, but foreground features like nocturnal habits, sleeping, eating, and sex habits should coincide or be compromisable.

Put differently, large personality differences may still be the basis for clicking well in roommating, ticking, and sticking together so long as the little things don't get in the way, like the sound of sawing logs through a paper-thin bedroom wall or grinding teeth while reading together in the shared living room.

The feelings that are ancillary to love—liking, trusting, and respect—become important in friendship and very important in other consorting relationships. In fact they are the main sentiments accompanying such relationships when they are short of love itself.

The more specialized the purpose of a coupling of people, the more specialized should the common background be. For instance, traveling companions ought to be matched in pattern of movement. It won't do for a zigzagging dawdler, stopping every few minutes to gaze, gawk, and finger merchandise, to travel with a speedy point-to-pointer who looks neither right nor left till she gets there. Although astronauts are probably self-selectively matched in terms of their philobatic (large-space-loving) and levitational propensities (determinable from samples of their sleep dreams), they should also be matched for self-discipline and the absence of a restlessness that usually accompanies this type.

FRIENDSHIP AND OTHER CONSORTINGS

For the purpose of description and study man must divide things artificially and then classify. In real life, things merge into a whole ball of wax. Consequently, types of consortings shift into one another as the purposes of relationships change. In any one space of time, many of the more intimate consortings, like a partnership, rooming or traveling together, can escalate into friendships. Similarly, in a segment of time and space a friendship can lose its purity of purpose or anima value and become expedient and instrumental. Thus the artificial barriers between it and consorting may disappear.

This is particularly apt to happen in an age such as ours, which has seen a proliferation of secondary relationships—with the rise in social complexity and the service industries—and an equal multiplication of transient acquaintanceships, along with an explosion of social roles—the many hats an individual wears. Parallel with this change are the consequences of a prolonged, effective and healthy life, the ability to pursue, serially if not concomitantly, different jobs and avocations as well as serial loves. The result is what scientists call a "noise effect"—a confusion. Sometimes we no longer know who our friends are—or our loves for that matter—or indeed whether we have any friends or loves, though we cannot escape entirely the concept of consort. In order to bring some order out of this chaos, we must ask ourselves divisive kinds of questions and attempt to answer them. For instance, the question arises whether one necessarily must have a best friend, especially if there's a group of them and more especially if it's a group of old good friends—a sorority or a fraternity. Many people, especially the people-minded, the sociable extroverts, and the evenly balanced (extrovert and introvert) popular types, deny that they choose or could choose a best friend. They will tell you that their choices depend on the purpose and nature of consorting, rather than on the degree of friendship; some friends are better for sports and parties, other friends are better for conversations, confessions, and working with. In this respect the utility of friends merges with that of other consortings short of friendships—traveling pals, locker-room buddies and that sort.

Theoretically, however, one ought to have a best friend for two reasons brought out in this book: the monogamous nature of love in general and the exclusivity of optimal matching by contrasting opposition in particular. In terms of the monogamous nature of love, people are generally quite limited in psychic energy. Therefore they are capable of investing most of it in only one *kind* of love object at one time: one member of the opposite sex, one child even, one friend, and even just one member of the family, parent or sibling. So this question of "best" friend is very much related to one heterolove at one time (monogamy) and perhaps even to loving only one leading member of each of the two sets of compulsorily close relationships—the original and the acquired family.

We have already advanced the arguments supporting the idea of the monogamy of heterolove. With regard to friendship and even family, let us take two admittedly abnormal extremes on this range in order to see where the golden mean, or the norm, falls. There are people professing a great love for humanity, for animals and/or for individuals. And there is one argument, advanced by no less a person than myself, that favors the idea of expanded love. This is the law (Cappon's) of appetites extended to both psyche and soma. It says that the more you do something like sleeping, eating, drinking and having sex (the appetites) or like exercise (the soma) or like being kind (the psyche), the more you want to do it. The appetite, the muscle, the heart expands accordingly. Competence increases with use and it establishes preferences. The opposite is also true—the less you do, the less you want to do—and everything shrinks accordingly and eventually everything becomes extinct, as in aging and finally in death. By analogy, love should be equally expandable and accommodate more and more objects, not necessarily ranked in order of priority. So far well and good. But these are extremes and there is a golden mean. The stomach expander becomes obese; the muscle expander, a fitness nut and a narcissist. And the love expander loses credibility as to whether she/he really loves anyone or anything, at one extreme point. And this is corroborated by clinical observation. The "mankind lover," wanting to save people and souls and distributing pamphlets at street corners or even fighting for the greater good of mankind with all he's got, rarely has the time, ability, or motivation to actually bestow personal love focused on *anyone.*

At the extreme range such people are eccentrics and fanatics ultimately loving only themselves even if they protest they love God above all. And I'm very aware of animal fanatics who wouldn't flinch at strangling a human being (because I've met and treated them). Very well. So everything, even love, flourishes in moderation. This reduces the number of love objects and the intensity or forces of love to an exclusive order.

But there's more, in coupling, in any dyadic relationship like heterolove and friendship, there's got to be a two-way-street. I've already argued the greater virtue of allowing oneself to *be loved* in proportion to loving. Allowing oneself to be loved and relying on this is far riskier than loving. Also, usually the people with a big heart, with lots of love to give, are not very good at accepting love, for the many reasons already given. Thus, where a gross imbalance exists it is doubtful that healthy heterolove or friendship exists.

Now at the other end of the scale, there are many people who can love only one person at a time. They can only love a friend if they discard another close one. They even discard their best friend when they've achieved a satisfactory degree of heterolove. Worse, they can love only one of their own children at one time, while they reject and hurt the other(s). They often set one love object against another so they can then choose the better—the winner or loser. Obviously such people are overlimited, sickly, often sadomasochistic, and it is doubtful whether they, as well as their neurotic extreme opposites, can love anyone.

So this brings the optimal range back to the middle ground. There is, however, one more confounding factor here that many readers might confuse. This is disguising the perhaps secret inward feeling of discriminatory love and potential action so as to show fairness and affection. It is perfectly possible and highly desirable not to show favor among one's children, or even among one's parents, siblings, or friends. But it is far more difficult to actually love them equally for a whole set of reasons to do with the laws of coupling. You saw how some one thousand variables had to be perceived and order-ranked, however subconsciously, and how the fearful symmetry of the personages of the inner self had to be aligned inwardly for heterolove to develop from clicking to ticking to sticking. Obviously, given a wide range of choice, some person—but very, very few people—will produce a best fit. This is the essential mechanism for the monogamy of heterolove (however temporary) and the choosing of a best friend. Both mental economy and the best fit for clicking favor exclusivity and order-ranking in loving and in liking.

Perhaps all these arguments put together do not discredit the experience of the very few who can rightly claim having more than one "best" friend, and similarly those who claim an equal love of children and other family members. Where does this leave the strong and powerfully validated arguments and experience of one heterolove at one time? I suggest that those who cannot or will not distinguish a best friend from the rest, for whatever reason, after having submitted themselves to the full impact of the above analysis, are either exceptional, or self-deceived. Or they confuse friendship with the instrumentality or pragmatism of other consortings, as described in this chapter; for utility and pragmatic purpose distinguish other consortings from the altruism of heterolove and friendship.

A TEST OF COMPATIBLE CONSORTING

For group read "person" as plural. Answer by checking one response to each question.

	Yes	Somewhat	No

1. Does your prospective consort share with you a common purpose?

2. Do you possess similar backgrounds *or* else similar personalities? (Answer *NO* if the similarity applies to both background and personality.)

3. Do you recognize right away the possibility of achieving a sense of familiarity with that person (or the majority of those forming a group)?

4. Do you like the person or feel you could (or the majority of a group)?

5. Do you trust the person or feel you could?

6. Do you respect the person or feel you could?

7. *At the same time,* does the person present a challenge to you in the sense of a childlike exuberance or devilment or a similar set of traits you wish you could express yourself?

8. Do you think you could live with that person in close quarters without clashing in daily habits or lifestyle?

	Yes	Somewhat	No

9. Do you feel the person has certain qualities you lack yet admire?

10. Do you think that the differences between you and that person could dovetail in a complementary fashion applicable to work, play, or pleasure?

Scoring
Score 2 for Yes, 1 for Somewhat, and 0 for No.

Interpretation

18–20	Highly compatible—go ahead.
15–17	Likely to be compatible.
10–14	Maybe, just maybe.
5–9	Very doubtful.
0–4	Don't bother, unless you're a masochist.

9

A Guide to Intimacy

Periods of human happiness
are the empty passages of history

—HEGEL

This observation is consistent with the law of entropy in physics, with ecological principles, and with Toynbee's theory of challenge in history, which, roughly speaking, state that life is a conflict of contending tensions and interests. When movement discharges tension, conflicts resolve, and the Big Ache disappears, life ends. Happiness is but a temporary balance—a momentary satisfaction—the pause between turbulence, the trough in a wave. Chasing it is like chasing a rainbow.

Certainly love, marriage, friendships, and close relationships are punctuated by moments of reward and happiness, but their substance is a constant to and fro, push and pull, presided upon by a myriad of feelings, good and bad, positive and negative, things to talk about, to think about, to ache about, to complain about, and to bless.

Those who are afraid of any of this, those who want to avoid challenge and strain, those in pursuit of the tranquil happiness, are eschewing life itself and hurry to find the peace of the grave. Certainly they are sidestepping love. Well, you might say, why not? There's enough tumult and tension one's compelled to meet; why seek more voluntarily? Because it's there. Because missing out on it, consciously or unconsciously, leaves a big gap, even in the weak-hearted. But mostly because you cannot get away with this avoidance. It carries with it the same penalty as does sin—the sin of not even trying to fulfill one's own potentials; the sin of not doing one's best with the gift of life. The penalty consists of regrets, the deep dissatisfaction of a cowardice one can't afford, restlessness, and greater pain in the end. Those are the wages of neurotic avoidance. So those who feel they "cannot stand the hassle," are harrassed and hassled into the ensuing purgatory of life till the peace of the hereafter.

The "me first and me last" ethic doesn't work. For one thing, coupling of any kind is biologically, psychologically, and socially ordained. It's in the service of life itself.

Assuming then that we've disposed of such rationalizations by the hordes of people indulging in them nowadays, assuming that they haven't been put off by the difficulties described in this tome and that, on the contrary, their psyches are redirected toward love, I ask myself what problems might they have out there that a guide would help solve. They can't be very different from the questions I've dealt with daily with patients over the years, or those of relatives and friends, as well as my own.

Take first the normative bunch of concerns that people have all over the world like: How can I tell that the person I'm getting to know is the right one for meaningful sex, for conjugal partnership, for love, for friendship, for business partnership, for consorting, rooming with, traveling with, or even asking to an important dinner party?

All these questions have been answered, to a degree, in the sections of this book. The questionnaire-tests should help you compute some of the answers. And reading between the lines and into your own psyche should give you the confidence of insight. Specifically, you should be able to sketch out your own psychoarchitecture by an inner vision of the personages dwelling in your mind. You should be able to assess your motivations and relate them to your experience of life thus far. Most important, you should be able to clear the tracks of your perceptions so as not to distort things by angular or tubular vision, by skewing the evidence of your sight, ears, and touch. And you should know whether you can trust your intuition.

If you cannot be sure of having done a good cleansing job

on your psyche, you can at least make allowances for the biases you possess, the eradicable prejudices in your system. Furthermore, the inventory of items to be matched—the guide to the processes of clicking, ticking, and sticking, the laws governing coupling—should help you assess the other person and the kind and quality of relationship you have or are about to make.

Next comes the *problematique,* not so much abnormal intrusions as normal sets of problems. Is late love valid? Have I got a worthwhile union? Are my marriage, friendship, or other consortings worth salvaging? These too have been answered, in part, in the various sections of this book. And you should be able to put the answers in the context of self-knowledge as suggested above.

But now we come to anomalies, to such questions as: "Am I capable of love?" I guestimate that millions of people fret about this one. The answer to this question is like that about insanity. In general, those who torment themselves with this question and agonize over the answer (unless they've had the evidence of a long-established pattern of not clicking or ticking with anyone) are perfectly *able* to love (just as the lyssophobics fearing insanity are perfectly sane) though they may have a block in the system. Whereas the people who lack the sensitivity to even question their capacity to love (just like those real crazies who feel they're sane at all times while they say that the whole world is quite wacky) are sometimes completely bunged up—incapable of love. The patterns of their abortive relationships, particularly the lack of closeness, should tell the tale.

Surprisingly, people worried about their capacity *to* love and those who exhibit obvious difficulties rarely if ever ask themselves a question that may be much more pertinent to their problem. This is "Do I have what it takes to allow myself to *be* loved?" I find that fear and distrust of this passive mood of love are quite common, though they may be *unconscious.* The person avoids closeness for that reason rather than the incapacity to give. It's being loved they can't handle.

Often this whole question is obscured by a degree of difficulty in *demonstrating* love or closeness, in being affectionate in words, touch, and deeds. Yet such people feel love and feel bonded. Their problem is *expressive* rather than experiential, rather like the people who feel and think a lot, and do it well, but they can't communicate it to others—a form of dumbness, if you like, but not a lack of loving. We'll come back to two essential points here; (1) how do you tell the difference between being able to love and being able to express it, and (2) what causes these blocks?

Close to this problem is the fear or the outright inability or the quite conscious and determined unwillingness to commit oneself to the entire process of loving in terms of any one of its elective objects—parental, heterolove, friendship, and so forth. Insofar as this might be avoidance of a "hassle," we've already dealt with part of that. An outright inability to actually commit is close to or coincidental with an incapacity to love. The premier person thus afflicted is the narcissist: Over-attracted to his own physical and/or mental self and virtually unable to escape himself, he cannot turn his libido to another object, to any degree of altruism. Narcissus, quite rightly, drowned himself in the pool reflecting his beautiful image. So the narcissist always gets his comeuppance from altruism. Love of another pays better than a sick self-love.

Rarely are people so hesitant because of an obsessive neurosis or because of a phobia of making a mistake that they will not commit themselves to love because of such a mental handicap.

In the crevices of uncertainty in this context of committal to a person, there is a subtle and ticklish problem often encountered by people "unlucky in love." They may have wasted considerable time in bad relationships or love affairs turned sour. And now they're around thirty-five years of age and between potential mates. They have doubts, perhaps well-founded, about the person(s) they're going out with, about a good fit. Should they risk committing not so much themselves as their precious "remaining time" to a doubtful relationship or let the bird in the hand fly away? Such people should have found most of the answers in these pages, in the first five chapters. But I would remind them that they need a fine judgment in order to hit somewhere between overreaching—having a shopping list a mile long of expectations and forgetting what they have to offer—and selling themselves short—settling for less than enough for fear of missing out altogether.

As for the philosophers of nonintimacy who decide that heterolove is a "hassle" that they can do without, along with such trappings as marriage; that friendship, brotherhood, and sisterhood, and the given family will suffice; that they've grown up enough, thank you, without unions or marriages, and that they need no spouse or child to keep them warm in the cold, dark, and dismal days . . . all I'd say to them is good luck! We've already pointed out that indeed you lose some and you win some through love—you pay your union dues. Perhaps the biggest and most unwarranted dues of a union were estimated by a lady who said (with objective justification), "I had lost so much of me in my marriage that I found I couldn't do anything alone afterwards."

But, in this writer's opinion, the wages of coupling are worth it. Perhaps not for some, though. The only thing I'd say to these people is: Are you sure you're actually *free* to love, to relate closely to the opposite sex? Can you do it? Have you a valid proof of this to satisfy the most astute judge, perched on your own shoulder? Or are you covering up, lying to yourself? Because if you *can't* do it—and ninety percent of those people I heard argue like that couldn't—you mustn't pretend that it's your choice, that you're doing what you really want, and certainly you can't argue that singlehood is the ideal best for you. You can only say that you're acting the only way you are able to act, with no apologies *or* rationalizations.

By the way, the funniest line these people use is a giveaway: "I want to keep my options open!" they say. What options? And their answering-service tape says, "I'm out for lunch. Leave your name and phone number, babe! But remember: I'm not *into* involvements."

As for conflicts between love objects, should you choose a spouse ahead of a friend; a partner ahead of marriage; one consort ahead of another? In part we've dealt with these questions too. Usually love hypertrophies the heart so that there's room for all and more. It's just like the way time dilates with good usage. That's why it's said that if you want something done you always ask the busy man.

The opposite is certainly true: If there's room in the human heart for *one* object only, especially if that object is exalted at the agape level—such as love of humanity or of God—then there's no love there at all.

Generally, psychosocial necessity has ordained that there be room at least for one of each kind of coupling, as in Noah's ark. But when there isn't, when there's virtually nothing there, or when it's so blocked that nothing is manifest, or when it exists in feeling but not in demonstrable fact or behavior, how can you tell? What has made it so and how do you tell the difference?

Let us first distinguish the input from the output, an expressive paralysis of love from its absence. How does the undemonstrative person himself know that he loves if he can't express it, and how can he keep on loving when the feeling and the bond require continuous reinforcement by demonstration of affection? Let me say at once that the extremely undemonstrative person is himself confused about that and often doubts his love, even if he feels *something* (we've already argued in Chapter 1 that you can never be *sure* that it is love because you can never compare it *subjectively* with the love of someone else)—especially if he's told often, "You don't love anybody but yourself." The undemonstrative are usually distant, introverted, ascetic, alabaster-skinned ectomorphs of few words and gestures. That's the constitution of a type of being capable of great courage and deeds but reluctant to show feelings, not trusting of emotions (quite rightly, if you review the arguments about the value of emotions as described in this book). They believe emotions to be an inferior aspect of Homo sapiens, as the golden Greeks of yore taught. But such people will show their love in meaningful deeds, even sacrifice, though they may fall short of demonstrating the ten tenets of conventional love (see Chapter 1). They're even more embarrassed by affection shown *to* them than by affection shown *by* them to others. Yet here's the crunch that distinguishes them from those who feel unworthy of *being loved* and cannot accept it graciously or trust it: These dour people have no such attitude. They know their own worth. It's just a fear of expending the cheap coin of "mush" that holds them back.

Next to these constitutional ascetics, who if they are physical isolates usually love to distraction yet dumbly, the cultural stoic is a dumb animal. Physically she/he may be any body type, raised behaviorly to stay aloof from the common muck of uncontrolled emotions. This is the Nordic as well as the Asiatic variety of inscrutability. They tend to treat the sexes quite differently. They exhibit a spartan attitude toward men and boys and a watchful aloofness toward girls—who are the mother's responsibility for raising—and toward women. Their boys must not be sissified by affection.

Though men exceed women by a large margin in both these varieties and in this general attitude of equating the display of affection with weakness and embarrassment, women can be like this, too. To mistake such people with those who cannot or will not love is a grave error, because, in fact, their feelings of love *do* run deep; they filter pure love in the layers of their unconscious. Their feelings are dammed up higher than those of extroverts, who discharge their affections profligately. Stoics require little overt positive reinforcement to sustain their love yet, most strikingly, they usually select the extrovert pourer-of-feeling in a union. You might ask why, if they need so little back? Because in the wisdom of their unconscious they know that their tendency should be counteracted by a warm and loving partner, especially for the procrustean bed of parenthood. When two seemingly cold inscrutables of the same kind marry and bear children, the result indeed may be disastrous, namely childhood autism. It's much more interesting to ask the rarer question: Why do effusive extroverts choose the other kind of person to live with when invariably they complain later of their partner's coldness and show eventual dissatisfaction? Because they feel shallower than their mate—and often are; because they themselves remain unconvinced by their incessant emotional displays and protestations of love; and most of all because they are the controlling givers and know deep down that their love *receptors* are narrow or partially blocked. They choose intuitively what they need, even though they may bellyache forever afterward. And of course, these bellyaches drive the introvert further in—just as nagging drives the obese further out—and reinforces the situation.

The people fearful of committal—those who will not risk showing affection—are very different again. To start with, they're neither of the constitutional body type described, necessarily, nor the cultural genus of stoics. Instead they've been hurt more than they can bear. And here's the catch; they might bear very little hurt. Small-hearted and anemic, they're emotional cowards foolishly overprotecting themselves. This block can be removed with a difficulty commensurate with the degree of hurt previously endured, and especially in keeping with the size of their libido and psychic energy. The lily-white anemics, overindulged as children, spoiled, conditioned to receive but to give little, come close to the narcissists, who are relatively imprisoned in themselves.

What are some of the everyday tests to separate undemonstrativeness from lovelessness? Rate of taking initiative in sex or phoning their partner is not, because there may be reluctance in being obtrusive or showing dependency. But subtle signs of pining, of suffering because of one's absence or remoteness, are. But you have to be able to read these signs. The undemonstrative loner may look cold and distant but is vigilant, alert to your real needs, thoughtfully helpful in deeds, which he hates to trumpet around. He is not withdrawn, in blue moods—or depressive—or in pink reveries like the schizoid.

What would cause an incapacity to love, then? Is it hereditary or constitutional? Not directly, except through the environment created by unloving parents. It's imprinted early in life through infant abuse (undiscovered child-battering) or, much more likely, through deprivation of infant handling and gentling (for the child abuser is often very passionate). It may be due to "hospitalism" (prolonged stay there) and to deprivation of parental affection; or due to indirect deprivation through having parents who don't or can't love one another, or who didn't want children; or who didn't want that particular child, or didn't like or accept that particular child—for whatever reason ranging from his being an ugly duckling to his being dumb. Certainly demonstration of affection is learned in myriad situations, generally by being cuddled, kissed and talked to as infants and children, by displays of tenderness between parents no less than toward children, animals, and even toys. Such microbehaviors run the gamut of love, from sensuousness through sexuality to love itself (see Chapter

1). If you're an only child, if you've been handled by strangers in early life, if you've been deprived of gentling parents and affection, if you've never felt and seen love until it was almost too late, it is difficult to *show* it though you may still feel it instinctively. If love has been blocked by violence, its display will be sadomasochistic rather than normally tender. If it has been blocked by the deep freeze, it will be similarly stultified in demonstration.

Sometimes, not too often, entirely external events can block the loving. In one such case a person felt that whomever they touched with loving got the "kiss of death," so she withheld out of this fear.

Marjorie was an only child, loved by both parents, but her father died suddenly in her arms and her mother died prematurely when she wasn't quite an adolescent and when she needed her most. Both her sets of grandparents died when she was young and her adoptive parents split up. Her first boyfriend crashed a plane. Thereafter she developed a phobia about any involvement. She spent her efforts and her devotion on people in need. She would risk rejection in pursuing an unattainable man, but the moment he showed her any signs of affection, she fled.

Such cases, of course, are much more easily healed by analytical therapy than those whose souls are destroyed rather than just bruised.

But what will kill love outright, you ask? We've already seen what will kill half of it—the acceptance of love—things like a deep feeling of unworthiness, a distrust that it can be genuine. We know that the narcissist can't give it out to another. Beyond that, prolonged, totally inhibited demonstrations of affection from day one to postadolescence will weaken the plant through lack of nourishment. Thereafter it will take very little to kill it off altogether, especially if the plant itself is constitutionally weak (low libido). Cool, early rejection will do that job best—not passionate violence but response with indifference to whatever immature or misread overtures you made.

And what's to be done about it? Very little when it's late, in adulthood. The person survives as an infirm person, one of the many mutilated by the hazards of life. It would take quite a Florence Nightingale (or her male equivalent) to nurse such a person to a weak semblance of normalcy, and the question will always arise, why should she (or he) do it? The motive must be relatively neurotic, masochistic martyrdom, and the achievement at best can hardly ever be the two-way-street of love we've described—it has to be imbalanced forever. Analytical psychotherapy, being more powerful than love itself (see the source of power of therapeutic transference, Chapter 1) can do more, but not much more.

All the personages of the inner self are singed by love-burn. The *eternal child* is melancholy and dares not risk the display of innocent vitality. The hominus and femina are all but extinguished, as they were by ascetic Christian martyrs. The ideal self is virtually not of this world, but one of a person in a state of suspended animation, devoid of feeling. The key, as usual, is in the shadow. Whatever passion it may retain could be turned into love. The anima may be burning with unearthly spirituality but its objective, at best, is at the high-agape level of abstracts, of symbols.

You're now in position to be guided through whatever problem you might have with close relationships and intimacy. The various chapters and tests in this book should have answered most of your questions in whatever category of problem you find yourself. Perhaps the only thing not yet covered is a self-diagnosis regarding not so much the evidence of a problem in loving as the cause of an incapacity to love or show love. This test follows.

WHY CAN'T I LOVE?

Answer each question by checking one response to each question.

	Yes	Somewhat	No
1. I'm your common garden-variety lean and hungry (ectomorphic) kind of introvert.			
2. My parents weren't loving toward one another.			

3. My parents weren't loving toward their children.

4. I was short one parent much or most of my early childhood.

5. I lacked a parental substitute to take the place of the parent I lacked physically, or to make up for the absence of love from one (or both) parent(s), such as grandparents.

6. I was not wanted or accepted when I arrived.

7. I felt I was not loved as a child.

8. I felt much rejected as a child.

9. I think I was abused as a child.

10. The relationship between me and my brothers and sisters (between them) was and still is poor; or else I'm an only child.

11. Whenever I tried to show love to somebody or even to some thing (animal), I lost out.

12. I'm embarrassed by a display of affection either way, giving or taking it.

13. I feel love but have difficulty showing it.

14. I've schooled myself not to miss anybody.

15. I'm afraid of showing affection because I might be hurt or rejected or feel foolish.

	Yes	Somewhat	No

16. I don't trust being shown affection because I feel it's insincere or undeserved, or I feel that deep down I'm not at all what I seem.

17. I don't believe in a show of emotion of any kind because it shows lack of control, or weakness, or something like it.

18. I feel that the returns from committing myself to heterolove would not be worth what I would have to put out.

19 I feel the same (as above) about close friendships.

20. I feel that *any* close relationship would cost me something of myself or hurt me more than I can endure.

Scoring
Score 2 for Yes, 1 for Somewhat, and 0 for No.

Interpretation

35–40	You've got it bad; I'm afraid you cannot love.
30–34	You have a major block in loving that would take much professional help and devoted people to rectify.
25–29	It's a flip between cannot and will not risk loving, either way. Try it; you'll like it.
20–24	You've got a reasonable block in loving—a little dab of courage ought to do it.
10–19	So you haven't had it easy but that's no reason to beg off—you deserve only a little sympathy.
0–9	What the heck are you doing taking this test? You're no worse off than the rest of us. Go out there and do your stuff or else take all the punishment you deserve.

10

Why Love?

For I dipt into the future
Far as human eye could see
Saw a vision of the world
And all the wonder that could be

—TENNYSON

We saw that the psychology of love, both between the sexes and in friendship, was in the service of biology, of personal and species survival. The prototype of love obeys the principle of contrasting opposition or, more accurately, the magical formula, a carefully balanced proportion of commonality and differences. This formula provides a guide to the selection and matching of intimates so that both sexual mates and friends would be acceptably (tolerably) complementary. Heterolove spearheads the genetic improvement of the stock, while friendship engenders social survival. Commonality in the background of heterolove is eugenically salutary because it insures continuation of an endowment already achieved and bids for enrichment by complementary characteristics offsetting weaknesses and balancing strengths. Commonality in friendship and consorts is socially salutary because it makes for a common cause, while complementarity helps to achieve it.

The dichotomy of offsetting or balancing polar characteristics, both in terms of likes and differences, reflects an apparent polarity that holds throughout the natural universe and in all man-made phenomena. To mention but a few in the physical universe, there are the negative entropy of high potential tension corresponding with growth, development, anabolism, life itself; and positive entropy corresponding with decline, degeneration, catabolism, and death. There are the two vectors of electromagnetism—the positive and negative. In cybernetics there's positive and negative feedback; in space there's up and down. There's God and the Devil, good and bad, love and hate, the yin and the yang. There's matter and antimatter in every element of nuclear physics (like protons and electrons).

In ecology there is succession and the steady state; in genetics, myosis and mitosis, the genotype and the phenotype, dominant and recessive. In the biosphere generally there is nature and nurture, pathogens and antigens, host and parasite, and the two sexes and so on *ad infinitum.*

In man-made things and in man himself, there's the left cerebral hemisphere (rational and thinking) and the right (creative and imaginative), the binary system of odds and evens, the adversary system in justice, and in governance the dialectic tension of dialogue in politics, the body- and the field-centered, the introvert and the extrovert, and so forth.

So the world seems divided in twain. This dichotomy in the physical universe, reflected in life and in human nature, is further reflected in religions, which then mirror back the phenomena of the objective world. The Manichaeans, for instance, who nearly swamped out Christianity in the third century A.D. divided the whole of the physical universe into two camps, first symbolically and finally literally. In their view all inanimate objects were actual and partisan. Light was good, darkness evil; the spirit was God-given, the flesh the Devil's gift. Altogether the material world was evil and the immaterial, the allegorical world beyond death, was most highly priced. Polarity then is the basis for all rudimentary structures.

Consequently the laws of selection of intimates based on contrasting opposition conform with the perceived shape of the world.

But then there is an overriding principle to this oversimplification; this is the necessary balance to be produced by the tension of opposites, of push and pull. This golden mean is celebrated throughout human purview: the entropic state in physics, the steady state in ecology, homeostasis in the biochemistry of the human body, maturity at the plateau of development, compatibility, health, harmony, symmetry, and love itself. In this book we see this balance both in the magical-formula seeking of contrasts against commonalities and in the activities of love—the tension of opposites, the Big Ache, and the union as a culmination of the three phases of coupling.

Also everything in the universe develops to a climax, then dies down, from the first Big Bang in space to the last tango into the black hole; from the white star and the expanding galaxies to the red star and their collapse; from the first daughter cell of a fertilized ovum to the three layers of tissues complexifying into the human body; from the seeming *tabula rasa* of the infant mind—its bud—to the mind of a mature adult. This is evolution. Similarly, it happens with love's progress from clicking to sticking.

Now while it's perfectly true that science admits to no teleology, no immediate or ultimate purpose, while its limited objective is the continuous description of phenomena, of how the world works, an understanding chiefly to be gained through deductive reasoning, the scientist and every other knowledge- and wisdom-seeking person are in constant search of purpose, to discover the reason for being.

In this respect the reasons for love of all kinds are amply demonstrated. Heterolove catalyzes the completion of a single person, who cannot be an island to himself or herself, into a couple necessitated by the essential incompleteness of humans and of all things. Moreover, coupling in its sexual attraction and its selectivity for long-term union serves both nature and nurture simultaneously. Nature in the individual is served in the biological imperative of sexuality, and in the species it's served genetically by the use of its magic formula for sexual selection. Nature is served by parental coupling.

Clearly we're a society in transition. Sexual selection is being carried out by a mixed strategy that must insure the quality of our species in the genetic pool as well as the quality of the life of mating adults. The same selective process determines the pristine human environments of infants. This function increases the importance of quality matching and mating in depth, as described in this book.

In looking systematically at the one thousand elements to be matched in love and particularly at the several constellations of personages, we refine our precision regarding the interacting forces of love. When we have it all categorized and described and see the purposes and functions, we shall have a workable model of love capable of being promoted, but never truly determined by a computer programmed accordingly. The complexity of clicking, ticking, and sticking reflects the complexity overlaying the universal structure of polar opposites, the function of balance, the development of matter to life and to intelligence, and conforms to the complexity of the web of things, both inanimate and animate.

In summary, the laws of love conform with the laws of the universe: Attraction is based on polarity; the union of close relationship depends on balance; its goodness relies on symmetry and an offsetting fit; and its development follows an evolutionary path analogous to that of universal animates and inanimates and the law of entropy.

The model for all close relationships is heterolove in that ideal initial selection and the subsequent clicking, ticking, and sticking in all intimate relationships, from friendship to travel mating, are based on the magical formula of an adjustable balance between contrasting opposites or differences (usually in the foreground) and commonalities (usually in the background).

Sex is the chief divider between heterolove and other couplings. The electromagnetism of sex, again conforming to the general laws of nature, is based on libidinal (psychic energy) drives directed by the perception of complementary differences (or opposites); it starts at the surface of sensuality and eroticism and ends at deeper personality levels (the hominus/femina attraction).

The chemistry of attraction and liking between people is based on a further psychological extension of this complementarity.

At the deepest level of the human psyche, at the interface of the collective and personal unconscious, where all things are fundamental, dwell the archetypal images of the personages of the inner self. They comprise the secret alchemy of love. They also obey the universal laws of nature, which rule the manifest world of matter and of life, in that these personages relate to one another in contrasting opposition. In coupling, the personages of the inner self bond in opposite symmetrical polarity so that the inner (intrapsychic) and outer (manifest) perspectives of a union crystalize into perfect replicas of one another.

No wonder then that the mystery of sex and love has eluded us for such a long time! Things that are perpetually under our noses always elude us for the longest time because they are always with us and thus dull our critical perception. This is true in science and generally in all knowledge begetting. But there is another cause for this protracted elusion beyond the invisibility of constant environments and of the mind.

As we ascend from matter to mind—both ultimately invisible—the complexity of *form* increases, although the universal laws governing them are essentially the same. And this complexity of psychological forms is bewildering, as we saw when we examined the mutuality of perception in some of the thousand or so perspectives of the elements of love being unconsciously selected, aligned, and bonded in clicking together and subsequently.

Furthermore, when everything functions smoothly, we're not inclined to study things; we just admire them, the wonders of nature and of love. Fortunately things don't always function smoothly. In fact, in human affairs they frequently don't function and break down. Thus, thanks to "patients" and problems in close relationships like marital breakdowns and to the need for better social technology in living—working and playing—we are forced to study the "abnormal." This is when things become obtrusive and simplified; hence the importance of Passages (Chapter 6), which describes the *problematiques* of intimacy. This is where the clinical insights built themselves up in my experience to burgeon into this book attempting to describe the normal (ideal) and normative (average) aspects of love. This is also whence the power of my prediction rose so that I could forecast the nature and fate of imperfect human bonding and whence the knowledge came in understanding the normal phenomena of love. As a result of this lifelong study, it will be possible to program computers and match people far better than ever before for all essential purposes, from love to the creation of a President's cabinet.

In this chapter, adumbrating the epistemology of love, I tried to go beyond the usual limits of science, of observation, classification, description of relationships, and prediction and outline the purposes of love—a speculative, teleological exercise. Clearly love serves the dictates of survival, individually and collectively, biologically (genetically in heterolove) and socially, in all couplings and in small, well-knit groups.

It is obvious that in this book, largely aimed at the practical, at recipes for close relationships, at tests designed to enlarge awareness, at an almanac of love, I have tried to go further and deeper. I have tried to explain scientifically the nature of things to do with love and their purpose and thus to expand the definition of life itself. In these days of a thirst for future projection, it is not satisfying enough to stop here. So why not go a wee step further?

Beyond love, what about a "vision of the world and all the wonders that could be"? What about inventing the future of love? The real historical question is whether scarcity, always with us, and aggressive competitiveness, one of its sequels, are relatively incompatible with love or not, and whether self-sufficiency, an equitable distribution of goods, and the pacific co-operativeness that has never quite been with us would be more compatible with love. My impression of the pendular swings between poverty and plenty, between ignorance and enlightenment, love and hatred is that they go together or at least they follow each other in quick succession. Affluence and boredom don't seem to have helped the Greeks and Romans gain any final or lasting dimensions in love or create a higher ledge for psychological and social well-being than had the times of scarcity. On the contrary, decadence, regressions, and cruelties always followed success and affluence. And much the same can be said of contemporary Western Europe, of Scandinavia and Britain, and certainly of North America. As McLuhan said, "Nothing fails like success." And Toynbee pointed to the need for challenge in civilization.

We are entering an era of scarcity again, and this will bring out the best *and* the worst in us, as usual. The hope is that the best it will bring will amount to a quantum leap in love and therefore in personal and social well-being. What precisely will do that? Well, we've analyzed (in Chapter 1) some of the causes of social decline, and why love is on the shrink. Many of these directions will be reversed.

Energy shortages will force us to conserve, to do more with less; technological advances will bring shorter work weeks and perhaps a revolution in our patterns of sleeping and waking behavior. Communication may well replace human transportation so people will be in touch audiovisually. Zero population growth will diminish crowding and heighten the quality of life. Man may evolve into a classless society—or into nonwarring, homogenous regions where different kinds of people will mix with maximal tolerance and understanding toward each other. The uplifting of individuation, of regionalism, of neighborhoods, of multielites, of pluricultures (standing in patterns of contrasting opposition to each other) will enhance the biosocial imperative for diversity; while central structures and socialization will insure continuity, orderliness and balance. And if this looks and sounds vaguely familiar to you, it's only because it is. Sure, the design is no more or less than the magical formula for the selection process of close relationships. What else? You see, if each microcosm, like heterolove, reflected truly the best of the realities of the macrocosm (as this chapter showed you that it can) and then again, if the macrocosm also reflected truly the best microcosms, then love indeed would permeate everything and all would be well.

Given this scenario and a life span of two hundred years or so on a planet with a stable population of four or five billion, I would imagine that sex will no longer bring any conflict and will be enjoyed in as much variety as gourmet food; that three or four times in a lifetime sex will ascend to heterolove of a far better quality than has ever been achieved before, because of improved selection and the improved nature of lovers. I'd imagine that in heterolove all personages of the inner self will have been given full play and been savored. They will have multiplied and rotated in the psyche in relation to the various close relationships.

I also imagine, with due humility, that when the essential facts in this book become refined into measurements these will be programmed into microprocessors (the miracle chip), and human matching will become a science.

By now you might have smelled a rat. I know I have. Something's missing. The picture's too good to be true—too utopic—instead of being like the usual human scene—like dystopia or disturbia. It's misery that's missing; also, the un-foreseen, the element of surprise, the total break from the past, which always happens in the future.

Well, let's inject these. There will always be the threat of cataclysms. Virulent viruses introduced from outer space are a likely source. Result: epidemics decimating the global pop-ulation. A reversal in the earth's magnetic poles may switch the globe's electromagnetic fields. But the most likely source of misery, in each short run into the future, is the faulty hu-man brain.

I suspect the real misery will come trom tampering with life and, particularly, with death. Wholesale body transplants and the deep freeze will have made us last for a long while, in bits and pieces. Genetic engineering and extra-corporeal gestation will have played havoc with the genetic basis of heterolove and the social basis of family life. It's possible that gerontological studies will have brought us to the brink of immortality and then there'll be mischief between the immortal overlords and the mortal slaves. That ought to do it for misery.

Who could then portray the many faces of love?

Meanwhile I invite you to join me in the *construction* of our last questionnaire, which is on the love status of future terres-trials.

	Yes	Partially	No
1. Are you an immortal?			
2. Have you made love deep under the earth's crust, inside the ocean, and in deep space?			
3. Have you matched yourself be-yond the anima to the level of the mandala archetype?			
4. Have you. . . .			

Glossary

Acnophile: small-space lover.

Alloplastic: change environment to adapt to self.

Anima: the core of the self, soullike quality.

Archetypal imagery: images of the (old) collective unconscious.

Archetypes: primordial images generated by the collective unconscious (ancient archaeological strata of the mind).

Assortative mating: homogeneous or similar pairing.

Autoplastic: change self to adapt to the environment.

Binary (system): odd and even numbers.

Collective unconscious: beyond personal experience, at the deep experience level of the human species.

Commensal (relationship): mutually beneficial.

Complementary (relationship): balancing differences.

Compulsory or obligatory (relationship): family or blood-bonded.

Concordant: in agreement with.

Congruent: fitting.

Consonant: in tune with.

Dichotomized: divided into two.

Dissortative: heterogeneous or dissimilar (pairing).

Duality: system of two.

Dyad: the intimate (sex) pair.

Dynamics: the effects of motivation.

Elective or facultative (relationship): freely chosen.

Empathy: identify with and feel for.

Epicine: pertaining to both sexes.

Femina: a man's image of ideal womanhood.

Givens: characteristics not chosen.

Heterolove: love between the sexes.

Hominus: a woman's image of ideal manhood.

Ideal self: one's ideal image for oneself.

Individualization: the process of acquiring the uniqueness of a person.

Individuation: fulfilling one's potentials.

Intrapsychic: inside the mind.

Making closure: completing the perceptual picture.

Parasitic: dependent and feeding on host.

Persona: the social image one projects.

Philobat: large-space lover.

Polarity: on opposite extremes or ranges.

Problematique: the knots caused by a pattern of ordinary problems.

Proxemics: the study of spatial relationships between people.

Psychoarchitecture: the structure of the mind.

Puer aeternus (and *puella aeterna*): the image of the eternal child manifest inside oneself.

Self: the totality of the individual comprising all the images or personages of the inner self.

Shadow: the inferior or hidden image of oneself in sharpest contrast to the persona.

Social profile: the social variables or groupings to which a person belongs, like race, creed, and culture.

Succession (of love): sequence or stages.

Supplementary or extending (relationship): based on likes.

Synetics: brain-storming (group).

Valency: positive and negative charges (or directions).

Index